Mary J. Ainslie is Assistant Professor of Film and Media at the University of Nottingham; she is based at the university's Ningbo campus in China. Her research interests include Southeast Asian culture and media, in particular relating to Thailand and Malaysia. She is the editor of a special edition of the *Horror Studies* journal, as well as the collection *The Korean Wave in Southeast Asia: Consumption and Cultural Production* (2015). She is currently working on a project on the Southeast Asian gothic.

Katarzyna Ancuta is a lecturer at the Faculty of Liberal Arts, King Mongkut's Institute of Technology Ladkrabang (KMITL) in Thailand. Her research focuses on the multidisciplinary, contemporary gothic and horror genre, currently with a strong Asian focus. Her recent publications include chapters in *A New Companion to the Gothic* (2012), *Globalgothic* (2013), *The Cambridge Companion to the Modern Gothic* (2014) and *Ghost Movies in Southeast Asia and Beyond* (2016), as well as two co-edited special journal issues on Thai (2014) and Southeast Asian (2015) horror film.

'At last! A much-needed book of essays on contemporary Thai cinema and auteurs has arrived! Within, you'll discover many fantastic and often politically subversive films. Anyone with an interest in digital and cinematic screen culture will find these pages historically informative, imaginative and thought-provoking.'

– Boreth Ly, University of California, Santa Cruz

TAURIS WORLD CINEMA SERIES

Series Editors:
Lúcia Nagib, *Professor of Film at the University of Reading*
Julian Ross, *Research Fellow at the University of Westminster*

Advisory Board: Laura Mulvey (UK), Robert Stam (USA), Ismail Xavier (Brazil), Dudley Andrew (USA)

The *Tauris World Cinema Series* aims to reveal and celebrate the richness and complexity of film art across the globe, exploring a wide variety of cinemas set within their own cultures and as they interconnect in a global context. The books in the series will represent innovative scholarship, in tune with the multicultural character of contemporary audiences. Drawing upon an international authorship, they will challenge outdated conceptions of world cinema, and provide new ways of understanding a field at the centre of film studies in an era of transnational networks.

Published and forthcoming in the World Cinema series:

Allegory in Iranian Cinema: The Aesthetics of Poetry and Resistance
By Michelle Langford

Animation in the Middle East: Practice and Aesthetics from Baghdad to Casablanca
Edited by Stefanie Van de Peer

Basque Cinema: A Cultural and Political History
By Rob Stone and María Pilar Rodriguez

The Battle Lines of Beauty: The Politics, Aesthetics and Erotics of West African Cinema
By James Stuart Williams

Brazil on Screen: Cinema Novo, New Cinema, Utopia
By Lúcia Nagib

The Cinema of Jia Zhangke: Realism and Memory in Chinese Film
By Cecília Mello

The Cinema of Sri Lanka: South Asian Film in Texts and Contexts
By Ian Conrich and Vilasnee Tampoe-Hautin

Contemporary New Zealand Cinema: From
New Wave to Blockbuster
Edited by Ian Conrich and Stuart Murray

Contemporary Portuguese Cinema:
Globalising the Nation
Edited by Mariana Liz

Cosmopolitan Cinema: Cross-cultural
Encounters in East Asian Film
By Felicia Chan

Documentary Cinema: Contemporary
Non-fiction Film and Video Worldwide
By Keith Beattie

Documentary Cinema of Chile: Confronting
History, Memory, Trauma
By Antonio Traverso

East Asian Cinemas: Exploring
Transnational Connections on Film
Edited by Leon Hunt and Leung Wing-Fai

East Asian Film Noir: Transnational
Encounters and Intercultural Dialogue
Edited by Chi-Yun Shin and Mark Gallagher

Film Genres and African Cinema:
Postcolonial Encounters
By Rachael Langford

Impure Cinema: Intermedial and
Intercultural Approaches to Film
Edited by Lúcia Nagib and Anne Jerslev

Latin American Women Filmmakers:
Production, Politics, Poetics
Edited by Deborah Martin and
Deborah Shaw

Lebanese Cinema: Imagining the Civil War
and Beyond
By Lina Khatib

New Argentine Cinema
By Jens Andermann

New Directions in German Cinema
Edited by Paul Cooke and Chris
Homewood

New Turkish Cinema: Belonging, Identity
and Memory
By Asuman Suner

On Cinema
By Glauber Rocha
Edited by Ismail Xavier

Palestinian Filmmaking in Israel:
Narratives of Place and Identity
By Yael Freidman

Performing Authorship: Self-inscription
and Corporeality in the Cinema
By Cecilia Sayad

Queer Masculinities in Latin American
Cinema: Male Bodies and Narrative
Representations
By Gustavo Subero

Realism in Greek Cinema: From the
Post-war Period to the Present
By Vrasidas Karalis

Realism of the Senses in World Cinema:
The Experience of Physical Reality
By Tiago de Luca

The Spanish Fantastic: Contemporary
Filmmaking in Horror, Fantasy and Sci-fi
By Shelagh-Rowan Legg

Stars in World Cinema: Screen Icons and
Star Systems Across Cultures
Edited by Andrea Bandhauer and
Michelle Royer

Thai Cinema: The Complete Guide
Edited by Mary J. Ainslie and Katarzyna
Ancuta

Theorizing World Cinema
Edited by Lúcia Nagib, Chris Perriam and
Rajinder Dudrah

Viewing Film
By Donald Richie

Queries, ideas and submissions to:

Series Editor: Professor Lúcia Nagib –
l.nagib@reading.ac.uk

Series Editor: Dr. Julian Ross –
rossj@westminster.ac.uk

Cinema Editor at I.B.Tauris, Maddy Hamey-
Thomas – mhamey-thomas@ibtauris.com

Thai Cinema

The Complete Guide

EDITED BY
MARY J. AINSLIE AND
KATARZYNA ANCUTA

I.B. TAURIS
LONDON • NEW YORK • OXFORD • NEW DELHI • SYDNEY

Published in 2018 by
I.B.Tauris & Co. Ltd
London • New York
www.ibtauris.com
Paperback edition published 2025

Copyright editorial selection © 2018 Mary J. Ainslie and Katarzyna Ancuta
Copyright individual chapters © Mary J. Ainslie, Katarzyna Ancuta, Patipat Auprasert, Benjamin Baumann, Brian Bernards, Linnie Blake, Natalie Boehler, Peter Braeunlein, Anchalee Chaiworaporn, Graiwoot Chulphongsathorn, Palita Chunsaengchan, Chanokporn Chutikamoltham, Yossapol Chutipanyabut, Rayna Denison, Brett Farmer, Arnika Fuhrmann, Jelka Günther, Andrew Hock Soon Ng, Dredge Kang, Liew Kai Khiun, Adam Knee, Bogna M. Konior, Mikel J. Koven, Kom Kunyosying, Pasoot Lasuka, Philippa Lovatt, Daniel Martin, Jovan Maud, Natthanai Prasannam, Wikanda Promkhuntong, Raphael Raphael, Jesse Sessoms, Sophia Siddique, Lalita Singhasri, Patsorn Sungsri, Rebecca Townsend, Noah Viernes

The right of Mary J. Ainslie and Katarzyna Ancuta to be identified as the editors of this work has been asserted by the editors in accordance with the Copyright, Designs and Patents Act 1988.

All rights reserved. Except for brief quotations in a review, this book, or any part thereof, may not be reproduced, stored in or introduced into a retrieval system, or transmitted, in any form or by any means, electronic, mechanical, photocopying, recording or otherwise, without the prior written permission of the publisher.

Every attempt has been made to gain permission for the use of the images in this book. Any omissions will be rectified in future editions.

References to websites were correct at the time of writing.

Tauris World Cinema Series

ISBN HB: 978 1 78831 141 0
PB: 978 1 35054 336 2
eISBN: 978 1 83860 925 2
ePDF: 978 1 83860 926 9

A full CIP record for this book is available from the British Library
A full CIP record is available from the Library of Congress

Library of Congress Catalog Card Number: available

Contents

List of Illustrations	xiii
List of Contributors	xv
Introduction	1
1 Key Directors	7
Nonzee Nimibutr	7
Ratana Pestonji	9
Prachya Pinkaew	11
Banjong Pisanthanakun	13
Pen-Ek Ratanaruang	14
Wisit Sasanatieng	16
Yuthlert Sippapak	17
Cherd Songsri	19
Apichatpong Weerasethakul	20
Chatrichalerm Yukol	23
2 Key Early Productions	27
Miss Suwanna of Siam / Nang Sao Suwan (1923)	29
Double Luck / Chok Song Chan (1927)	31
A Fable from an Uncle: The Magical Ring / Nithan Khong Lung Rueang Waen Wiset (1929)	32
The King of the White Elephant / Phrachao Changphueak (1940)	33
Santi-Vina (1954)	35
Country Hotel / Rong Raem Narok (1957)	37
Mae Nak Phra Khanong (1959)	38
Black Silk / Phrae Dam (1961)	39
Money Money Money / Ngoen Ngoen Ngoen (1965)	41
Sugar Is Not Sweet / Namtan Mai Wan (1965)	42
Ngu Phi (1966)	44
Pisat Saneha (1969)	45

Contents

Monrak Lukthung (1970)	47
Golden Eagle / Insi Thong (1970)	49
Tone (1970)	51
Ghost of Guts Eater / Krasue Sao (1973)	52
His Name Is Khan / Khao Chue Kan (1973)	54
The Scar / Phaenkao (1977)	55
Mountain People / Khon Phukao (1979)	56
The Adventure of Sudsakorn / Sudsakorn (1979)	58
Son of the Northeast / Luk Isan (1982)	59
Butterfly and Flowers / Phisuea Lae Dokmai (1985)	60
The Elephant Keeper / Khon Liang Chang (1987)	62
Boonchu Phu Narak (1988)	63
Ban Phi Pop (1989)	64
Song of Chaophraya / Nong Mia (1990)	66
Somsri #422R (1992)	67
A Couple in Two Worlds / Khu Thae Song Lok (1994)	68
Muen and Rid / Amdaeng Muean Kap Nai Rit (1994)	70
Red Bike Story / Chakkrayan Si Daeng (1997)	71

3 New Thai Cinema — 75

Fun Bar Karaoke / Fan Ba Karaoke (1997)	77
6ixtynin9 / Rueang Talok 69 (1999)	78
Tears of the Black Tiger / Fa Thalai Chon (2000)	80
Transistor Love Story / Monrak Transistor (2001)	81
Mekhong Full Moon Party / Sip Ha Kham Duean Sip Et (2002)	83
Last Life in the Universe / Rueang Rak Noi Nit Mahasan (2003)	85
Citizen Dog / Ma Nakhon (2004)	86
Invisible Waves / Khamphiphaksa Khong Mahasamut (2006)	88
Ploy (2007)	89

4 Heritage / Nostalgia — 93

Dang Bireley's and Young Gangsters / 2499 Anthaphan Khrong Mueang (1997)	94
Bang Rajan: The Legend of the Village Warriors / Bang Rajan (2000)	95
Behind the Painting / Khanglang Phap (2001)	97

Contents

	Jan Dara (2001)	98
	The Legend of Suriyothai / Suriyothai (2001)	99
	My Girl / Faen Chan (2003)	101
	The Overture / Hom Rong (2004)	103
	The Siam Renaissance / Thawi Phop (2004)	105
5	**Nang Phi / Nang Sayong Khwan / Horror**	**107**
	Nang Nak (1999)	109
	Buppha Ratri: Flower of the Night / Buppha Ratri (2003)	111
	The Unborn / Hian (2003)	113
	Sars Wars / Khun Krabi Phi Rabat (2004)	114
	Shutter / Shutter Kot Tit Winyan (2004)	116
	Zee-Oui (2004)	118
	Art of the Devil 2 / Long Khong (2005)	120
	Scared / Rap Nong Sayong Khwan (2005)	122
	13 Beloved / 13 Game Sayong (2006)	123
	Dorm / Dek Ho (2006)	125
	Ghost Game / La-Tha-Phi (2006)	126
	Ghost of Valentine / Krasue Valentine (2006)	127
	The Unseeable / Pen Chu Kap Phi (2006)	129
	The Victim / Phi Khon Pen (2006)	130
	Alone / Faet (2007)	132
	Body #19 / Body Sop 19 (2007)	133
	The House / Ban Phi Sing (2007)	135
	Coming Soon / Program Na Winyan Akhat (2008)	136
	Phobia / Si Phraeng (2008)	137
	The Screen at Kamchanod / Phi Chang Nang (2008)	139
	Meat Grinder / Chueat Kon Chim (2009)	140
	Slice / Chuean (2009)	142
	Ladda Land (2011)	143
	Pee Mak / Phi Mak Phra Khanong (2013)	145
6	**Muay Thai / Action**	**147**
	Killer Tattoo / Mue Puen Lok Phra Chan (2001)	149
	Beautiful Boxer (2003)	150
	Ong-Bak: The Thai Warrior / Ong-Bak (2003)	152
	Born To Fight / Koet Ma Lui (2004)	154
	The Bodyguard / Bodyguard Na Liam (2004)	155

Contents

The Protector / Tom Yum Kung (2005) — 157
Dynamite Warrior / Khon Fai Bin (2006) — 158
Muay Thai Chaiya / Chaiya (2007) — 160
Chocolate (2008) — 161
Raging Phoenix / Jeeja Due Suai Du (2009) — 163
Red Eagle / Insi Daeng (2010) — 164
The Gangster / Anthaphan (2012) — 166

7 Comedy / Romantic Comedy — 169

OK Baytong (2003) — 171
Sayew (2003) — 172
M.A.I.D.: Mission Almost Impossible Done / Chaeo (2004) — 173
The Holy Man / Luang Phi Teng (2005) — 175
Metrosexual / Kaeng Chani Kap I Aep (2006) — 176
Noo Hin: The Movie (2006) — 177
Seasons Change / Phro Akat Plianplaeng Boi (2006) — 178
Bus Lane / Mel Narok Muai Yok Lo (2007) — 179
E-Tim Tai Nae (2008) — 181
Bangkok Traffic Love Story / Rotfaifa Ma Ha Na Thoe (2009) — 182
Hello Stranger / Kuan Muen Ho (2010) — 183
30+ Single On Sale / 30+ Sot On Sale (2011) — 185
SuckSeed / SuckSeed: Huay Khan Thep (2011) — 186
ATM / ATM: Er Rak Error (2012) — 187
I Fine... Thank You... Love You (2014) — 189
Freelance / Freelance: Ham Puay... Ham Phak... Ham Rak Mo (2015) — 190

8 Queer Cinema — 193

The Iron Ladies / Satri Lek (2000) — 194
The Adventures of Iron Pussy / Huachai Thon Nong (2003) — 196
Bangkok Love Story / Phuean Ku Rak Mueng Wa (2007) — 198
Haunting Me / Ho Taeo Taek (2007) — 199
Love of Siam / Rak Haeng Siam (2007) — 200
Me... Myself / Kho Hai Rak Chongcharoen (2007) — 201

Contents

	This Area Is under Quarantine / Boriwen Ni Yu Phaitai Kan Kakkan (2008)	202
	Yes or No / Yes or No: Yak Rak Ko Rak Loei (2010)	204
	It Gets Better / Mai Dai Kho Hai Ma Rak (2012)	205
	Supernatural (2014)	207
9	**Animation**	209
	The Blue Elephant / Khan Kluay (2006)	210
	Nak (2008)	212
	Yak: The Giant King / Yak (2012)	213
10	**Independent Cinema**	215
	Mysterious Object at Noon / Dokfa Nai Mue Man (2000)	217
	Blissfully Yours / Sut Saneha (2002)	218
	One Night Husband / Khuen Rai Ngao (2003)	220
	Tropical Malady / Sat Pralat (2004)	221
	Syndromes and a Century / Saeng Satawat (2006)	222
	Wonderful Town / Mueang Ngao Son Rak (2007)	224
	Mundane History / Chao Nokkrachok (2009)	225
	Uncle Boonmee Who Can Recall His Past Lives / Loong Boonmee Raluek Chat (2009)	226
	Eternity / Thirak (2010)	228
	Hi-So (2010)	229
	36 (2012)	231
	In April the Following Year, There Was a Fire / Sin Me Sa Fon Tok Ma Proi Proi (2012)	232
	Mekong Hotel (2012)	234
	Concrete Clouds / Phawang Rak (2013)	235
	Mary Is Happy, Mary Is Happy (2013)	237
	Paradoxocracy / Pracha Thip'Thai (2013)	238
	The Last Executioner / Phetchakhat (2014)	240
	Bibliography	243
	Index	247

List of Illustrations

1. Kangwan in his shiny suit on business in India in *Pisat Saneha* (1969).   47
2. The cast of *Monrak Lukthung* (1970) in one of their many musical numbers.   48
3. A confused and unnerved Tum after mistakenly receiving a noodle box full of money in *6ixtynin9* (1999).   79
4. Paen and Sadao's idyllic country romance in the early parts of *Transistor Love Story* (2001).   82
5. A disillusioned Pod contemplates life as a factory worker in *Citizen Dog* (2004).   87
6. The gang of boys in 1980s provincial Thailand in *My Girl* (2003).   102
7. Close friends Jeab and Noi Na, the young protagonists of *My Girl* (2003).   103
8. A ferocious Nak lashes out at the tormentors who would send her back to the dead and away from her family in *Nang Nak* (1999).   110
9. A subdued Nak sits in her grave and says goodbye to her husband Mak under the watchful eye of the monk in *Nang Nak* (1999).   111
10. The dead Buppha stares down at her next victim in *Buppha Ratri: Flower of the Night* (2003).   112
11. Standing next to jars of preserved creatures in the university biology lab, Jane attempts to take a photograph of the ghost she believes is haunting her and her boyfriend Thun in *Shutter* (2004).   117
12. The ghostly Natre appears at the end of Thun's bed in *Shutter* (2004).   118
13. Miss Panor enacts her brutal revenge in *Art of the Devil 2* (2005).   121

14	The sinister Miss Somjit patrols the near-derelict mansion in the atmospheric *The Unseeable* (2006).	129
15	The stoical Ting reclaims Thai masculinity and virtue in *Ong-Bak: The Thai Warrior* (2003).	153
16	Hero Siang rides to the rescue on top of a rocket in *Dynamite Warrior* (2006).	159
17	The complex noir-esque protagonists of *The Gangster* (2012).	166
18	The recreated 1950s Thai cinema in *The Gangster* (2012).	167
19	The triumphant volleyball players of *The Iron Ladies* (2000).	196

List of Contributors

Mary J. Ainslie is Assistant Professor at the University of Nottingham Ningbo campus, China. She has published widely on Thai cinema and was a visiting professor at Chiang Mai University, Thailand, in 2015.

Katarzyna Ancuta is a lecturer at the Faculty of Liberal Arts, King Mongkut's Institute of Technology Ladkrabang in Bangkok, Thailand. Her research interests oscillate between the interdisciplinary contexts of contemporary Gothic/horror, more recently with a strong Asian focus.

Patipat Auprasert is a Thai writer whose by-line appears in academic and journalistic publications. His research interests focus on gender studies in both Thai and Chinese contexts.

Benjamin Baumann is an assistant professor at Humboldt-Universität zu Berlin's Institute of Asian and African Studies. His research focuses on the links between popular religion and sociocultural identities in the Thai-Cambodian borderlands.

Brian Bernards is Assistant Professor of East Asian Languages and Cultures at the University of Southern California and specializes in Chinese and Southeast Asian literature, cinema, and postcolonial studies.

Linnie Blake is Head of the Manchester Centre for Gothic Studies and the Principal Lecturer in Film at Manchester Metropolitan University, UK. When not watching Korean TV drama, she writes extensively on the Gothic's intersection with neoliberal economics.

Natalie Boehler researches and writes on cinema and other media, with a focus on East and Southeast Asia, independent transnational cinema, and the globalization of culture.

List of Contributors

Peter Braeunlein is currently Professor for the Study of Religion at the University of Leipzig, Germany. His research interests include film and media studies, ghosts, spirits and the uncertainties of modernity.

Anchalee Chaiworaporn is an independent researcher, travelling around Asia and the world to discover Asia-based film theory. Her main focus includes genre, women's films, transnational cinema, film festivals, and film criticism.

Graiwoot Chulphongsathorn is a PhD candidate at Queen Mary University of London. His thesis explores the roles of cinematic forest in global art cinemas. He also works as a film curator.

Palita Chunsaengchan is a PhD student in the Department of Comparative Literature at the University of Oregon. Her research focuses on comparative media aesthetics with a particular interest in early Thai cinema and transnational modernism.

Chanokporn Chutikamoltham is a lecturer at Thammasat University in Bangkok, Thailand. Her research interests focus on Thai cultural history as seen through the lens of cultural studies.

Yossapol Chutipanyabut is a lecturer at Assumption University, Thailand. He has worked as an editorial staff member and writer at *Computer Arts Thailand* magazine and was a judge on the sub-committee for ADFEST.

Rayna Denison is a senior lecturer in Film Studies at the University of East Anglia, UK, doing research and teaching in the areas of contemporary Asian film and animation.

Brett Farmer is a research fellow of Chulalongkorn University in Bangkok, Thailand, and an independent scholar who has been published widely in the fields of film, media and sexuality studies.

Arnika Fuhrmann (Asian Studies, Cornell University) is an interdisciplinary scholar of Southeast Asia who works at the intersections of the region's aesthetic, religious, and political modernities.

List of Contributors

Jelka Günther is a lecturer and PhD student at Georg-August University in Göttingen, Germany. Her research concentrates on mobilities (especially domestic tourism) and urban-rural dynamics in Thailand.

Andrew Hock Soon Ng is Associate Professor in Literary Studies at Monash University Malaysia. His latest book is *Women and Domestic Space in Contemporary Gothic Narratives: The House as Subject* (2015).

Dredge Kang is Assistant Professor in Anthropology at University of California San Diego. His research interests include love, beauty, sex, and violence in inter-Asian and Asian diasporic contexts.

Liew Kai Khiun is Assistant Professor at the Nanyang Technological University, Singapore. His research interests include the transnational circulation of popular entertainment in Asia.

Adam Knee is Dean of the Faculty of Fine Arts, Media & Creative Industries at Singapore's Lasalle College of the Arts. He has published widely on Asian and US popular cinemas.

Bogna M. Konior is a scholar, a curator, and an artist. She is currently based in Hong Kong, where she is completing her dissertation on activist art through the lens of decolonial and post-humanist theory.

Mikel J. Koven is Senior Lecturer in Film Studies at the University of Worcester, UK. His books include *La Dolce Morte: Vernacular Cinema and the Italian Giallo Film* (2006) and *Film, Folklore and Urban Legends* (2008).

Kom Kunyosying, an independent scholar, has published essays on the relationship between images and metonymy in ecological media, the rise of geek culture, and the popularity of hyperreal hillbilly protagonists.

Pasoot Lasuka is a lecturer in literary and cultural studies at Chiang Mai University, Thailand. He is interested in the power of audiovisual narratives in relation to consumption culture.

Philippa Lovatt is Lecturer in Media and Communications at University of Stirling, UK, and PI on the AHRC-funded Southeast Asian Cinemas Research Network: "Promoting Dialogue Across Critical and Creative Practice."

List of Contributors

Daniel Martin is Associate Professor of Film Studies at KAIST in South Korea, and the author of *Extreme Asia: The Rise of Cult Cinema from the Far East* (2015).

Jovan Maud is a lecturer at Georg-August University in Göttingen, Germany. His research focuses on popular Buddhism in the Southern Thai borderland and, more recently, on online religiosity.

Natthanai Prasannam is an associate professor of Thai literary and cultural studies at Kasetsart University in Bangkok, Thailand. His research interests include modern Thai literature, adaptation studies and memory studies.

Wikanda Promkhuntong is a lecturer at the Research Institute of Languages and Cultures of Asia, Mahidol University, Thailand. Her interests are in East Asian film cultures including star-auteurs and fan/cinephile practices.

Raphael Raphael lectures at the University of Hawai'i at Mānoa. His interests include transnational film and celebrity, genre, disability and technology. His scholarship is also informed by his practice as a filmmaker.

Jesse Sessoms is formerly a lecturer at Burapha International University, in Bang Saen, Thailand. He is currently taking time off to pursue his passion for writing.

Sophia Siddique is an associate professor and chair of the Department of Film, Vassar College. Her research interests include genre theory (global science fiction and horror), Singapore cultural studies, representations of trauma and memory in Cambodian, Indonesian, and Thai cinema, and the impact of new media on Southeast Asia's moving image culture.

Lalita Singhasri is an independent scholar and Thai language instructor based in Los Angeles who is interested in critical mixed-race theory, issues of body as text, and in/authenticity politics.

Patsorn Sungsri is a lecturer at Rajamangala University of Technology Thanyaburi in Pathum Thani, Thailand. Her research focuses on the representation of nation, religion, and monarchy in the development of Thai national cinema.

List of Contributors

Rebecca Townsend received her PhD in Southeast Asian History at Cornell University. Her research focuses on the international political economy of gender in Thailand during the Cold War.

Noah Viernes is Assistant Professor at Akita International University in Akita City, Japan. His current research focuses on collectivity and political expression in poetry, cinema, and photography.

Introduction

The days in which Southeast Asian cinema was absent on global screens are over. Today, alongside Japan, South Korea, China, India and other major East and South Asian nations, we now see the emergence of Malaysia, Singapore, Indonesia, Vietnam and other Southeast Asian cinematographies taking their place on DVD racks around the world and in major global film festivals. However, while this region continues to grow in international film prominence, it is Thai cinema that has been the most consistent Southeast Asian presence on the global cinema screen. Spurred on by the success of Muay Thai films such as *Ong-Bak* (2003), the international remakes of horror films such as *Shutter* (2004) and *13 Beloved* (2006), the festival success of *kathoei* comedies such as *The Iron Ladies* (2000), and the substantial awards collected by avant-garde auteur Apichatpong Weerasethakul, Thai film has now taken centre stage among national industries and is arguably the most prolific and fastest growing industry from this region, as well as the most popular internationally. While academic analysis of Thai and Southeast Asian film was previously "tacked on" to collections more focused upon East Asian film, research addressing media within this particular region is now increasing, and the next decade is likely to see a glut of emerging collections, both scholarly and popular, addressing Thai cinema.

Alongside such international proliferation, there is increased demand for more insight into Thai filmmaking and its rich history from both Thai and non-Thai audiences. For the non-Thai viewer, the cinematic traditions of this nation can seem perplexing, and beg the need for more explanation. Traditional genre categories can also seem inadequate when faced with the generic blending typical of Thai film, and indeed it is difficult to place the horror comedies of Yuthlert Sippapak, among others, and the much remade ghostly love story of Mae Nak within these foreign generic parameters. Likewise, while film now enjoys a much more central position as a part of the nation's heritage, filmmakers and studios still hold a problematic relationship to the state, and the confines of unclear and subjective guidelines together with successive and ongoing changes of government has left an industry reeling from uncertainty and confusion.

Despite the increased saturation of international markets with Thai cinema, Thai and non-Thai film enthusiasts still struggle to access detailed information and scholarly analysis of Thai filmmaking. Even many high-grossing Thai films do not travel outside of the country and are difficult to source, while few are released with non-Thai subtitles. Similarly, some Thai independent films play exclusively to foreign festival audiences and are never theatrically released, or find a distributor in Thailand. There are also those that have incurred the wrath of government censors and have been significantly cut or banned from screening in the country. Let us also not forget that there is still a lack of book-length English language resources or guides to Thai film. Online sources, which tend to be incomplete, are often the only source of information available to those who take an interest in this growing industry. Existing literature overwhelmingly focuses upon the most readily available post-millennial Thai films, meaning many scholars and fans are unable to access Thailand's equally rich cinematic past.

Thankfully the history of Thai cinema has been largely documented due to a handful of determined individuals at the Thai film archive, who have gathered a wealth of resources over the decades and to whom Thai heritage owes a significant debt. Indeed, the archives and their attached museum have done much to preserve the rich history of filmmaking and film-going within the country that might otherwise have been lost. For cinephiles no trip to Bangkok is now complete without a bus ride to

Introduction

the well-kept museum and archives in the suburbs, which has likewise expanded dramatically over the past decade, and finally been delivered some long-sought-after and much-deserved funding.

In light of increased interest in this national cinema, this book seeks to partially address the substantial space created by this general lack of information and so offer limited insight into Thai filmmaking and the Thai industry for scholars and cinephiles within and outside Thailand. Gathering together a host of Thai and international academics at various stages in their careers, this collection will provide a detailed guide to major Thai films and filmmakers in Thailand. All of the contributors in this volume have a specific interest in Thai cinema, be it from a Thai cultural studies perspective or from a film studies background. A number of authors also have specific practical links to Thai filmmaking, and bring particular insight to the position of such productions within the contemporary industry. Others are historians and understand the complex development of media within a context that placed specific industrial, technological and political constraints upon such cultural products, shaping this form of entertainment in unique ways.

Given the proliferation of Thai cinema and the changes undergone in the industry since the millennium, the majority of the collection focuses upon this contemporary industry, with a separate smaller section addressing key productions from earlier in the twentieth century. This is also motivated by the fact that such newer films are more easily available today for both Thai and non-Thai audiences. Older Thai films can rarely be found in DVD shops both locally and internationally, and while many of them can be accessed at the Thai film archive, the copies usually do not include non-Thai subtitles. Moreover, many early Thai films, including films from the prolific post-World War II 16mm era, are today considered lost, or exist in limited out-of-print editions of such poor quality (usually formatted as VCDs) that they are almost impossible to watch.

Contemporary productions introduced in this book have been divided into separate sections designed to distinguish between the various genres present in Thai filmmaking. Ultimately such genre divisions are problematic and rely upon decisions that are highly subjective, with many films able to cross such boundaries with ease, such is the nature of Thai cinema.

Likewise, while some genre categories, such as Horror and Comedy, will be familiar to international viewers, others, such as New Thai Cinema and Heritage/Nostalgia, may be more puzzling. Each section therefore contains an introduction that gives an explanation as to the nature and development of these categories and provides some justification for the inclusion of the titles therein.

Films are listed by the year of release and, whenever possible, priority is given to English titles. Thai filmmakers, as well as Thai scholars, are listed by their surnames rather than first names, which is common in Thai referencing systems, to avoid unnecessary confusion for non-Thai readers. The Thai film titles in the book (as well as any terms in the Thai language) have been transliterated in accordance with the Royal Thai General System of Transcription, or RTGS, in order to standardize the spelling. At this point it is necessary to mention that both the titles of Thai films and the names of actors and directors follow multiple spellings and are often recorded differently on posters, in the film credits, on DVDs, and in various film databases. While RTGS is a locally and internationally accepted system of transliteration of the Thai script, most commonly Thai names are just transcribed as anyone sees fit resulting in the same films and filmmakers being inevitably referenced under multiple titles and names. This is additionally complicated by the fact that Thai films frequently change their Thai and English titles between theatrical release and DVD distribution.

The presence of Thai films in the IMDb online database has increased significantly over the last few years but given that the data is inserted by the filmmakers or producers themselves, no transliteration rules apply. In fact, some of the film directors have several profiles under different names, and some have managed to change the spelling of their names several times within the last decade. While we do acknowledge the importance of IMDb as the most readily accessible online source for those who want to learn more about Thai cinema past and present, which also includes academic researchers, it is also important to mention that it is an incomplete and inconsistent source that has been known to provide misleading information. Faced with an impossible task of organizing such incompatible data, we felt that unifying the transcription of the film titles may be a small step in this direction. The names of the Thai actors and directors have been kept in the current spelling provided in the IMDb database, since this is how they are usually promoted internationally.

The structure of the book acknowledges the most commonly held critical opinion dividing Thai cinema into pre-1997 and post-1997 productions, with the 1997 release of Nonzee Nimibutr's film *Dang Bireley's and Young Gangsters* considered to be the film separating the New Thai cinema from the Old. The first section of the book, Key Early Productions, introduces selected significant films made before 1997. While this short section certainly does not give justice to almost a century of Thai filmmaking, the selection includes works which proved particularly influential for later filmmakers.

The discussion of contemporary cinema begins with the introduction of New Thai Cinema, two categories that reflect profound economic and cultural changes taking place in Thai society at the turn of the millennium and in the aftermath of the 1997 Asian Crisis. This includes the promotion of nationalistic discourses of Thai-ness tinged with nostalgia for a perfect imagined community of the past. This is followed by three sections addressing Thai reconfigurations of the more universal cinematic genres of horror, comedy, and action. The collection also features a very short section on Thai animation to acknowledge its presence within the Thai industry as an emerging film form. Last but not least, the book addresses two categories most familiar to festival audiences outside of Thailand, Thai Queer and Independent Cinema, both largely a product of the twenty-first-century changes within the Thai industry.

While the reviews of films comprise a large part of the book, the collection also includes a short section addressing key directors in Thai filmmaking (also listed alphabetically), singling out those whose contributions have been deemed particularly significant in light of their artistic merits and stylistic consistency. This section is regrettably short due to word limit, and focuses largely on the older generation of Thai filmmakers. Given the fact that in the recent years we have seen the appearance of promising young talent, it is of no doubt that the future will bring to light many more contributions worthy of inclusion.

As always, due to word count it has not been possible to include all the films that deserve mention and to acknowledge all filmmakers who deserve recognition. We are particularly regretful that we did not manage to include sections on Thai documentary, as well as short and experimental films that are among the most interesting recent productions. Instead, editors were left with the unenvious task of distinguishing the individuals and films that best allow us to map the current condition of Thai cinema. We hope that such choices will at least meet the approval of readers and so provide some insight into this dynamic and impressive national cinema.

Mary J. Ainslie and Katarzyna Ancuta

1

Key Directors

Nonzee Nimibutr

A Thai film director, producer and screenwriter, Nonzee Nimibutr was born on 18 December 1962 in Nonthaburi, a neighbouring province of Bangkok. Nimibutr pursued his higher education at Silpakorn University (formerly known as the University of Fine Arts) and attained his bachelor's degree in visual communication design in 1987. Nimibutr's early career was related to television documentary production, yet over the years he crafted scripts and edited television shows before moving to Rotfai Dontri (Music Train) Company. He first worked as a producer, then a creative director, of music videos, radio spots and television shows, founding Buddy Film and Video Production Company during the early 1990s producing concerts, mini-series and commercials for advertising agencies.

Nimibutr is considered a key director in the New Thai Cinema era. His début, *Dang Bireley's and Young Gangsters* (1997), was a hit at the domestic box office before going on to screen at Vancouver and other film festivals. The film responded to nostalgic discourses of the time by combining depictions of Buddhism and references to Hong Kong gangster films set during the Cold War era. This was the beginning of Nimibutr's *Thai-thae* or vernacular Thai aesthetics that appealed to both national and international audiences. In 1999, acclaimed Thai heritage film *Nang Nak* was released, a film that reconstructed a much more realistic version of "old Siam" and revitalized Thai folk tales as a new form of horror film. *Nang Nak* received a hugely positive reception among film audiences and film studies scholars in Thailand and beyond, winning the best film award at the Asia-Pacific Film Festival that year.

Continuing this fascination with a very lucrative version of Thai nostalgia, in 2001 Nimibutr adapted the period erotic novel *Jan Dara* into a film. This also introduced the director to transnational collaboration, as Hong Kong actress Christy Chung played a character in the film. Likewise, in 2002, Nimibutr filmed *The Wheel*, produced by his own Cinemasia Company, a segment of the film *Three* (2002) which also included segments from Hong Kong and Korean directors. This development echoed the "Pan-Asian" and transnational elements favoured by the New Thai directors.

Nimibutr then shifted his interests to the Southern Thai situation, making *OK Baytong* (2003), which told the story of a Buddhist monk who has to take care of his Muslim niece. The film transformed ethnic and religious controversy into a "feel-good" story. Likewise, *Queens of Langkasuka* (2008) which was partly funded by the transnational "Nova Group," was adapted from a renowned writer's novel and portrays a fantasy representation of the history of the Pattani Kingdom of Thailand's South. Nimibutr's experimental spirit was then shown in *Distortion* (2012), a crime film and psychological thriller for which he also was a producer.

Nimibutr worked as a film producer for several films, including on Wisit Sasanatieng's renowned *Tears of the Black Tiger* (2000), Pen-Ek Ratanaruang's *Transistor Love Story* (2001) and *Last Life in the Universe* (2003), as well as Ittisoontorn Vichailak's *The Overture* (2004). He also produced Pha-un Chanthonsiri's *The Letter* (2004) and later filmed its sequel *Timeline* (2014). The famous teen stars who perform in the film are also reminiscent of Nimibutr's former career beginnings as a music video director.

As a key New Thai Cinema director, Nimibutr is a renowned and respected figure in the Thai industry. He chaired the Thai Film Directors

Association before receiving the Silpathorn Award from the Thai Ministry of Culture in 2008. In recent years he also turned to directing Thai television series', including *The Four Elements* (2009), *Above the Cloud* (2010) and *The Sorcerer* (2012), so continuing to play an active role in the Thai media industries.

Natthanai Prasannam

Ratana Pestonji

To scholars of Thai film history, Ratana Pestonji needs little introduction. Variously called the "father" of Thai film, the "pioneer" of Thai cinema and even "the man who died for his art," Pestonji, for many, remains symbolic of all that is wrong with Thai cinema's ongoing difficult relationship with the Thai state. For filmmakers and cinephiles who lament the lack of official support for filmmaking and the overwhelming presence of foreign films in the country, Pestonji takes pride of place in Thai film history as a rare early Thai auteur untouched by the trappings of commercial filmmaking and bravely fighting against the monopolizing Hollywood system. Indeed, the recent interest in and recognition of Pestonji's films speaks of the need to reclaim an alternative and artistic thread in Thai film history besides that of the mass produced 16mm productions which, despite their innovation, still bear the stigma of rampant commercialism and Thai lower-class preferences. Pestonji's films are now favourites at international festivals and provide global cinephiles with a rare perspective on Southeast Asian film history.

Yet given this hugely symbolic status in Thai film history, it is at times difficult to separate the man from the mythology and to identify Pestonji's role and place as an actual filmmaker. Born in 1908 to Persian immigrants, Pestonji's talents are evident in any exhibition of his available work, including his skill as a still life photographer, which is often overlooked in favour of his films. Pestonji originally studied engineering in the UK but seems to have retained a strong interest in film and photography, becoming a salesman of film stock upon his return to Thailand. A number of Pestonji's early short films received accolades at festivals, with the 1937/38 film *Tang* resulting in a much touted photograph of Pestonji with Alfred Hitchcock, and which sources point to as the first time in history that a Thai film won a foreign award.

Yet while Pestonji remains a strong symbol of resistance against the influx of foreign films, the filmmaker's actual history and relationship with the Hollywood studios in Thailand is complex. After becoming a cinematographer, Pestonji worked closely with American filmmakers in Thailand in the 1950s, as such foreign support and cooperation would have enabled the director to work with the best facilities and equipment available in the country at the time. However, this entirely logical and understandable integration is often overlooked in favour of the later more nationalistic role he occupies as a struggling artist expressing strong criticism of "predatory" foreign films in Thailand. Indeed, this earlier role is not so well documented and remains shrowded in mystery. Hollywood studios were connected to the importance of cultivating filmmaking as a means of pushing anti-Communist propaganda in East and Southeast Asia. Around a minute of film exists depicting Pestonji working with Hollywood writer Robert North, the vice-president of the newly formed "Far East Film Ltd" (also known as Hanuman Film) of which Pestonji was the president. Sources indicate that North and his wife were in contact with Richard Nixon and regularly expressed anti-Communist concerns, though there is as yet no evidence directly connecting Pestonji to such activities.

North's sudden and untimely death in 1954 meant that such cooperation quickly ceased, and Pestonji continued his passion alone, though he is mentioned in Hollywood sources at the time. The filmmaker continued making his own films in 35mm film stock throughout the 1950s and 1960s, constantly lamenting Thai authorities' lack of support for local filmmaking right up until his own untimely death in 1970. It is during this period that Pestonji's talent as a filmmaker is most evident. The tragic storylines, stylish and compelling *mise-en-scène* of productions such as *Country Hotel* (1957), *Black Silk* (1961) and *Sugar Is Not Sweet* (1965) are all outstanding and impressive, even if their lack of commercial success makes the actual role of such productions in Thai film development at the time probably negligible. The noir-esque qualities of both film style and storylines display an awareness of international filmmaking that is undoubtedly unique in Thailand at this time. However, working apart from both the international and internal film systems was undoubtedly difficult and frustrating, and although the true state of his health at the time is unknown, it is certainly understandable that Pestonji's untimely death in 1970 is often attributed to such pressure and dissatisfaction. Perhaps fittingly, his fatal heart attack occurred during a speech given to Thai government officials about the need for more support for Thai filmmaking, so sealing his fate as a tragic artist forevermore.

Mary J. Ainslie

Prachya Pinkaew

As the producer-director of such internationally renowned Muay Thai blockbusters as *Ong-Bak: The Thai Warrior* (2003), *The Protector* (2005) and *Chocolate* (2008), Prachya Pinkaew is heavily associated with both the action genre and the Thai film revival since 1997. However, the attachment to this specific genre and films means that Pinkaew's very weighty overall contribution to Thai film development throughout the earlier period of the 1990s is too often overlooked, along with his very capable and durable presence behind the scenes as a driving force behind Thai filmmakers and the filmmaking industry.

Possibly the most generically versatile out of all the current active directors in Thailand, Prachya Pinkaew offers a rich and varied body of work since his advertising beginnings in the early 1990s. As part of the teen movie industry before the 1997 resurgence of Thai cinema internationally, Pinkaew's films embodied the sentiments of this time, with Pinkaew's directorial debut, *The Magic Shoes* (1992) and his later teen romance thriller *Dark Side Romance* (1995), both seminal films in the immediate pre-1997 teen movie era.

Indeed, Pinkaew's skills, honed in his advertising and teen era music video origins, are evident in the short takes, extreme angles and striking soundscapes of his later fast-paced blockbusters such as *Ong-Bak* and *The Protector*. Combined with his notorious insistence upon making fight scenes as realistic as possible, it is perhaps not surprising that it is within the Muay Thai genre that the director derives most of his high level commercial success and his international reputation. Pinkaew was also arguably responsible for the revival of the Thai action genre after successfully highlighting the cinematic potential of the impressive performances of future key players such as martial arts star Tony Jaa and martial arts choreographer Panna Rittikrai to Thai film studios. Thanks in part to Pinkaew, material that was previously relegated to low budget VCD action flicks became a defining and highly profitable part of the new Thai film industry. After the international success of *Ong-Bak*, Pinkaew's repertoire largely remained within Muay Thai productions, and the director expressed some frustration at being expected to stay within this genre. Working within such studio expectations however, Pinkaew was able to experiment creatively with this genre, directing *Chocolate*, his only Muay Thai film with a central female character.

Notably, it is in Pinkaew's position as a producer that his influence is most apparent. As the owner of Baa-Ram-Ewe Production Studio, working in close cooperation with Sahamongkol Film, he has been the driving force behind many commercially successful Thai productions. His expertise stretches across both the commercialized and sensational appeal of *Ong-Bak* to that of smaller art and horror productions. As a producer, Pinkaew turned to comedy (*Sayew*, 2003, *The Sperm*, 2007), horror (*Sick Nurses*, 2007, *Opapatika*, 2007) and romance (*Midnight My Love*, 2005, *Love of Siam*, 2007), and his frequent partnership with younger more inexperienced directors speaks of Pinkaew's personal effort and desire to further cultivate the Thai industry, to the extent that he appears often content to stay out of the limelight. Such collaboration ensures that smaller Thai films and lesser known Thai directors are often given international exposure and opportunities that would not otherwise be available, as Pinkaew is particularly adept at mixing local preferences and tastes alongside the global standards required and expected by international festivals and cinephiles. Indeed, Pinkaew remains one of the few Thai directors known for his international collaborations, including *Elephant White* (2011), starring Djimon Hounsou and Kevin Bacon, and the Korean co-production *The Kick* (2011).

As a continuing presence within the Thai industry and a strongly influential figure, Pinkaew's impression upon Thai cinema should not be underestimated. Yet this importance is also underlined by the director's willingness to grapple with authoritarian constraints. Pinkaew was an open critic of Thai censorship regulations during the 2000s, questioning both the merit and motivations of such a system, particularly around the more draconian code proposed in 2007. Indeed Pinkaew has been involved in some controversial films, as producer for *Abat* (2015), a Buddhist-themed horror film that was originally pulled days before its release by the Thai Film Board, who then relented after some shots were removed from the final edit.

Mary J. Ainslie

Banjong Pisanthanakun

Representing a new and younger generation of Thai filmmakers, Banjong Pisanthanakun could be called the most successful commercial director Thailand has ever had. Holding a degree in film from Chulalongkorn University, Pisanthanakun made waves with his directorial debut, *Shutter* (2004), which he co-directed with Parkpoom Wongpoom. Telling the story of a ghost who exacts revenge upon her abusers through a haunted camera, *Shutter* remains the best known Thai horror film in the world and the first Thai film to be officially remade in Hollywood, as *Shutter* (2008), and (perhaps not so officially) in Bollywood, as *Click* (2010). In 2007, Pisanthanakun and Wongpoom returned as co-directors with another successful horror movie, *Alone*, this time scaring the world with the story of conjoined twins and their fatal separation.

Pisanthanakun's love of horror made him embark on several joint projects with Thai and international directors. He directed short segments for both *Phobia* (2008) and *Phobia 2* (2009). The first, *In the Middle*, tells a story of a group of friends who go hiking in the woods only to get haunted by a ghost of their friend who died in a camping accident, while the second, *In the End*, takes place on a movie set where the crew suspects that one of the actresses may in fact be a ghost. Both of these short films offer their audiences a well-balanced combination of scares and laughter, where the comedy is mostly dialogue driven and enhanced by effective performances from the actors.

While Pisanthanakun's contributions to the *Phobia* horror omnibuses may be short, they mark a significant point in his career as they cemented his association with the GTH studio and so forecast his turn away from horror and towards comedy. Released in 2010, *Hello Stranger* was the first of Pisanthanakun's romantic comedies, engaging with the ever growing influence of Korean popular culture in Thailand. The film follows an unlikely couple on a trip to Korea where they gradually grow closer only to eventually part ways. In 2016, Pisanthanakun returned with a similar story in *One Day*, this time taking his protagonists to Japan. Just like before, the love affair depicted in the film comes with a termination date. Now, a lonely IT worker takes a chance to spend one day with the girl he loves, exploiting the fact that she suffers from temporary memory loss and believes him to be her boyfriend. The film was released to launch the GDH 559 production house, following the breakup of GTH. Romantic comedy is also part of Pisanthanakun's most commercially successful film to date: *Pee Mak* (2013) is a ghost love story which returns to the tale of Mae Nak, the beloved Thai ghostly wife. Retelling the story from the perspective of Nak's husband Mak, this was notably the first adaptation in which Mae Nak's transgressive romance had a happy ending. The film broke all records and became the top grossing Thai film in history as well as an international phenomenon.

Katarzyna Ancuta

Pen-Ek Ratanaruang

Since his directorial debut in the late 1990s, Pen-Ek Ratanaruang has remained one of the most significant and consistent directors of contemporary Thai cinema, a status that has already earned him international recognition as an auteur. His early films, *Fun Bar Karaoke* (1997), *6ixtynin9* (1999), and *Transistor Love Story* (2001) were among productions that redefined Thai filmmaking and contributed to the formation of what is known today as New Thai Cinema. While not describing any coherent artistic movement, this label was originally applied to the films that appeared in the late 1990s and were characterized by higher production values and broader, more complex themes. This change is generally attributed to the emergence of a new generation of directors with backgrounds in art and design, and experience in commercial advertising, of which Ratanaruang is no exception.

Born in 1962, Ratanaruang studied at the Pratt Institute in New York in the early 1980s, also working as a designer and illustrator. In 1993, he started work at The Film Factory, a production company mostly known for television commercials, which also helped produce some of his films. He debuted in 1997 with *Fun Bar Karoke*, the story of a girl who falls in love with a hitman sent to kill her father. Depictions of the unsavoury yet ordinary world of mobsters, contract killers, and bar hostesses living their mundane lives alongside other equally invisible professions, seem to be a recurring motif in Ratanaruang's films: *6ixtynin9* focuses on a woman who finds herself running from gansters after picking up a delivery that was mistakenly left at her door; *Invisible Waves* (2006) makes crime international, following a Japanese gangster (Tadanobu Asano) on the run from Macau to Thailand; while *Headshot* (2011), based on a novel from a Thai author Win Lyovarin, introduces a contract killer whose life is literally turned upside down because of a bizarre medical condition that affects his vision.

Other recurring motifs include accidental encounters between people that result in their lives changing course, indeed in Ratanaruang's films human life is full of choices and "what if" moments. In *Transistor Love Story* a young, simple country boy is given a chance to become a star only to learn that not all dreams are perhaps worth chasing; in *Last Life in the Universe* (2003) a suicidal Japanese man finds comfort in an unlikely companion who seems to be his exact opposite; *Ploy* (2007) ponders over the death of a relationship, as a disillusioned married couple meet strangers who act as vehicles of sexual desires, jealousy, and dangerous obsessions; while *Nymph* (2009) makes use of the forest spirits to portray how bad relationships can get.

Ratanaruang is among the most critically acclaimed Thai directors and has received a fair share of awards and nominations within the Thai industry. His films are regularly screened at notable film festivals, including Cannes, Berlin and Venice, and three have been sent as Thailand's official entry for Oscars. Despite the fact that his films are often promoted as arthouse, Ratanaruang insists that they are first of all commercial, stating "they need to play in the cinema, they need to make money back, and they need to relate to the audience" (quoted in Ancuta, 2011, p. 216). Perhaps the largest challenge to this claim came in 2013 with the release of *Paradoxocracy*, a sociopolitical documentary on Thai politics and the democratization of Thai society since 1932, all of which reflected upon the country's deep political divisions in the contemporary era. Heavily censored, the film had a short limited run in selected Bangkok cinemas and made history as the first Thai film to be screened while the cinema was simultaneously denying that the screenings were taking place and refusing to sell the tickets. Given the reluctance of Thai filmmakers to openly address political topics due to harsh censorship rules making open debate impossible, *Paradoxocracy* remains a tough act to follow and a testament to the director's integrity.

Katarzyna Ancuta

Wisit Sasanatieng

Born in Bangkok on the 28th June 1963, Wisit Sasanatieng is a prolific Thai film director and screenwriter. His creativity was honed at the Faculty of Decorative Arts, Silpakorn University where he earned his undergraduate degree. As with so many New Thai filmmakers Sasanatieng began his career making television commercials, but this changed when he joined with his classmate Nonzee Nimibutr and wrote the screenplays for Nimibutr's *Dang Bireley's and Young Gangsters* (1997) and *Nang Nak* (1999).

Sasanatieng is considered one of the key New Thai directors of the post-2000 era, with his signature saturated "chromophilia" represented since his feature film début *Tears of the Black Tiger* (2000). His films are often referred to as *nang naeo* or alternative films, the term *naeo* being associated with postmodern characteristics recognized by film scholars. Notably the materials used in Sasanatieng's films are "vernacularly" Thai but are also intertwined with representations of foreignness, marking an intertextual and postmodern style of filmmaking. A nostalgia for past "Thai-ness" is combined with humour, with *Tears of the Black Tiger* a true exemplar of this. This film is a heavily melodramatic version of the Western, but also contains references to post-war Thai cinema, the Thai star system and Buddhism. Similarly, *Citizen Dog* (2004) was a magical realist fantasy that also criticized urbanisation and consumerism in the millennial era. Another vernacular Thai film was *The Unseeable* (2006), a Gothic-inspired horror film which again referenced Thai film history, particularly the ten-*satang* (one-baht) graphic horror novels. Likewise, *Red Eagle* (2010) also paid homage to the legacy of Thai action-adventure films of the late 1950s and the great post-war Thai actor Mitr Chaibancha. This film was also influenced by Hollywood superhero films: the villains are part of a transnational crime organization and the hero is a psychologically damaged and conflicted individual. In recent years Sasanatieng has continued to make films and has also branched out into writing, following his spouse Siriphan Taechachiadawong who wrote the novel versions of *Tears of the Black Tiger* and *Citizen Dog*. In 2015, his teen film *Senior* was screened, another *naeo* film which fused horror and romance and also included references to Japanese horror.

Many of Sasanatieng's films were not commercially successful with Thai audiences, instead his films were designed to *go inter*, to appeal to international rather than domestic audiences. *Tears of the Black Tiger* was screened at the Cannes Film Festival and the Vancouver International Film Festival, where Sasanatieng won the Dragons and Tigers Award. *Citizen Dog* screened at the Berlin Film Festival, the Toronto International Film Festival, the San Francisco International Asian American Film Festival and even some commercial cinemas in France. This international recognition also resulted in Sasanatieng being awarded the Critics Prize from the Deauville Asian Film Festival, the Silver Prize for Most Groundbreaking Film and the Bronze Prize for Best Asian Film at Fantasia Festival in Montreal, Canada, all of which demonstrate Sasanatieng's significance as an international contemporary filmmaker. As a result of such recognition, Sasanatieng also received the Silpathorn Award sponsored by Thailand's Ministry of Culture in 2006.

Natthanai Prasannam

Yuthlert Sippapak

To a large extent, Yuthlert Sippapak embodies the creative energy of the contemporary Thai film industry. Outside of Thailand, he has gained critical attention for his striking visuals, surreal storylines, and daring genre mixing, all of which have been hailed as innovatory. At the same time, those familiar with the history of Thai film will clearly recognize Sippapak's stylistic debt to earlier generations of filmmakers, particularly those active in the post-World War II 16mm era. Often focused on a group of protagonists rather than an individual hero, these early films propagated a type of filmmaking that escaped the confines of cinematic genres, revealing the plot through a series of fragmented narratives and spicing every story with a large dose of laughs. Indeed, Sippapak's films fit snuggly into this tradition.

Born in 1966, Sippapak entered his cinematic career alongside the giants of New Thai Cinema – Nonzee Nimibutr, Wisit Sasanatieng and Pen-Ek Ratanaruang. In their company, however, Sippapak appears to be the underdog, his early attempts at filmmaking notably marked by studio rejections of his minimal scripts. Yet things have changed greatly since the release of his debut film *Killer Tattoo* (2001), a bizarre comedy about a group of aged and mentally unstable hitmen who find themselves on the wrong end of the contract. This film began a long-lasting association with the colourful world of Thai comedians, who Sippapak often chooses to cast in dramatic roles. This dissonance between the personalities of actors and the roles they are meant to portray has become a trademark style of Sippapak.

Sippapak's films can often be considered quintessentially Thai, utilizing the formula known locally as *talok-phi-kathoei*, demanding a necessary inclusion of slapstick elements, ghosts and transsexuals into any film plot regardless of the genre. This pattern is perhaps most visible in his 2007 film, *Ghost Station* which puts together elements of horror, Western and gay romance in a bizarre Thai tribute to *Brokeback Mountain* (2005). The director's persistent return to the dysfunctional world of gangsters and petty crooks speaks volumes about his fascination with mid-twentieth-century Hong Kong action cinema, whether depicting gun-slinging hitmen as in *Friday Killer* (2011), or the martial-arts trained assassins of *Bangkok Kung Fu* (2011).

Sippapak gained much of his fame thanks to a series of films featuring the ghost of a broken-hearted student who refused to be removed from her rented apartment. *Buppha Ratri* (2003), *Buppha Ratri Phase 2: Ratri Returns* (2005), *Buppha Ratri 3.1* (2009), and *Buppha Ratri 3.2* (2009) can be seen as a Thai response to the cinematic Japanese long-haired ghosts, and it was

Ratri who represented Thailand on the global horror stage before anyone had heard of *Shutter* (2004). Other notable contributions of Sippapak to the world of Thai ghost films include *Ghost of Valentine* (2006) which tells the story of a nurse working at a derelict hospital who transforms into the iconic Thai spirit *phi krasue*, depicted as a flying head detached from a body trailing its internal organs behind. Likewise, *Haunting in Japan* (2016) is an intertextual nod towards the Japanese horror films that remain so infuential in the region. Despite being penned as a director of comedies and horror films however, Sippapak does not shy from more serious matters. His second film, *February* (2003) told the story of a dying woman who suffers memory loss and embraces her new life, all the while not knowing it is about to end. The more recent *Fatherland* (2012) also tackles the much politicized issue of the violent unrest between Buddhists and Muslims in the Southern provinces.

Katarzyna Ancuta

Cherd Songsri

Often called the "master" of Thai film, Cherd Songsri's career is a rarity in Thai cinema; spanning five decades of filmmaking, Songsri's productions straddle the many varied incarnations of Thai film throughout history. Working in 16mm during the 1960s right up to the big budget New Thai industry of the 2000s, Songsri was a continuous presence in Thai filmmaking. Even more unusual, was his international proliferation and success during these early periods, with films such as *The Scar* (1977) and *Muen and Rid* (1994) shown overseas in Japan, Europe and even South America, long before the interest shown today.

Songsri's experience studying filmmaking abroad in the US caused him to turn inwards, recognizing that exploring and depicting national symbols was the best way to distinguish oneself locally and globally onscreen. As such, Songsri's films are filled with traditional representations of Thailand that, at times, border on the stereotypical. These recognizable representations of Thai culture include many depictions of fantastical and lavish historical periods (*The Siam Renaissance*, 1990, *House of the Peacock*, 1996), traditional dancing (*Norah*, 1966) and songs (*Lampoo*, 1970), which garnered much success and popularity both within the country and without. However, while such films, on the surface, can appear very nationalistic in their display of "Thai-ness," Songsri did not shy away from depicting difficult and problematic situations caused by issues such as inequality, poverty and the pressure of social obligation. Indeed, Songsri's topics bear the hallmarks of Thailand's difficult and divided society, addressing lovers separated across social divides, as well as the difficult world of prostitution, the restrictions of parental control and the often tragic consequences of challenging such inequality.

Despite his central role in these previous eras of Thai cinema, Songsri's filmmaking continued into the birth of the contemporary industry, and he remained an active part of Thai filmmaking. A familiar figure at film festivals in Thailand, Songsri's unwavering and constant presence in the Thai film industry ensured he remained a figure of reassurance for younger contemporary directors and a comforting connection to the traditions of old for those otherwise divorced from previous eras. His last film, *Behind the Painting* (2001), was an adaptation of a controversial yet highly acclaimed novel that addresses the tricky topic of class divisions, and has been interpreted in the Marxist sense as representing the breakdown of such older class divisions in the 1930s, again illustrating Songsri's hunger for difficult social topics. After his death from cancer in 2006 aged 74, Songsri's obituaries spread across the global filmmaking community, with accolades arriving from around the world. Thai filmmakers, meanwhile, were faced with the unthinkable situation of continuing without the constant presence of the "master" of Thai cinema.

Mary J. Ainslie

Apichatpong Weerasethakul

One of the most influential directors in contemporary Thai cinema, Apichatpong Weerasethakul has had a profound impact on the development of independent Thai cinema in the last two decades. After receiving his bachelor's degree in Architecture from Khon Kaen University in the Northeast of Thailand, the director obtained a master's degree of Fine Arts in filmmaking from the School of the Art Institute of Chicago.

Weerasethakul then returned to his homeland and immersed himself in the art scene and cinephile community in Bangkok. The director participated in and showcased his works at local art exhibitions and the Thai Short Film and Video Festival organized by the Thai Film Foundation, which has since cultivated a growing pool of young Thai filmmakers who are interested in making films outside the studio system.

Unlike the previous generation of Thai directors who largely emerged from local film studios and the marketing industry, Weerasethakul has been part of a network of East Asian directors at international film festivals who were supported by film funding initiatives and award recognitions. His first feature *Mysterious Object at Noon* (2000) was awarded the Hubert Bals Fund from the International Film Festival Rotterdam, a rare early success for Thai independent cinema, as the festival sought to reach out to directors across the developing world. Uniquely combining Western avant-garde traditions and documentary filmmaking with stories of working class people across Thailand and the fantasy worlds they construct, the high level of critical interest in the film paved the way for the director's later international collaborations and filmmaking career.

Weerasethakul's subsequent films were largely funded by art patrons and European film funding platforms. *Blissfully Yours* (2002), *Tropical Malady* (2004), and *Syndromes and a Century* (2006) form an oeuvre of jungle reverie that has become the director's signature. This motif was established from memories of growing up with his doctor parents in Khon Kaen city in the Thai Northeast, a region and people who have been politically and historically marginalized by the Thai state. The combination of folklore spectacle and brutal realism have attracted interest from diverse critics and scholars in both history and Thai studies who discuss the films' portrayal of identity, body and geopolitics. Likewise, Weerasethakul's transcultural cinematic experimentation appeals to cinephiles globally, who draw attention to the director's effective play of light, sound and colour.

Weerasethakul's global auteur status was effectively solidified after winning the prestigious Palme d'Or award from the Cannes International Film Festival in 2010 for *Uncle Boonmee Who Can Recall His Past Lives*. This success allowed the film and Weerasethakul's earlier works a much wider international distribution beyond the niche market of film festivals and the art world. Developed as part of the larger multimedia project called "Primitive," the work also highlights Weerasethakul's dual career as a visual artist and a filmmaker who fuses multimedia art form with diverse filmmaking traditions. Significantly, his body of work coincides with the resurgence of art cinema globally, a medium that seeks to blur boundaries between film and art practices, lowbrow and highbrow culture, and local and global politics.

As Thailand sank into political crisis and increased censorship during the mid to late 2000s, Weerasethakul also chose to reflect upon these circumstances in his art and filmmaking. His early works, *Blissfully Yours* and *Syndromes and a Century*, were subjected to censorship by the Thai Film Censorship Board which led to the organization of the campaign to "Free Thai Cinema" and promote freedom of expression. As Thailand has been under the military junta since 2014, the director declined to submit his most recent film *Cemetery of Splendour* (2015) to authorities. He also spoke of moving to Latin America, which has similar political history with Thailand and other Southeast Asian countries, possibly marking a new era of Weerasethakul's career.

Weerasethakul's identity and body of work are fostered through his relationship with people and places in Thailand. These include his mother and home town in Khon Kaen, his muse Janjira Pongpas and her life along the Mekong river, as well as the director's current home in Chiang Mai. Yet Weerasethakul also spends half of the year overseas where the majority of his audience are, so leading a dual existence as both a full-time transnational filmmaker and a local artist based in Thailand. In this capacity Weerasethakul creates personal features, short films, music videos, and commissioned artworks for corporate and art institutions in various countries.

As cinema celebrated its centennial anniversary, Weerasethakul's works have been referred to on various occasions as an exemplar of the past decade of cinema. In 2014, the Rotterdam International Film Festival's celebration of the 25th Anniversary of the Hubert Bals Fund commemorated their success in supporting innovative filmmakers around the world through the retrospective programme entitled "Mysterious Objects," named after Weerasethakul's first feature. Through his own international networks and a strong community of independent Thai filmmakers, the director also co-established a sales and distribution company, Mosquito Films, which works to support a new generation of Thai filmmakers, as well as engaging in film curation for festivals and museum exhibitions.

Despite this monumental recognition in the film and art worlds, Weerasethakul is careful to reflect upon the discourses imposed upon him as a Thai or international film director. In various short films and print publications, his self-portrait is represented through images of the director at work, looking away or staring straight into the camera, rather than being portrayed as a conventional celebrity-auteur. When talking about his life and work, including a public lecture at the Tate Modern in the UK during the major retrospective of his features and short films in early 2016, Weerasethakul has chosen "mirages" as the title of his talk, which resonates with the temporal process of image-making. On various occasions, Weerasethakul also spoke of a wide open future of cinema, and about freeing himself from a specific medium to engage with any new tools that would allow him to capture and express his imagination.

Wikanda Promkhuntong

Chatrichalerm Yukol

Prince Chatrichalerm Yukol, also known as Than Mui, was born on 29 November 1942, the son of His Royal Highness Prince Anusornmongkolkarn and Mom Ubol Yukol. The Prince was educated at Geelong Grammar School in Australia before pursuing a degree in geology at the University of California Los Angeles. Film was his minor subject and during his studies the Prince was able to cultivate a close connection with future Hollywood directors Francis Ford Coppola and Roman Polanski, who were his classmates. As well as his distinguished directing career the Prince has also published behind-the-scenes books and film production notes, and is also an acclaimed scientific author, writing *The Blue World* (1984) and *The World of Animals* (1992), which received an award from the Siamese Environment Club.

Prince Chatrichalerm Yukol was familiar with film production from a young age as his parents were pioneers of early Thai cinema and founded the Lawo Film Company in 1936. Working with his father, the Prince began his career as a photographer for *Paradise Island* (1969) and *Mae Nak in the City* (1970). In the late 1960s he founded Prommitr Film (later known as Prommitr Production Co., Ltd.), producing both film and television series. He directed series such as *Pink Room* (1969), *Little Mermaid* (1972) and *Shaman* (1973). His first feature film was *Out of the Darkness* (1971), an experimental film which unfortunately was not well-received.

The 1970s was a transitional period in Thai film history, marking a shift from the dubbed 16mm era to the synchronized sound of 35mm. During this period Prince Chatrichalerm and his contemporaries, Piak Poster and Sakka Charuchinda, were regarded as "new wave" directors who developed filming techniques and materials. As Prince Chatrichalerm was in the US during the New Hollywood period of the 1960s, a similar cinematic attention to social problems began to mark his signature in his second film *His Name Is Khan* (1973). The film criticized corruption in Thai bureaucracy and gained significant public attention, as a result the Prince received the *Tukkata Thong* Award (Saraswati or the Golden Doll Award) for best director in 1974.

Several months after the release of *His Name Is Khan*, the political uprising of *14 tula* (14 October 1973 event) erupted. The corresponding wave of social realism in art and cultural productions impacted upon and informed Prince Chatrichalerm's social problem films. *Hotel Angel* (1974) focused upon human trafficking and was a hit at the box office. It also arguably launched the careers of film stars Sorapong Chatree and Wiyada Umarin. This was then followed by *Angel Who Walks on the Ground* (1976) which addressed drug problems and teenage crime.

Prince Chatrichalerm then moved into making 'ethnographic' social problem films such as *Taxi Driver (Citizen)* (1977) and *Before the Storm* (1980), both of which attempted to give voice to the subaltern in Thai society. His ethnographic concerns were also articulated in *Gunman* (1983), the source material of which was developed from real gangster communities in Petchaburi and Chonburi. Similarly, *Teacher Somsri* (1985) was a semi-biopic blended with fieldwork data collected from slum areas in Bangkok and *The Elephant Keeper* (1987) shared the same inspiration. *The Elephant Keeper* in particular was celebrated by international audiences, and was one of 35 foreign language films shortlisted for an Oscar in 1987. Another successful social problem film was *Daughter* (1994) which won several *Tukkata Thong* Awards. Its sequel, *Daughter 2* (1996), was praised by film institutions though it was less financially successful. This dichotomy of success and failure typifies the Prince's career, indeed he once mentioned these two extremes in an interview as a "God vs. Dog" dynamic. However, a certain reconciliation with popular culture and mass consumption can be found in some of the director's romantic comedy, drama and action-adventure films, such as *Last Love* (1975), *Falling in Love with You* (1976), *Kama* (1978), *Detective, Section 123* (1984), *Powder Road* (1991) and *Salween* (*Gunman 2*) (1993).

The New Thai industry of the late 1990s marked a transition between Prince Chatrichalerm's former films and the more recent ones. *The Box* (1998) was his last experimental film before the director shifted to make national epics. The landmark Thai film *The Legend of Suriyothai* (2001) depicted a sixteenth-century Siamese queen's heroism and even reached international audiences due to Francis Ford Coppola editing an international version of the film. *The Legend of Suriyothai*'s success in Thailand foregrounded Prince Chatrichalerm's career and the director was celebrated as a Thai national artist (performing arts) by the Ministry of Culture in 2001. Under the wind of royal-nationalism, the Thai public was again moved by the six part film series *The Legend of King Naresuan* (2007–2015). Two parts of the series were funded by Thai Khemkhaeng (Stronger Thailand Project) at the Ministry of Culture. Boosting the Thai heritage film industry, this "epic" filmmaking was later repeated in *Phan Thai Norasing* (2015) which was later serialized on television in 2016.

Natthanai Prasannam

2

Key Early Productions

Given the international success and domination of the post-1990s Thai industry today, it is easy to overlook the long and rich history of Thai cinematic development throughout the twentieth century. Yet such history demands analysis, and the recent popular trend towards discovering and documenting local film history in Southeast Asia certainly means that more formerly "lost" productions continue to be uncovered, and more aging film stars and filmmakers are lifted from obscurity and awarded the respect and gravitas they deserve.

The history of Thai cinema began in June 1897 with an exhibition taking place in Bangkok less than two years after the famous Lumière brothers' Paris showing of "Moving Picture" images in 1895. This followed a similar path in-keeping with the majority of film worldwide, in which a national cinema took time to become established and recognisable as a film form and industry. Yet Thailand has its own unique history of cinematic development throughout the twentieth century, one shaped by the competition of Western and Eastern powers over Southeast Asia, and the internal development of Thailand itself.

Similar to the rest of the world, this new "moving pictures" entertainment proved to be successful in Thailand, and before long cinemas had begun to appear, with the first crude buildings set up by Japanese entrepreneurs and then various other companies that established (first in 1919) more permanent buildings. This new form of entertainment, at first dubbed *nang yipun* "Japanese shadows" later changed to *nang farang* "foreign shadows" (a name which continues today) grew quickly due to its immense popularity. In the 1920s cinemas are recorded to have spread outside of Bangkok to outer provincial towns and by the late 1930s it is estimated that there were around 120 cinemas in Thailand, most to be found in Bangkok. What is considered by some to be the first Thai production *Miss Suwanna of Siam* (Henry Alexander MacRae, 1923), actually directed by an American though starring only Thai performers, appeared in 1923, and the first completely indigenous Thai production *Double Luck* (Kun Anurakrathakarn, 1927) in 1927. More followed (the vast majority of which are now lost) including various productions by the Thai aristocracy and a number of co-productions between Western filmmakers and the Thai elite that were concerned mostly with state propaganda.

Foreign pictures also poured into the country, the majority from Hollywood, ensuring that the exhibition sector received early heavy investment from Thai businesses and entrepreneurs as the key to financial success in Thai cinema. Major Hollywood companies opened up offices in Bangkok, and while such investment squeezed out under-funded and under-equipped local filmmakers, the concentration of Hollywood-funded cinemas in urban areas meant that travelling cinemas targeting rural consumers were free to carve their own niche audiences and productions upcountry. Indeed, when the Japanese occupation of World War II prevented the import of Hollywood productions, Thai filmmakers were quick to fill this space, resulting in an upsurge of local productions, though ones which were recorded on silent 16mm film stock and live dubbed in cinemas. The post-war era then saw the emergence of significant stars such as Mitr Chaibancha, Petchara Chaowarat and Sombat Metanee, all of whom participated in a record-breaking number of action-packed saturated cowboy-esque productions which formed the "golden age" of Thai film production. After the success of the musical *Monrak Lukthung* (Rangsi Thatsanapayak, 1970) however, synchronized sound was soon standardized, and the milestone production *Tone* (Piak Poster, 1970) then capitalized upon the new urban Americanized culture that was sweeping Thailand during the Vietnam War.

Yet commercialized cinema was not the only outlet for filmmakers. The 1970s saw the brief yet significant appearance of "social problem" films, ones which remain an integral part of Thai film nostalgia for Thai cinephiles today. Likewise, the increase in urban immigration attracted by the economic upturn in the 1970s and 1980s then led to a new urbanized audience made up largely of teenagers. This very profitable (and often overlooked) industry of teen orientated productions then quickly laid the foundations for a network of urban cinemas that was to prove the eventual stepping-stone towards the post-1990s internationally competent industry today.

It is this long and complicated development that has resulted in the contemporary big budget Thai industry. While the various development stages may seem disconnected from the lavish historical epics, graphic horror, avant-garde and slapstick romantic numbers associated with Thai cinema in the contemporary era, there are significant aesthetic and formal connections which mark an entirely Thai style of filmmaking. Through examining and analyzing such productions in light of their historical and cultural context, we can begin to understand the various genres, audiences and film styles that characterize Thai cinema today.

Mary J. Ainslie

Title:	*Miss Suwanna of Siam / Nang Sao Suwan*
Director:	Henry Alexander MacRae
Studio:	Universal Studios
Year:	1923

Miss Suwanna of Siam was written and directed by Henry Alexander MacRae, an American, in 1923. The film holds a significant place in the history of Thai cinema as the first feature film made in Thailand since *nang farang* or "Western shadow theatre" arrived in the country in 1897, as well as the first Hollywood production ever made in and about Siam.

Siam Sakkhee newspaper indicates that the film was first screened under the title *Suwan Siam* at cinemas owned by the Siam Niramai Company.

Text after the title also affirms that the film is an authentically Thai film (*Thai-thae*) with a completely Thai cast and no *farang* (Westerners), conveniently glossing over MacRae's (and Hollywood's) involvement. A silent film seven reels in length, *Miss Suwanna of Siam* depicts the romantic story of the young woman Suwanna, searching for her true love while also overcoming her conservative father's disapproval. *The Bangkok Daily Mail* newspaper published a brief synopsis of the film on Monday, 25 June 1923, which reads as follows: "The story itself has all the necessary features of melodrama, love, hate, revenge, injured innocence, false accusation, manslaughter, etc., and it all ends up nicely and pleasantly with the long-lost heir coming to his own and the lovers wandering off hand in hand into the bright future."

Evidently an entertaining and melodramatic film, *Miss Suwanna of Siam* was also a means through which to promote the scenic backgrounds and tourist sites of Thailand. This latter objective was part of a favour requested by King Rama VI of the Chakri Dynasty, indeed an early letter from Prince Kampaengphet suggests that the King wanted to provide the American production team with support and facilities from the Royal State Railways Department and the Department of Royal Entertainment in return for a copy of the film. The letter indicates that the copy would be sent to the Royal State Railways Department, for the authorities to use motion pictures in promoting modern Siam at that time.

Unfortunately, this crucial piece of Thai film history is considered lost and there is no record of any copies made available to the public since MacRae's return to America. Some available stills were made into postcards and together with some photographs of the production team filming at the Temple of the Emerald Buddha in Bangkok these are all that remains of this early attempt to promote Thai culture. It is still not clear why this highly regarded authentic Thai film disappeared so completely without leaving any records. Thai film scholars still search for clues about the film itself, and some query whether the loss of the film may have been connected to its depiction of certain controversial issues, such as the public execution of Thai prisoners.

Palita Chunsaengchan

Key Early Productions

Title: *Double Luck / Chok Song Chan*
Director: Kun Anurakrathakarn
Studio: Bangkok Film Company
Year: 1927

Double Luck holds a special place in Thai film history as the first fully Thai-produced feature film. The production originated from a group of Siamese noblemen who worked in publishing and whose interests involved motion pictures and cinematographic technology. One such nobleman, Luang Konkarnjenjit, the director of the Topical Film Service of the Royal State Railways Department at the time, invited Luang Boonyamanop (Saengthong) to write a fictional melodrama for the film, a highly popular genre among the Thai public. The Wasuwat Brothers, owners of Sri Krung Press and some of the few people outside of the Thai royal family to have participated in filmmaking in Siam during this early period, were also asked to be part of the film as producers and editors. Kun Anurakrathakarn (Pleng Sookviriya), who already had experience in filmmaking for official purposes from the Royal State Railways Department, served as director of the film while Luang Konkarnjenjit worked as director of photography while filming.

Similar to so many other silent films around the world from this early period, the six reeled *Double Luck* is today considered a lost film; indeed, many film historians attribute the loss of such early Thai films to the lack of preservative skills specifically required for this type of fragile filmstock combined with the all-year tropical weather in the region. Nevertheless, The National Film Archives of Thailand were able to recover a few fragments of the film, including a seconds-long scene of a rape attempt and a minute-long car-chase scene between the hero and the villain, who has abducted the heroine. Due to the missing original footage, scholars have to rely upon local newspapers, posters, leaflets and other short writings from the period for further information about this crucial moment in Thai film history. Local newspaper *Khao Pappayon* (The Moving Picture News) states that the first public screening was on 30 July 1927, informing us that the film was well received by local viewers, a reaction that is not surprising considering the growing number of cinemas in many big cities around the country and the increasing familiarity of the Siamese public with motion pictures as a new form of public entertainment.

Posters, film reviews and advertisements in newspapers, as well as some photographs of the crew, also raise further observations and questions, specifically regarding what kind of information was shown and advertised as part of the film's promotion, and what was left out. Surprisingly, surviving posters indicate that the name of the director was not considered central to the public's interest, and instead such images seem to focus upon identifying actors and characters, and giving a clear justificatory explanation as to who is good and who is bad. The heroine in particular seems to be highlighted in both promotion and the existing fragmented footage, suggesting the film had a strong focus upon the behaviour and position of women in society, a theme that continues throughout Thai filmmaking up to the present day.

Palita Chunsaengchan

Title:	*A Fable from an Uncle: The Magical Ring* / *Nithan Khong Lung Rueang Waen Wiset*
Director:	**Noi Sorasak**
Studio:	**Aumporn Cinema**
Year:	**1929**

A Fable from an Uncle: The Magical Ring was produced and directed by King Prajadhiphok (King Rama VII) under a pseudonym Noi Sorasak in 1929, only two years after the successful public screenings of the first fully Thai-produced film, *Double Luck* in 1927. Cinematography first came to Siam in the late nineteenth century under the royal patronage of King Chulalongkorn (King Rama V of Chakri Dynasty), thriving among the Thai ruling class and elites. Despite this royal support, only *The Magical Ring* was actually made by one of the kings, with the actors also from the royal family and no record of any public involvement in the production.

The Thai word *nithan* translates as "fable," and includes imaginary and magical characteristics, all of which are evident in *The Magical Ring*. The film is a morality tale of five loving children who rebel against their abusive stepfather. One of the children is given a magical ring by a female spirit and casts a spell on the stepfather for abusing his little brother. However, after regretting his actions the son later undoes the spell and the stepfather then begins to appreciate how much his children love him, thus changing into a good loving father. Similar to most fables, the film ends with a reductive and simplistic portrayal of human characters: the punished stepfather who has been tamed and regrets his previous evil deeds, and the forgiving goodness of the children.

With its simple story and moralistic message, *The Magical Ring* initially seems somewhat unremarkable as a text, yet the film's technical style is noteworthy as director King Prajadhiphok seems to favour a strong sense of realism that rejects the expected conventions associated with such a fantastical story. An abundance of long shots and takes foreground Thailand's scenery, with very little editing, giving the film realist conventions paradoxically alongside a story of magic and spirits. Given such notable cinematography, *The Magical Ring* thus offers insight as to how early Thai filmmakers sought to adapt traditional stories to the capacity and techniques of this newly imported visual entertainment. Together with its strong visual verisimilitude, this early filmic representation of a strictly fictional Thai genre makes it highly significant to both the history of Thai cinema and of Thai literature.

Palita Chunsaengchan

Title: *The King of the White Elephant / Phrachao Changphueak*
Director: **Sunh Vasudhara**
Studio: **Pridi Productions, Thai Film Studio**
Year: **1940**

As the oldest surviving Thai feature film in complete form, *The King of the White Elephant* would command a significant place in any chronicle of Thai cinema. However, the film also demands historical and critical attention for many other reasons. Produced in 1940 by leading public intellectual and the then Minister of Finance, Pridi Bhanomyong, from his self-penned novel of the same name, *The King of the White Elephant* was as much a political production as a cinematic one. Indeed, the nascent People's Party constitutional government had already financed several motion pictures as part of a broader project of populist nation-building. Yet unlike other state propaganda films of the era – such as *Blood of Thai Soldiers* (1935) and *Heart of the Navy* (1937) – which were essentially works of parochial militarism, *The King of the White Elephant* can be distinguished by its progressive discourse of internationalist pacifism.

Made at a time when Europe was already at war and the threat of Japanese imperialism was looming in the region, *The King of the White Elephant* was Bhanomyong's impassioned plea for Thai neutrality. A left-leaning pacifist, Bhanomyong had been instrumental in negotiating a series of multilateral non-aggression pacts and *The King of the White Elephant* was a clear cultural expression of his political agenda. The film's titular hero, King Chakra (Renu Kritayakon) is a fictional monarch of the Ayutthaya period who finds himself embroiled in growing tensions with the neighbouring kingdom of Hongsa in Burma, a favoured "villain" of Thai cinematic nationalism. Despite his best efforts at brokering a peace deal, King Chakra is forced into battle where, after the inevitable climactic victory, he reasserts his commitment to peaceful diplomacy and neutrality.

Written and produced entirely in English – a first for Thai cinema and a rarity even today – *The King of the White Elephant* was clearly geared for international rather than local reception. An opening prologue uses maps and select shots of modern day Bangkok to contextualize the story for foreign audiences and project a flattering image of the young Thai nation as cosmopolitan and up-to-date. Despite its historical setting, the film is infused with modernist ideologies. King Chakra is an embodiment of Bhanomyong's own liberal humanist world-view, a progressive reformist committed to principles of social justice and democratization. In one of many anachronisms, he even rejects the courtly tradition of polygamy for the modern ideal of egalitarian companionate marriage.

Ultimately however, *The King of the White Elephant* was too "foreign" for local Thai tastes and too aesthetically "primitive" for international audiences. A review in the *New York Times* condescendingly dismissed it "as an amusing cinematic oddity" of "unintentional humor" that seems like "a home-made movie turned out by a bunch of precocious kids." Ironically though, it was the film's thwarted internationalist ambitions that proved its historical saviour. Hoping for foreign success, Bhanomyong registered the film for US copyright with the Library of Congress. That print in turn became the sole surviving copy of *The King of the White Elephant* and the reason we have the film today.

Brett Farmer

Title: *Santi-Vina*
Director: Thavi Na Bangchang
Studio: Far East Film, Hanuman Film
Year: 1954

For a long time, *Santi-Vina* was regarded as the "Holy Grail" of lost Thai films. The winner of the 1954 Asia Pacific Film Festival in Tokyo (a festival originally entitled, The Southeast Asian Film Festival), the film was considered lost apart from a few still images, a badly degraded piece of film stock that was virtually unwatchable, an old script and several reviews from international film magazines. Privately confident that a print existed somewhere given the film's international prominence at the time, the Thai Film Archive resolutely pursued the film until finally, in 2014, forgotten prints of *Santi-Vina* were located in various archives in Russia, China and the UK.

As with so many "lost" works of art, the danger that the surrounding mythology would overtake the actual quality of the film loomed large. Such concern was well-founded given the US support which engineered *Santi-Vina*'s creation and success at the festival, itself an event created largely to demonstrate and retain US control over filmic content in East and Southeast Asia, rather than a genuine attempt to cultivate local filmmaking.

The film tells the story of an impossible romance between two village sweethearts, the blind and poor boy Santi (Poonpan Rangkhavorn), and Vina (Rayvadi Sriwilai), a girl who has taken on the role of Santi's protector since early childhood. Santi's father sends his son to live with the local monk hoping that devotion to the Lord Buddha may bring about a miracle and restore his sight. When Santi and Vina meet several years later they inevitably fall in love, yet Vina's parents disagree with the match and hastily arrange a more socially convenient marriage.

An ambitious undertaking at the time, *Santi-Vina* represents significant cooperation between American and Thai filmmakers at the beginning of the Cold War period and was made specifically for this American-backed festival. Indeed, the company Far East Film Ltd (under the trademark Hanuman Film) was founded by Thai filmmaker Ratana Pestonji together with Robert North, a former writer for Twentieth Century Fox, who was the company's vice-president. *Santi-Vina* was to be the first high quality 35mm production of many, and Pestonji (who also served as *Santi-Vina*'s cinematographer) even travelled to Hollywood to buy 35mm equipment, illustrating the close entwinement of American and Thai activities during this period. Some sources even consider the company to have been one of the many fronts for American CIA activities in Thailand, a relationship that would have been neither surprising nor unusual in the country at this time, yet one for which there is (as yet) no real concrete evidence. Notably, *Santi-Vina*'s strongly apolitical religious story is also markedly different to the many anti-Communist Thai-American propaganda films made by the US Information Service (USIS) and shown in up-country areas around this time, suggesting that filmmakers did not explicitly see themselves as part of this organization and efforts.

Despite *Santi-Vina*'s festival success, Robert North's sudden and untimely death in 1954 coupled with a general lack of enthusiasm for such expensive productions from all involved put an end to such cooperation, and Pestonji continued his efforts without foreign support. Thai filmmaking quickly resorted to the cheap mass-produced live-dubbed 16mm productions, forming the Thai cinematic "golden age" of the 1960s, while Hollywood companies monopolized urban audiences by screening blockbusters in their purposely built 1000 seat air-conditioned cinemas. *Santi-Vina* therefore remains a testament to regional politics at the time, and one of the many "what ifs" in Thai film history.

Mary J. Ainslie

Key Early Productions

Title: *Country Hotel / Rong Raem Narok*
Director: Ratana Pestonji
Studio: Hanuman Film
Year: 1957

Commonly rendered *Country Hotel* in English but literally meaning "Hell Hotel," *Rong Raem Narok* is a landmark film in the career of fabled director Ratana Pestonji, the oft-dubbed "father of contemporary Thai cinema." Born in Thailand to a family of Iranian descent and university educated in the UK, Pestonji brought a decidedly transnational perspective to his work and was keen from the outset to help move Thai cinema onto the global stage. Establishing his own production company, Hanuman Films, in 1953 with the express purpose of making quality Thai films of distinction, Pestonji worked as producer-cinematographer on a number of features before graduating to full artistic control as director on *Country Hotel*.

Positioned in the middle of Thai cinema's first century, *Country Hotel* is a crossroads text that draws from the rich native traditions of Thai film and folk cultures, while also pointing to new currents ahead. In keeping with Pestonji's commitment to international best practice, the film was shot on 35mm film stock with synchronized sound rather than post-dubbed 16mm, the industry standard of the time. Like many of the filmmaker's other efforts, *Country Hotel* is daringly artistic. Inspired by Alfred Hitchcock's *Rope* (1948), Pestonji shot the film on a confined studio set, using a single camera with long takes and minimal cuts. The resultant effect is a bit stilted and stage-bound but it imbues the film with a formalist self-consciousness rare in Thai cinema of the period.

However, if *Country Hotel* has one foot in the realm of international "quality" cinema, its other is firmly planted in the local traditions of popular Thai film. The film draws centrally from the era's star system with familiar actors like Chana Sri-Ubon as the hero, Sutasit Satayawon as the villain and, making her charismatic screen debut, Sarinthip Siriwan as the feisty "femme fatale." It also follows Thai folk traditions of textual heterogeneity where elements of drama, comedy, romance, action, and even musicals are thrown together with little attention to the ideals of organic unity that govern classical Western narrative.

In fact, the film's first half plays much like a disjointed vaudeville revue as a cast of itinerant characters drift through the provincial hotel of the film's title offering a series of performative vignettes including Italian opera, Chinese classical singing, comic Thai boxing, and a Filipino lounge song. Even after the film has settled into its narrative groove – with parallel plotlines focussed on an evolving heterosexual romance and a marauding gang of bandits – *Country Hotel* makes repeated stylistic gear changes across conventions of the Western, thriller, romantic melodrama, and slapstick comedy.

Country Hotel's attempts to serve twin masters of international "quality" cinema and Thai populism arguably proved its undoing. Neither fish nor fowl, the film's artistic pretensions alienated domestic audiences, while overseas viewers were befuddled by its carnivalesque genre-mixing. Nevertheless, it is precisely its unapologetic hybridity that makes *Country Hotel* such a fascinating text and has helped fuel its latter-day re-appreciation.

Brett Farmer

Title: *Mae Nak Phra Khanong*
Director: Saneh Gomarchun
Studio: Saneh Silp Pappayon
Year: 1959

Mae Nak Phra Khanong has the distinction of being the first of many films dedicated to the Mae Nak legend of Thailand. Arguably one of the most faithful cinematic renditions of this traditional tale about a wife whose profound love for her husband transcends death, its foundational scenes would also set the narrative directions for future adaptations, the most important of which is the climactic confrontation between Nak and a Buddhist monk.

Unlike later versions, this early adaptation contains substantial depiction of Nak (Preeya Rungreuang) when she was still human, before her death. Such scenes stress her devotion to wifely qualities and womanly perfection, ideals to which Thai women should aspire, yet also depicts her less desirable characteristics, such as her flirtatiousness. Likewise, in displaying Nak's fallibility, the film also does not spare the monk, who in this version is not as powerful as he is usually (and subsequently) depicted. In this version,

Nak's punisher shows no qualms in resorting to trickery in order to defeat his adversary, and it is such indiscriminate representations of both Nak and the monk (metonymically, Buddhism) that directly underscores *Mae Nak Phra Khanong*'s link to the most successful contemporary cinematic retelling of the folktale: Nonzee Nimibutr's version of *Nang Nak* (1999), another depiction without clear ideological fidelity to its source material.

The role of Nak was assumed by Preeya Rungreuang in her first, and most famous, screen appearance that was also the last time she would play a lead character or protagonist. A household name in Thai cinematic history, Rungreuang's fame was largely anchored in "vixen" roles such as the "other" woman, the castrating wife, and the wicked mother-in-law. This development of Rungreuang's career is telling and, although impossible to prove, was probably indirectly related to her character in *Mae Nak Phra Khanong,* as part of a film that dared to attack two of the nation's most revered heritages: the Mae Nak legend and Buddhism.

Notwithstanding the film's unsophisticated effects and sometimes confusing narrative (due to multiple subplots), *Mae Nak Phra Khanong* remains a significant work in Thai cinema both historically and ideologically. The film not only provides a kind of narrative template for subsequent adaptations, but also refuses to glorify either the legend of Nak herself or the Buddhist order she challenges. *Mae Nak Phra Khanong* therefore allows for a unique comparison as to how the legend has been retold in modern times and, as such, encourages the viewer to carefully reconsider the foundational stories the nation tells itself.

Andrew Hock Soon Ng

Title: ***Black Silk / Phrae Dam***
Director: **Ratana Pestonji**
Studio: **Hanuman Film**
Year: **1961**

Black Silk was submitted and shown at the 1961 Berlin Film Festival, the first Thai film to do so. This "crime drama" is considered to be veteran Thai director Ratana Pestonji's finest work, and Thai film scholar Chalida Uabumrungjit labels *Black Silk* as "the film that pulled Thai film up to an international level in terms of both photography technique and substance" (2003, p. 45). This is certainly due to the film's location shooting and first ever use of Cinemascope to make widescreen possible, as well as Pestonji's insistence upon using 35mm film stock with synchronized sound for his productions at a time when the majority of Thai films were live-dubbed 16mm affairs. Yet *Black Silk* certainly goes further than Pestonji's other productions in terms of its storyline, *mise-en-scène* and cinematography, all of which was highly original in Thai filmmaking at the time.

The film tells the story of a gangster, Seni (Senee Wisaneesarn), who assumes the identity of his dead twin brother in order to avoid paying a debt. The gangster's henchman, Tom (Tom Wisawachart), is in love with a widow, Phrae (played by Pestonji's daughter, Ratanavadi Ratanabhand), who is in mourning and only wears black. When Phrae unwittingly becomes involved in (and witness to) Tom's criminal activities, Seni holds Phrae's baby hostage, causing Phrae to enter a nunnery upon the advice of a monk. The film details the loyalties that the henchman Tom is then torn between, as he attempts to build a life with Phrae and defeat his boss. In a tragic ending, which includes both the death of Phrae's baby as well as Tom's execution, the film finishes with a karmic warning read by a Buddhist monk about the consequences of one's actions.

The film has been interpreted as Thailand's first film noir, due in part to its heavy *chiaroscuro*, gangster storyline, flawed characters and tragic ending. Certainly, scenes involving the quietly dignified widow Phrae, who stays silently weaving silk in her traditional home as Tom confesses his love, are worlds away from the exaggerated displays of post-war Thai cinema. Likewise the low-key atmospheric lighting (complete with a red filter) renders Phrae's wooden home a sinister and frightening place when she is accused of assisting in murder.

Yet while *Black Silk* is often seen as very much apart from Thai cinema at the time, with its dark, ruthless and tragic story of murder, lost love and psychological torment, it also includes a surprising selection of music and dance numbers in the gangster's nightclub, along with fight sequences, all of which are depicted in an array of bright, saturated primary colours. The film alternates these scenes of music and dance within the tragic storyline, so following the generically blended narrative structure prevalent in Thai cinema at the time. Likewise, although Pestonji's use of unknown actors was also pioneering at a time when star images were a major draw, many of the performers appear to have retained the histrionic performances and typage associated with the 16mm post-war Thai productions. While *Black Silk* is therefore often depicted as a breath of fresh air in post-war Thai film-making, this outstanding work of cinema is also very much a part of Thai film culture at the time.

Mary J. Ainslie

Title: *Money Money Money / Ngoen Ngoen Ngoen*
Director: Anusorn Mongkolkarn
Studio: Lawo Films
Year: 1965

Made at the height of the so-called "American Era" when intensive US involvement in Thai politics and the economy sparked rapid social change, *Money Money Money* is a film heady with the breathless spirit of its time. With a title not unlike one of the jingoistic slogans coined by Field Marshal Sarit in praise of economic development, and a sprawling narrative about an unlikely group of provincial village musicians who find fame, fortune, and love as nightclub operators in Bangkok, *Money Money Money* mirrors the era's rising cultures of capitalist modernity and aspirational class mobility.

The film also signalled an ambitious new highpoint of technical and commercial confidence in Thai feature film production. Filmed in 35mm Superinescope with eye-popping Technicolor and fully synchronized stereo sound, *Money Money Money* offered local audiences, almost for the first time, a home-grown film with the glossy look and slick production values of an imported product.

True to these Hollywood-sized ambitions, *Money Money Money* trades centrally on the aesthetics of excess with a running time of over three hours, a hit-laden musical soundtrack with 14 full numbers, and a cast of sixty feature actors, including the era's golden star couple of Mitr Chaibancha and Petchara Chaowarat. Moreover, the film's *mise-en-scène* foregrounds a lavish showcase of American-style commodity consumerism with modish fashions, home interiors, motor cars, jet planes, and even backyard swimming pools in abundance.

If at times the net effect of this textual exuberance risks making *Money Money Money* seem like an overlong commercial, the film's integral sense of comic irony redeems it from mere ideological propaganda. From the start, with its humorous prologue about the "struggles" of modern life, the film signals a knowing ambivalence in its response to Thailand's new era of materialist progress. At once exhilarated by the possibilities of economic modernisation, the film remains troubled by the obverse costs of social upheaval and loss.

It's a tension possibly best exemplified in the film's conflicted generic profile. Like many Thai films of the era, *Money Money Money* is a sometimes jarring patchwork of competing genres and styles. Ostensibly a musical comedy, it also contains strong elements of romance, domestic melodrama, and even tragedy. Among the film's varied plot strands is not one but two parallel cross-class romances – a thematic staple of Thai melodrama even to this day – where the inevitable scenario of generational conflict and parental disapproval serves as a potent metaphor for macro-dramas of social change. That one of these romances ends tragically in death tempers any sense of the film as unproblematic in its narrative imaging of Thai social development.

Hugely popular upon its release, *Money Money Money* continues to exercise considerable cultural fascination. It has been remade several times both in film and TV formats and, most recently, resurfaced as a stage musical in 2007 showcasing a new generation of stars in this perennially popular comic meditation on life, love, and selfhood in an age of economic transformation.

Brett Farmer

Title: *Sugar Is Not Sweet / Namtan Mai Wan*
Director: Ratana Pestonji
Studio: Hanuman Film
Year: 1965

Sugar Is Not Sweet holds the eponymous title of Ratana Pestonji's last feature film before his death five years later in 1970. Similar to Pestonji's other productions, the film contains songs, musical numbers and a strong saturated colour palette, demonstrating how well Pestonji fits within the canon of Thai film at the time despite the production's obvious difference in filmic quality to conventional 1960s Thai cinema. However, *Sugar Is Not Sweet* is also distinguished by its far more lighthearted tone when compared to Pestonji's other more tragic productions, telling a very humorous story of familial obligation, cultural difference and the complications of arranged marriage, some of which (family members have speculated) is possibly based upon Pestonji's own personal experiences.

The film tells the story of businessman Chaokun Jaroenkesa, the wealthy Thai-Chinese owner of a business selling hair growth treatment for men. Jaroenkesa pushes his young and wayward son Manas (played by heart-throb Sombat Metanee) into marrying Sugar (Metta Rungrattana), the daughter of his Indian business partner whose genius formula was behind their successful product. Jaroenkesa feels a debt of gratitude to his business partner, even offering to pay Manas to agree to the marriage. Manas' lover, the stroppy and sexy Watchari (Preeya Rungreuang), agrees to his marriage on the condition that she will be paid half the money and that Manas will not sleep with Sugar but will remain loyal to Watchari, an arrangement that Sugar is, understandably, not happy about.

Yet while Jaroenkesa believes that the gentle and modest sari-wearing Sugar can turn his scoundrel son into a gentleman, Sugar herself proves to be a formidable opponent who is not easily humiliated, and works to get her own back on Manas and his shallow attempt to gain financial reward for himself through their marriage. Teaming up with Chaokun Jaroenkesa's friend and employee Mr Moti, Sugar gives the loutish Manas a lesson in humiliation and hard work, before Manas is eventually deserted by his mistress (who leaves to marry her own lover) and realizes the benefits of married life.

The film is also somewhat risqué at times, with drawn out kissing scenes between the lovers and an extended sequence in which a naked Watchari appears as a silhouette in the shower, spending much of the rest of the scene in revealing pink hotpants. Drunken karaoke at Manas' and Sugar's disastrous wedding then ends in a mass brawl involving the groom, the groom's father and a melee of guests. One particularly hilarious scene, which could certainly hold the potential to offend, depicts a perplexed and clearly disheartened Sugar arriving on a plane from India to be greeted by an uproarious welcome scene, in which guests are dressed up as stereotypical Indian characters, sing Indian songs and cover Sugar up to her forehead in traditional wreaths whilst she peeks out with incredulity.

Such scenes ensure that what could otherwise be a potentially tragic subject of cultural misunderstanding, bribery and forced marriage, quickly descends into absurdity and farce. In addressing such problematic social issues through humour, Pestonji is able to offer up a serious commentary upon race, culture and gender relations in Thailand at the time, one realized largely through the film's feisty no-nonsense heroine Sugar.

Mary J. Ainslie

Title:	*Ngu Phi*
Director:	Ratana Saetthaaphakdee
Studio:	Tepkorn Pappayon
Year:	1966

Ngu Phi is not only a highly enjoyable tale of deviant femininity and sexual temptation, but is also an interesting examination of the power awarded to women in Thailand through supernatural means. A somewhat overly erotic film for the period in which it was made, the story tells of a Phi Ngu, a spirit that can appear in either snake or human form, that is hiding in a local village woman and lusts after the hero.

The story begins with a couple who initially disturb a Phi Ngu living in a local cave. This transgression results in the death of the couple, with only their young baby girl Boonleua (Prim Praphaphom) surviving, who then unwittingly carries the Phi Ngu inside of her. After being adopted and raised by a local family, the adult Phi Ngu's full monstrosity soon becomes apparent, and government administrator Phrakit (played by the dependable Mitr Chaibancha) is sent to investigate the number of deaths in the village. Boonleua then exercises her own sexual desire and agency by bewitching and seducing Phrakit, imprisoning him in a cave far away from any familial or village influences. This remarkable sequence involves semi-clad dancers seductively surrounding Phrakit, who is seemingly rendered helpless by their charms. This deviant femininity also tempts men in a notable scene when Boonleua appears as a beautiful half-naked young woman swimming in a river, suddenly changing into a gruesome monster and killing her suitors. This ability to exercise such mobility and desire is depicted as destructive and terrifying in its control and manipulation of men, and only the virginal heroine (played by Petchara Chaowarat) can seemingly break Boonleua's hold over Phrakit, rescuing the hero from his trance in the snake-woman's cave after which the two join forces to eventually defeat her.

This very negative connection between the supernatural and the female is present in many Golden Age post-war Thai productions and speaks of the growing anxiety around the increased mobility and independence of Thai women during this period. Thanks to close cooperation between the Thai and US governments during the Vietnam war period, American money had enhanced rural development, and such infrastructure transformed both the "physical landscape and social and economic systems" of rural Thailand in the 1950s and 1960s, along with its people (Ruth, 2011, p. 5). Many of these migrant workers moving into cities were women, a transition that would have previously been unthinkable given the strong connection between Thai women and the home. It is no accident therefore, that monstrous and dangerous women are unnaturally mobile in post-war Thai cinema, exist outside of the family and the home and use supernatural means to enact power over men and bend society to their voracious sexual appetites. Defeating and destroying such women is largely up to the virginal heroine, who, as in *Ngu Phi*, embodies more traditional feminine qualities and must rescue the hero from these corrupting influences.

Mary J. Ainslie

Title: *Pisat Saneha*
Director: Pan Kam
Studio: Kaweechai Pappayon
Year: 1969

As a typical contribution to 1960s mass-produced Thai cinema, *Pisat Saneha* could be considered unremarkable in Thai film history. The film contains all the staple characters and scenarios associated with this Golden Age of Thai film. Genres are blended, with ghosts, romance, comedy and a soundtrack of *luk thung* country music, all of which takes place against a middle-class family setting in rural 1960s Thailand. The central hero and heroine are played by the famous acting duo of Mitr Chaibancha and Petchara Chaowarat, while the story is a familiar one of family strife, involving an evil step-mother and a battle against good and evil. Yet it is the inclusion of scenes from overseas in India that give the film an interesting sequence and set this production apart from other more "typical" 1960s Thai productions.

Beginning with two bumbling fools in a graveyard discussing their fear of ghosts before a phantom suddenly appears and scares them away, the story introduces the heroine Karaket (Petchara Chaowarat) as she is laying flowers for her dead mother. When she catches the eye of the handsome hero Kangwan (Mitr Chaibancha), a shy and chaste (yet intense) romantic number begins with Karaket telling Kangwan the story of her mother's death. As it becomes clear that the couple are fated for one another, Karaket's evil stepmother attempts to kill her step-daughter by putting a poisoned drink in Karaket's room, conniving with the gullible lower-class maid to manoeuvre Kangwan into marrying her own daughter Eau. Karaket's dead mother then sends minions to protect her daughter from the murder attempts, although she is unable to save Karaket when her daughter is finally bitten by a snake placed in her room. Trapped in the underworld with her mother, Karaket then appeals to Kangwan as a disembodied voice and a phantom-like figure, pleading for his help to bring her back to the world of the living.

It is this sequence that gives the film an extra layer of interest. At this point in the narrative, Kangwan travels to India on business, a trip in which he becomes the very personification of a jazzy new urban lifestyle, symbolized by his shiny tight suit, sunglasses and briefcase. This travelling is of course unthinkable for the virginal heroine, whose purity would be compromized by such a solo trip. As Kangwan walks around the Taj Mahal in India reacting with horror to Karaket's disembodied plea for help, we are treated to the spectacle of a sophisticated and exotic foreign location. The scene celebrates the spectacle of India and emphasizes Kangwan's impressive position within it, as well as his romantic devotion to Karaket (see Figure 1).

This use of spectacle continues in a notable romantic sequence involving Kangwan and Karaket on a river boat together. This elongated romantic

Figure 1 Kangwan in his shiny suit on business in India in *Pisat Saneha* (1969).

number serves no real narrative purpose, instead, over a traditional *luk thung* soundtrack, the characters smile endearingly at each other while they float along the river together. Such sequences also extend to supernatural numbers, many of which interject into the narrative freely, demonstrating the presence and acceptance of this belief system as a staple part of rural Thai social organization.

Mary J. Ainslie

Title: *Monrak Lukthung*
Director: Rangsi Thatsanapayak
Studio: Rising Sun Productions
Year: 1970

Upon its release in 1970, *Monrak Lukthung* caused nothing short of a cultural phenomenon. Hugely popular, it smashed all existing box office records to become the most commercially successful Thai film to date and enjoyed a record theatrical run of over six months in Bangkok theatres. Special daily coach tours were organized to ferry fans in from surrounding areas with many returning for multiple viewings. The film continued to circulate for years in provincial screenings, seeping into popular consciousness courtesy of a best-selling soundtrack of hit songs, many of them instant classics.

Monrak Lukthung's success is routinely ascribed to the fact that it was the last film made by iconic star couple Mitr Chaibancha and Petchara Chaowarat. Appearing together in a staggering 160 films between 1961 and 1970, "Mitr-Petchara," as they were affectionately known, were the undisputed sovereigns of the Thai star system with a visibility and popular devotion unmatched by any other public figure of the era outside the monarchy. Mitr Chaibancha's untimely death in an on-set accident in October 1970 unleashed an unprecedented wave of public mourning that undoubtedly added to the film's legendary status. However, *Monrak Lukthung* had been in theatrical release for several months prior to the beloved star's death and was already a smash success, so the extraordinary appeal of the film requires more thought.

From its opening sequence where Thai country music star Phraiwan Lukphet wanders the fields of rural Thailand singing the film's lilting title track about love and courtship among flowering acacias, lotus ponds, and rain-soaked rice paddies, *Monrak Lukthung* nails its colours firmly to the mast of romantic pastoralism. That the singer is shown wearing modern 1970s-era clothes while workers in the fields dressed in traditional garb further accentuates the film's investment in an arcadian vision of Thai rural life understood as both different from and increasingly lost to the modern observer (see Figure 2).

Figure 2 The cast of *Monrak Lukthung* (1970) in one of their many musical numbers.

Emblazoned in its title, the popular music genre of *luk thung* is pivotal to the film's textual ethos of bucolic nostalgia. Blending traditional folk music with modern Western instrumentation, and characterized by sentimental ballads about the simple pleasures of upcountry life lost and the pains of economic migration, *luk thung* (which literally means "child of the fields") emerged in the post-war period as the defining musical genre of Thailand's massive rural sector and a popular means of expression for its collective experiences of social dislocation under modernity.

Monrak Lukthung capitalizes on the bittersweet sentimentality of *luk thung* to offer audiences a romantic vision of timeless pastoralism and – through its stock melodramatic narrative of star-crossed lovers prevailing against the odds to achieve the inevitable happy ending – a fantasy of ideological reassurance in the face of a rapidly changing world. That *Monrak Lukthung* spawned two further big screen remakes in 1982 and 2005 respectively, as well as three hit TV series and several stage adaptations, is a testament to the continuing resonance of its bucolic fantasy on the popular Thai imagination.

Brett Farmer

Title: *Golden Eagle / Insi Thong*
Director: **Mitr Chaibancha**
Studio: **Somnuk Pappayon**
Year: **1970**

Golden Eagle has long been memorialized as the last film of the famous 1960s Thai superstar Mitr Chaibancha, who was accidentally killed in the final scene when he fell from a rope ladder hanging from a helicopter. A hugely famous and successful actor, it is thought that Mitr starred in at least 226 films from 1957 to 1970.

Part of an action genre known as *nang bu, Golden Eagle* is the last in a series of films following this particular superhero. The story was adapted from the last episode of the popular crime fiction series *Red Eagle* written by author Sake Dusit between 1955 and 1970 and follows the missions of Golden Eagle, a Thai superhero in the Cold War period. In this particular film, the Golden Eagle figure works with the police and the military to protect the Thai nation from an invasion of the communist *Pai Dang* movement, and the film therefore contains elements of action and violence while also encompassing a strong right-wing ideology. Agents of the state, such as the police and the military, are important groups which support the hero throughout, while sexy female stars and comedians play supporting characters. In traditional Thai style the film blends various emotions and reactions, including melancholy, excitement and comedy.

The film captures the atmosphere of Thailand in the 1970s, when Thai society was heavily influenced by American culture. This came to represent a new form of modernity for consumers. *Golden Eagle*, however, demonstrates that Thai people remained strongly conservative, with the film presenting a clear confrontation between older social values and those of a modern society. Indeed, the central figure of the film certainly protects such older values, following a mission to maintain peace and order in the Thai nation. The superhero rescues the senior noble scientist and his beautiful daughter from the *Pai Dang* movement, figures who become representative of institutions such as the monarchy and the nation state, as well as a symbol of times past, when the aristocracy was venerated and young women were submissive and coy. Modern society and lifestyle are also represented, through scenes set in a nightclub, the advanced technology of the *Pai Dang* movement and Wasana, the heroine, a figure who can fight side by side with the hero and so offers a potential new role for Thai women.

Traditionally films from the *nang bu* genre close with a happy ending in which all problems and conflicts are solved. The hero's triumph also encourages adherence to social order and champions the actions of such figures in reinforcing a peaceful nation. Unfortunately, due to the tragic accident in its final scene *Golden Eagle* could not maintain this equilibrium, and instead broke many Thai hearts with the death of the most famous Thai performer of his time.

Patsorn Sungsri

Key Early Productions

Title: *Tone*
Director: Piak Poster
Studio: Suwan Film
Year: 1970

The significance of *Tone* as a milestone in the development of Thai film cannot be underestimated. Together with *Monrak Lukthung* (1970), the film contributed towards standardizing the use of 35mm film-stock with synchronized sound in Thailand and lies at the crucial point when Thai cinema began to transform to a bigger and better organized industry. The film follows the story of Tone (Chaiya Suriyan), a young orphaned village temple boy who is in love with the richer girl, Kularb (Jaruwan Panyopas). When Tone saves a visiting city boy Aod (Sayan Chantaraviboon) from a group of bullies, he is invited to live and study with Aod in Bangkok.

Tone marked a dramatic turning point in the development of Thai film by embracing signifiers of American capitalism, both formally and ideologically, that flooded into Thailand in the post-war era. This was a result of the strong American presence in the nation, garnered by Thailand's uninhibited cooperation with the American military throughout the Vietnam War. Modern and consumerist American culture came to represent a freedom from the conservative village environment of old, one that the shy village boy Tone is simultaneously frightened of and attracted to.

The film style of *Tone* is correspondingly very different to the structural and thematic conventions of the earlier Thai films. Scenes contain more shots, takes are shorter and the camera is significantly more mobile. This is also coupled with a new urban and Americanized *mise-en-scène*. In Aod's birthday party sequence in Bangkok, revellers dance in psychedelic 1960s flares and short mini-dresses with hairstyles to match. The camera moves amongst them, using canted angles and zooms in and out to focus upon the moving bodies in their tight, bright outfits and long, bare legs. The musicians play rock 'n' roll music on electric guitars, saxophones and drums and the party is awash with Pepsi-Cola logos.

This new Americanized Bangkokian culture is also embodied in Aod's sassy sister Dang (Aranya Namwong), whose depiction breaks all conventions for Thai female characters. Dang is first introduced in a memorable scene that begins with a close-up shot of her hand putting on a rock 'n' roll record. The camera then moves slowly up her body as she dances, revealing her skimpy clothes and her bare midriff, while Tone stands transfixed and shocked. Despite her cavorting, Dang's lifestyle is presented as fun, exciting and desirable. The plot has been described as "anti-formulaic" (Chaiworaporn, 2001, p. 142): while Tone must save Dang from the gangsters she is involved with, the couple still eventually fall in love, a development that Chaiworaporn labels as "groundbreaking" for a Thai film plot.

The film stands symbolic of the ways American popular culture was transforming Thailand, its young people and its social norms. While such a transformation was deeply problematic in its varied impacts upon Thai society, *Tone* demonstrates the freedom and new opportunities for self-expression such importations represented for the Thai consumer. Even today with its scratched print and (at times) incomprehensible English subtitles, it still represents one of the most entertaining forays into Thai film history.

Mary J. Ainslie

Title:	***Ghost of Guts Eater / Krasue Sao***
Director:	**S. Naowarach**
Studio:	**Sri-Sayam Production**
Year:	**1973**

Usually depicted as a floating female head dragging an oozing mass of luminescent entrails behind it, *phi krasue* is one of the most iconic uncanny creatures of Thai folklore and occupies a special place in Thailand's contemporary popular culture, being generally known by young and old alike. Available (yet unfortunately still incomplete) Thai film history suggests that *Ghost of Guts Eater* is probably the first Thai film featuring this witch-like being as the major uncanny protagonist.

Given the fact that until very recently the film was considered missing in Thailand, the lasting pop-cultural impact of *Ghost of Guts Eater* is remarkable. The film played a central role in the creature's burgeoning and continuing popularity, adding some of the idiosyncratic but now generally accepted features to *phi krasue*'s ghostly repertoire. Most important in this respect are the drawn-out entrails that were largely unelaborated in Thai folklore but, due to the film's artwork and especially illustrator Thawi Witsanukon's imagination, soon became one of the creature's most important visual attributes in popular culture.

The film itself is a tragic love story with supernatural plot twists rather than a horror film in any conventional sense. Set in 1960s rural Thailand, *Ghost of Guts Eater* tells a story of conjugal obligation and karmic debt. The film targeted a rural audience and thus relies on elements from Thai folklore to enhance its narrative force. The plot revolves around Bua Kli (Pisamai Wilaisak) and her lover (later husband) Bun Mueang (Sombat Metanee). Bua Kli inherits the burden of becoming a *phi krasue* from her grandmother (Sulaleewan Suwanatat), who is killed by an angry mob of villagers. Becoming a *Krasue Sao* (juvenile *krasue*) she is doomed to nurture her grandmother's hungry ghost, which resides in a ring that is her only heirloom.

Contrary to oral tradition therefore, the film depicts Bua Kli's transformation into a *phi krasue* as a manifestation of karmic debt and filial obligation towards dead kin, rather than a self-inflicted form of supernatural punishment. The social message is thus utterly conservative, emphasizing that husband and wife need to stay together irrespective of the many obstacles a marriage may face. In *Ghost of Guts Eater* such obstacles include the wife's ghostly identity, interventions by local thugs, a black magician and his attempts to kill husband and wife, a girl's "love magic", the husband's second marriage and finally the death of the only child. The film's narrative emphasizes that jointly accumulated karmic debt binds Bun Mueang and Bua Kli together and the couple has to endure such suffering as an inevitable consequence of their karmic fate. These karmic teachings are usually delivered by one of the many figures from traditional folklore that appear throughout the film. Most tellingly in this respect is the conspicuous absence of the Buddhist monk, who is usually the moral authority in more recent Thai films. In the end it is marital fidelity and their joint endurance of karmic debt that subdues the evil spirit and finally frees Bua Kli.

Benjamin Baumann

Title: *His Name Is Khan / Khao Chue Kan*
Director: Chatrichalerm Yukol
Studio: Lawo Films
Year: 1973

As a young doctor walks along a dusty road, he passes an older woman and her daughter. The older woman puts her hands together in front of her chest in a respectful Thai *wai* (a Thai formal greeting). Her daughter crouches low to the ground, giving an even more respectful *wai* to the doctor. The doctor stops and returns the *wai* to the pair. As the mother and daughter continue, the daughter asks, "Why did he *wai* us?" The respect the doctor offers to common people, and the young girl's perplexity, is part of the controversial message of Prince Chatrichalerm's classic film *His Name Is Khan*.

Based on a story by writer Suwanee Kuhontha, the film tells the story of a young, poor doctor, Khan (Sorapong Chatree), who commits to serving a small rural community in Phitsanulok. Khan brings his Bangkok society wife, Haruthai (Naiyana Sheewanun), out to the countryside to live with him. Haruthai's mother, friends, and jealous ex-boyfriend Tomon, all doubt Haruthai's ability to survive without city luxuries, even though she initially follows Khan with a cheerful attitude. Soon however, Khan is faced with serious challenges from the community's isolation, environment, and official corruption, and becomes consumed by his work. Haruthai feels increasingly abandoned, and temporarily returns to Bangkok, where she rekindles her relationship with Tomon. Angered at her relationship with Tomon, Khan assaults Haruthai, but the act triggers her memories and Haruthai remembers her love for Khan, rejecting Tomon. Yet when Khan returns to the village he is fatally shot by a gambler, an incident in which the police and local village chief are then implicated.

His Name Is Khan was Prince Chatrichalerm's second film, and part of a corpus of Thai films from the 1970s in which Thai filmmakers chose to depict the dynamics of social, political, and economic change in Thailand. This movement sought to make high quality and socially aware films in order to distinguish Thai cinema from the "putrid water," or *nam nao* label associated with popular Thai film at the time. The film contrasts city and country life through gritty, chaotic depictions of Bangkok's streets and nightclubs, in opposition to the dusty, isolated countryside. The depiction of corrupt and murderous policemen and government officials was highly controversial and the film was only given a limited release under the authoritarian regime of Field Marshal Thanom Kittikachon. However, *His Name Is Khan* had a second release after the 1973 people's overthrow of the regime, and in 2013 was finally added to Thailand's National Film Heritage registry.

Rebecca Townsend

Title: *The Scar / Phaenkao*
Director: Cherd Songsri
Studio: Cherdchai Films
Year: 1977

Cherd Songsri should be regarded as one of the first directors to export "Thai-ness" to global film markets. Throughout his study of film production in America, Songsri was moved by the isolation of American senior citizens, who reminded him of his own grandmother in rural Thailand. Songsri was motivated to make *The Scar*, an adaptation of Mai Muengderm's 1936 novelette which was written in regionalist style, so serving as the perfect material for a film.

Despite its humble beginnings, *The Scar* became the biggest box office success in Thai film history and has attracted global attention since the 1981 Nantes Three Continents Festival. The film was later anthologized as one of the world's 360 classic movies by global film directors, critics and the British Film Institute and is included in the list of significant Thai films.

The film is set in Bang Kapi along the Saen Saep canal in the 1930s, and depicts the romance of protagonists Khwan (Sorapong Chatree) and Riam (Nantana Ngaograjang), whose relationship is obstructed by their family conflict. The pair make their vows to a local spirit shrine under a banyan tree and, enraged by his daughter's disobedience, Riam's father Kamnan Rueng sells her to Madame Thongkham, a land tycoon in Bangkok. Madame Thongkham finds Riam similar to her dead daughter and, in mingling with the upper classes, Riam is gradually transformed. Meanwhile Khwan, now complete with a scar from fighting to free Riam, fails to find love in Bangkok and later seeks to be ordained as a monk. After years in the city, Riam returns to Bang Kapi yet is forced to leave for Bangkok despite her promise to see Khwan again. The film ends in tragedy with the death of both protagonists, when Khwan is shot dead by a man from Bangkok and Riam jumps into the canal, using Khwan's dagger to commit suicide. In the ending shot, the water is dyed red as the star-crossed lovers are both sacrificed in the name of true love.

The Scar should be read as a key nostalgic text of the era; filmed after the age of development and political turmoil during the Cold War period, the urban-rural divide articulates the fear of modernization since the 1932 revolution and the corresponding democratic changes in Thailand. The regionalist style from the novelette is sustained throughout the film by Thai folk songs and recreations of agrarian society. The film score features melancholic melodies from Thai flutes and Thai country songs that are combined with the idyllic setting. Yet the overall Thai-ness of the film is strongly embedded within masculinity, represented by both the fearless fights and the faithfulness of Khwan.

Natthanai Prasannam

Title: *Mountain People / Khon Phukao*
Director: Vichit Kounavudhi
Studio: Five Star Production
Year: 1979

After decades of churning out populist 16mm genre films, Vichit Kounavudhi underwent a late career change in the 1970s and 1980s to become a leading figure of the social realist movement (*nang sathon sangkhom*). *First Wife* (1978) hinted at this shift, but it was *Mountain People* that gave the clearest indication of the filmmaker's stylistic reinvention.

Combining social-issue themes, slice-of-life storytelling, and a semi-ethnographic style, *Mountain People* exemplifies many of the defining hallmarks of Thai social realism. One of the first feature films to deal sympathetically with the "social problem" of marginalized ethnic minorities in

Thailand's mountainous Northeast border regions, *Mountain People* was shot entirely on location with a cast of mostly untrained actors to evoke a sense of gritty authenticity. The film's aesthetic realism was further bolstered by the strategic use of documentarian conventions such as voice-over narration, "authentic" regional music and dialect, and a naturalist *mise-en-scène*.

The film starts with a rather lengthy voice-over prologue that introduces the major ethnic hilltribes, detailing their cultural beliefs and historical struggles, before homing-in on the Akha or "Egaw" tribe as the film's narrative focus. What ensues is part ethnographic drama and part coming-of-age picaresque as the film follows the adventures of Ayo (Montri Jenaksorn), a young Akha man from Shan state in Burma. Ayo's girlfiend Amiyo (Suphavadee Tiensuwan) is pregnant and the couple marry. However, when Amiyo gives birth to twins, an inauspicious omen in Akha culture, the offspring are killed and the couple is forced into exile. They set off to make the arduous journey on foot to an uncle in Thailand but, in an attempted river crossing, Amiyo is drowned and Ayo swept miles off course. Wandering the mountains in desperation, Ayo proceeds to encounter a host of characters from Christian missionaries to Chinese drug-runners to kindly Thai policemen. In the process, he meets and falls in love with another young woman, Mei-Fin (Vailaikorn Paovarat) from a different hilltribe and the two battle discrimination and exploitation before finally achieving a happy ending.

As this brief synopsis might suggest, *Mountain People* continues the populist sensationalism of Kounavudhi's earlier 16mm films. Melodramatic flourishes remain in the form of gunfights, rapes, and even moments of sexual comedy. However, the film also seeks to create the sober "quality" aesthetics and serious tenor of social realism. To contemporary eyes, the film's depiction of hilltribe minorities and unquestioned endorsement of Thai state benevolence can seem disturbingly paternalistic. Nevertheless, its liberal message of tolerance for ethnic and cultural difference was a bold move for the time. In recognition of the film's historical significance, *Mountain People* was added to the Registry of Films as National Heritage by the Culture Ministry in 2013.

Brett Farmer

Title: *The Adventure of Sudsakorn / Sudsakorn*
Director: Payut Ngaokrachang
Studio: Jirabenterng Film
Year: 1979

Payut Ngaokrachang has been praised as the Walt Disney of Thailand, making a number of short animations before creating the first feature animation in Thai film history – *The Adventure of Sudsakorn* (1979). *Sudsakorn* is adapted from Sunthorn Phu's *Phra Aphai Mani*, one of the most popular literary tales in Thailand since the early nineteenth century. The film was particularly successful among young Thai audiences and was publicized and popularized by Thailand's Ministry of Education.

In terms of narration, the film does not focus upon Phra Aphai Mani (the protagonist in the source text) who appears only in the mermaid's recollection. Instead the film features the story of Sudsakorn, the son of Phra Aphai Mani and a mermaid. Raised by a hermit on the island of Koh Kaew Phissadarn, Sudsakorn is taught worldly and magical knowledge. With the hermit's magical objects Sudsakorn can tame a dragon-horse to ride, yet his real adventure begins when he decides to search for his true father. The protagonist travels across the ocean, encountering hungry ghosts and vampires, being tricked by a naked yogi and defeating, among other antagonists, an army of demonic butterflies. Though the film ends with the phrase "to be continued," Ngaokrachang never completed animating the entire epic. Instead, Sudsakorn's adventure has later been retold in other forms and continues to be referenced in Thai popular culture.

The film boasts well-crafted animating techniques of the age, showcasing dancing mermaids and the action scenes of Sudsakorn, all set to a film score dominated by Thai traditional music. Rather than pure entertainment, the film seeks "to delight and to instruct" its young audiences, as seen in its focus on the mother-son relationship and the didactic speech preached by the hermit. Interestingly, the literary conventions of the source text are entwined throughout the film, with excerpts of poetry merged into the narrating voice and dialogue. Such quotations and poetic descriptions are from lines canonized in Thai school textbooks and follow the conventions of Thai literary tales. Yet the film is also significantly "Disneyfied," depicting an owl who helps the mermaid give birth to her son and also watches over Sudsakorn's growth. As such, animated animal helpers appear to have become compulsory in adaptations of folk tales in Thai screen culture ever since.

Manifesting its pride as the first Thai animation, a short documentary on the production of the film is now available before the opening scene. This "paratext" depicts how to create and process a feature animation and begins by paying homage to Sunthorn Phu at his birthplace, Rayong province.

Natthanai Prasannam

Title: *Son of the Northeast / Luk Isan*
Director: Vichit Kounavudhi
Studio: Five Star Production
Year: 1982

Based on Kampoon Boontawee's award-winning 1979 memoir of his rural boyhood in Depression-era Isan, *Son of the Northeast* is a warmly rendered homage to the people and culture of Thailand's vast Northeast. Long marginalized as an underdeveloped backwater, Isan was culturally "rediscovered" in the 1970s/80s and recoded as a bucolic foil to Thailand's exploding urban modernity. *Son of the Northeast* was an important part of this recuperative project, but the film's innovative form and observational realism removes the production from merely sentimental nostalgia.

Son of the Northeast is the most explicit expression of director Vichit Kounavudhi's late-career move into social realist cinema. The film is shot entirely on location with untrained local actors speaking in Isan's local dialect, performers are also accompanied by a soundtrack that emphasizes direct diegetic sound and indigenous music. Aided by Porniti Virayasiri's handsome 35mm cinematography, the film constructs a richly textured visual and aural evocation of Isan's wide dry landscapes and scorching heat.

Upon this vast cinematic canvas, Kounavudhi weaves the film's simple tale of a small rural community in the grips of a drought-stricken season. Anchored through the narrational perspective of Koon, the eldest boy of a tightknit farming family, *Son of the Northeast* charts the family's daily struggle to eke out an existence from the unforgiving land. With a leisurely, almost contemplative pace that is peppered with moments of modest relief, the film depicts a wedding, a trip to town, a mongoose hunt and a rainmaking ritual. The effect is a slice-of-life ethnography where social observation and character study take precedence over narrative action.

The film's semi-ethnographic tenor is further enforced by the understated naturalism of the performances. Led by Ong-art Ponethon, a farmer and former Muay Thai boxer whose only other acting credit was the political docudrama *Thong Pan* (1977), the cast consists almost entirely of non-professional locals who speak authentic dialect, sing regional folk songs, and even play the *khaen* and other local instruments.

Upon its release, *Son of the Northeast* did reasonably well at the box office, though possibly not as much as might have been expected given the source novel's bestseller status. Many viewers struggled with the film's slow-paced formalism and Bangkok audiences were allegedly put off by the use of Isan dialect and consequent need for Thai subtitling. It was however a major critical success both at home and abroad. Awarded the Special Jury Prize at the Manila International Film Festival and another gong from the "Office Catholique Internationale du Cinema," *Son of the Northeast* was part of the rising wave of new Thai films to garner international recognition. In the intervening years, *Son of the Northeast* has grown in stature and is regularly cited as a formative influence on a whole new generation of Thai cinematic formalists, including Apichatpong Weerasethakul and Uruphong Raksasad.

Brett Farmer

Title: *Butterfly and Flowers / Phisuea Lae Dokmai*
Director: Euthana Mukdasanit
Studio: Five Star Production
Year: 1985

Butterfly and Flowers speaks of the legacy left over from the more radical Thai political atmosphere of the 1970s. The film is based upon a young adult novel first published in 1978 by "Nippan" Makut Oradee. As one of the few texts in wider society at the time to represent Thailand's Southern

Muslim population, the book won the Thai national book awards and was eventually canonized in reading lists for school students.

A story of hope amidst adversity, the film recounts the story of Hujan (Suriya Yaowasang) who, due to poverty, is forced to drop out of primary school. When selling ice cream one day, Hujan reunites with his female classmate Mimpee (Wasana Pholyiam) and the two travel by train to the Malaysian border to see how *Kong Tap Mot* (the ant army) smuggles rice across the border. When Hujan's father is disabled in a train accident, Hujan becomes the family breadwinner, and must work in the *Kong Tap Mot* to support his siblings' education. In this risky job Hujan matures and grows fond of Mimpee. Yet when a tragic accident kills Naga, one of the *Kong Tap Mot* fellows, Hujan decides to give up this job and he and Mimpee turn to planting and selling flowers instead.

Director Euthana Mukdasanit is known for his portrayal of the Thai social underclasses, with peasants, the proletarian and prostitutes all making up the main subject matter of his films before *Butterfly and Flowers*. This particular film explores the everyday life and culture of Southern Thai Muslims, a subject matter that was (and, in many ways, remains) underrepresented in Thai film. As an impoverished young Muslim boy in a rural part of Thailand, Hujan in particular is very much a subaltern subject, and the film follows the character's struggle to cope with his hastily enforced maturation whilst also remaining a "good person" in a difficult and exploitative environment. Such difficulties cause Hujan to question his own faith, and eventually it is Naga's death that functions as a divine signal, causing Hujan to turn over a new leaf and return to his faith and the Muslim community.

The mid-1980s was a time of significant growth for the Thai film industry, with more than 100 films produced and screened across Thailand in 1985 alone. *Butterfly and Flowers* was shown in cinemas alongside a heady mix of teen pics, horror, action-adventure and comedy genres. Within this however, *Butterfly and Flowers* was widely successful and won an array of *Tukkata Thong* Awards (Saraswati or Golden Doll) including Best Film and Best Director. A year later, the film also went on to win the Best Film award at the 5th Hawaii International Film Festival. Such success and notoriety continues into the contemporary age. A television adaptation was aired in

2010 and finally, in 2014, the Unify Thai Spirit Foundation included the film in its Royal Anthem music video, celebrating the royal institution, the diversity of Thai culture and this important cinematic memory.

Natthanai Prasannam

Title:	*The Elephant Keeper / Khon Liang Chang*
Director:	**Chatrichalerm Yukol**
Studio:	**Prommitr Film**
Year:	**1987**

Building on the success of his long line of "social message" films, *The Elephant Keeper* was director Prince Chatrichalerm "Than Mui" Yukol's most ambitious attempt to couple the highbrow seriousness of social realism with the populist appeal of narrative genre film. Like preceding efforts in the director's prodigious oeuvre, *The Elephant Keeper* addresses a topical issue – in this case, deforestation and environmental politics – by means of a dramatic narrative with readily legible themes, identifiable characters, and high production values.

Narrated in flashback by virtuous park ranger Chai (Ittisoontorn Vichailak), *The Elephant Keeper* recounts his experiences as a young cadet sent to the country's North to help battle an illegal logging operation in a national reserve. The criminal mastermind of the operation is Sia Hok, a dissolute Chinese timber baron who keeps the locals under his thumb through a combination of intimidation, corruption and blackmail. Caught in the web is Boonsong (Sorapong Chatree), the kindly mahout of the film's title who has been forced into Hok's service by a crippling loan that he incurred while paying for his beloved elephant's medical bills. Befriending the rangers and realizing the environmental threat posed by illegal deforestation, Boonsong is forced into an existential dilemma. All the while, his trusty elephant, Taeng On, remains by his side and ultimately proves Boonsong's saviour.

A clear exercise in environmental consciousness-raising, *The Elephant Keeper* draws from a range of cinematic traditions to evoke both the beauty and degradation of Thailand's natural resources. The opening prologue functions as a de facto educational film with Chai conducting a campfire lecture about deforestation, before shifting into nature documentary mode with pristine wilderness shots vividly rendered through the film's lush 35mm colour cinematography. A sudden jump to images of buzzing chainsaws and circling helicopters spells out the film's central message, while also pushing the film into action mode and the first of several gunfight sequences. As the film unfolds, other elements are thrown into the mix including family melodrama and romance. The film even references animal adventure films, as the bond between human and companion beast becomes a source of both emotional power and narrative agency. It is to Than Mui's directorial credit that he is able to incorporate these disparate elements so coherently.

The Elephant Keeper is also significant as a further entry in the long line of director-star collaborations between Than Mui and Sorapong Chatree. One of the era's most popular leading men, Chatree was an important part of the film's commercial appeal and gives a typically charismatic performance. Additional star power is provided on the film's soundtrack with a number of specially composed songs from popular "songs for life" (*phleng phuea chiwit*) rock groups Caravan and Carabao, with the latter's lead singer, Aed Carabao, even making a brief cameo appearance.

Brett Farmer

Title:	*Boonchu Phu Narak*
Director:	Bhandit Rittakol
Studio:	Five Star Production
Year:	1988

Boonchu Phu Narak's storyline is ultimately quite formulaic: a young man enters and has to survive in a chaotic capital city. In this new environment he makes new friends and with their support eventually achieves his goals. The film tells the story of Boonchu, a naïve young man from the countryside whose mother wants him to go and study for a college degree in Bangkok. Before he goes, Boonchu's mother asks him to do two things: to get a degree (so he will be the first graduate in the village) and to avoid falling in love (since it will distract him from graduation). Nevertheless, in Bangkok Boonchu quickly falls in love with Khun Mo, a pretty young lady who already seems to have a boyfriend and is also pursued by a local gangster. When Mo is kidnapped, Boonchu and his companions must rescue her.

The film employs several stereotypes: all people from the countryside are kind, sincere and dull, while most people in the metropolis are mean and careless (except for Khun Mo). Many characters are from different regions and employ a range of accents, adding to the comedic effect. Boonchu's companions include Vaiyakorn (a guy who has tried repeatedly and failed to enrol in the School of Medicine), Yoi (a talkative and funny overweight guy), Khammoon (an honest guy from the Northeast), Nara (a Southern Thai character who speaks very quickly), and Chuay (a Northern Thai character who speaks very slowly). Many of these performers were also college friends and made comedy TV shows together.

Despite the love story and action sequences, the film is overwhelmingly a comedy, and is neither intense nor realistic. The film also includes musical tracks sung by Thai legendary folk song artist Jaran Manopet. Although no performers actually sing, the lyrics of the music narrate the story from a third person perspective.

Written and directed by the late Bhandit Rittakol, *Boonchu Phu Narak* launched the famous on-screen coupling of Santisuk Promsiri (Boonchu) and Chintara Sukapatana (Khun Mo), who remained Thai favourites for the next decade. Loved by Thai audiences for its light-hearted humour and tales of innocent young love, the film generated over 10 million baht at the Thai box office, and produced seven sequels from 1989 to 2003.

Yossapol Chutipanyabut

Title:	*Ban Phi Pop*
Director:	Saiyon Srisawat
Studio:	Group Four Production
Year:	1989

Phi pop is arguably Thailand's most well-known uncanny creature. In rural folklore a *phi pop* emerges if a person dabbles in black magic and breaches one of the associated taboos. The magic then turns against the practitioner and transforms the person into a *phi pop*. Part of this uncanny transformation is an insatiable hunger for raw meat and human entrails, which the being tries to satisfy by entering fellow villagers during the night to feast on their internal organs.

Ban Phi Pop is the first installment of what would become Thailand's most successful ghost film series, with 13 episodes launched between 1989 and 2011. The first episode was produced as a B-movie with a minimal budget of 400,000 baht and shot in only seven days. The film's idiosyncratic blending of graphic scenes with slapstick comedy elements soon became iconic for the entire genre.

Yet despite its modern outlook, the film's social message remains profoundly conservative and bound to rural ideals. The plot emphasizes the ideal of the chaste and restrained village girl who fulfills her social role without asking. *Ban Phi Pop* is set in a remote village (*ban*) where grandmother Thongkham (Suchada I-Aem) hosts a *phi pop* and randomly preys on fellow villagers. The female protagonist Phlapphlueng (Trirak Rakkandi) continues to care for grandmother Thongkham, despite the rumours of her ghostly identity. When a group of young volunteer doctors from Bangkok accidentally arrives in the village, one of their party, Naret (Ekphan Banluerit), immediately develops a crush on Phlapphlueng. However, the village headman's seductive daughter Kradueng (Kaew Malako) also has her eye on the young and handsome doctor. Unlike the chaste Phlapphlueng, this woman approaches the young doctor quite explicitly, and while Naret rejects Kradueng, she still kills one of his female colleagues the moment she discovers that this woman loves Naret too.

In the meantime, it is revealed that the *phi pop* in grandmother Thongkham is a curse-like effect brought about by the mountain deity that used to be the village's guardian spirit. This deity became furious when a village girl named Ueangsai committed adultery with a soldier from Bangkok. When Ueangsai killed herself to protect her lover, the deity cursed the girl's soul by sending a *phi pop* to accompany the girl during her next lives. Thus we discover that Phlapphlueng and Naret are the reincarnations of Ueangsai and the soldier from Bangkok, both of whom have been brought back together to fulfil their karmic destiny. Kradueng's amoral behaviour also attracts the *phi pop*'s attention. Instead of sticking with Phlapphlueng, grandmother Thongkham transfers the *phi pop* to Kradueng and dies afterwards. This transfer via saliva is depicted in a graphic scene, which highlights the essentially sexual nature of Kradueng's misconduct and indicates how female agency and active sexuality are not only rebellious but also demonic. The chaste Phlapphlueng is then freed from the ghostly presence and heads off towards Bangkok together with Naret, while the village remains haunted by *phi pop* in the person of Kradueng.

Benjamin Baumann

Title:	*Song of Chaophraya / Nong Mia*
Director:	**Chatrichalerm Yukol**
Studio:	**Prommitr Film**
Year:	**1990**

Before his late-career drift into historical royal epics, Prince Chatrichalerm "Than Mui" Yukol was best known as a director of films with a strong social message, or what is often referred to in Thai as "social reflectionist movies" (*nang sathon sangkhom*). Inspired by the political idealism and student activism of the 1970s, these films formed part of a broad-based arts movement colloquially dubbed "art for life" (*sinlapa phuea chiwit*). The principal aim of the movement was to use artistic production of all kinds – film, literature, music – for social commentary and political consciousness-raising. *Song of Chaophraya* was made at the height of Than Mui's social reflectionist period and arguably presents his most stylistically mature work.

Based on an earlier 1978 film directed by Than Muis' father (Prince Anusorn Mongkolkarn) *Song of Chaophraya* tells the kind of country-town morality tale beloved of popular Thai melodrama. Saeng (Chatchai Plengpanich) is a hardworking boatman trying to eke out a living on the mighty Chao Phraya river, selling sand to construction sites. He lives aboard a small weather-beaten boat with his wife Prang (Passorn Boonyakiart), their infant son, and Prang's young teenage sister, Tubtim (Pattamawan Kaomoolkadee). Dissatisfied with the mundane toil of river life, Prang jumps ship for the bright lights of Bangkok where she falls prey to unscrupulous characters in a prostitution racket. Sick with worry, Sang goes off in search of Prang, leaving Tubtim in charge of the baby and the boat. With the aid of a cynical but ultimately kind-hearted taxi driver, Sang scours the city's seedy red light districts, falling foul of criminal henchmen and policemen alike. After a series of dramatic struggles, Prang, duly chastened by her experiences, makes her repentant way back to the boat and the family is reunited.

The story of rural innocents lost in the wicked city is hardly original. However, one of the great distinctions of *Song of Chaophraya* lies in the way it uses the aesthetics of social realism to breathe fresh life into its stock melodramatic content. From its opening shots of dilapidated river boats and sweat-sodden workers together with an ambient soundtrack of noisy machinery and the wail of crying babies, *Song of Chaophraya* offers an unflinchingly gritty vision of working class poverty. The naturalistic performances of the central leads augment the film's powerful authenticity, while at the same time signalling a lyrical optimism of emotional strength. Far from merely melodramatic ciphers, the central characters are deeply human figures with unexpected subtleties and contradictions. Rounding out the film's social realist credentials is its select use of music from original "songs for life" folk group, Caravan.

Song of Chaophraya was a major commercial and critical success in Thailand, winning several awards, notably for Than Mui as director and Chatchai Plengpanich as lead male actor. The director-star duo would reunite on a string of later productions up to and including the director's recent *Naresuan* series. *Song of Chaophraya* was put forward as the official Thai entry for the Best Foreign Language Film at the Academy Awards, but was not selected as a finalist.

Brett Farmer

Title: *Somsri #422R*
Director: Narong Charuchinda
Studio: Five Star Production
Year: 1992

Directed by veteran television and filmmaker Narong Charuchinda, *Somsri #422R* could be categorized as a science fiction film, as the story explores artificial intelligence and in doing so raises questions about life and spiritual values. However, despite these themes, *Somsri #422R* remains overwhelmingly a comedy. The film features Santisuk Promsiri and Chintara Sukapatana, the most popular on-screen celebrity couple at the time, who play a motorcycle taxi driver and Somsri the cyborg maid. Two sequels were released: *Somsri Program B* (1993) and *Somsri Program D* (1995), demonstrating the popularity of the film.

The story follows Somsri, a young and pretty female-appearing cyborg who was created by university professor Ter to assist his wife with housekeeping and childcare. Being new to the world and not perfectly programmed, Somsri unintentionally causes trouble, though is still loved by everyone in the family including Krit, a motorcycle taxi driver who falls in love with her at first sight. However Ter's eldest teenage daughter is not fond of Somsri, and a meddling neighbourhood couple who do not know that Somsri is a robot also try to figure out who the new member of Ter's family really is.

Despite its central science fiction theme, the tone of *Somsri #422R* is very similar to a television soap opera, being a family-oriented film that addresses coming-of-age issues. The plot is very simple and there is little dramatic intensity. Indeed, the antagonistic characters in particular are one-dimensional types similar to those found in traditional forms of Thai stage entertainment. As a genre science fiction is rarely produced in Thailand, and even though *Somsri #422R* focuses upon a robot, the film takes place in the present and gives no explanation as to how the robot has been created.

Yossapol Chutipanyabut

Title: *A Couple in Two Worlds / Khu Thae Song Lok*
Director: Udom Udomroj
Studio: Tai Entertainment
Year: 1994

In the late 1980s and early 1990s Thai film was dominated by the oft-derided "teen industry." This very successful body of films gave rise to the backbone of urban cinemas that was to later enable the post-1997 rise of Thai film nationally and internationally. However, not only was this overlooked period actually crucial to the later development of Thai film and its filmmakers, such films actually offered far more complex social commentary than is often realized. In particular, this corpus generated several underexplored hybrid genres, among these the "vampire teen pic" realized in *A Couple in Two Worlds*, a subject matter more often associated with contemporary America than early 1990s Thailand.

A Couple in Two Worlds recounts the romance between Ken (Saharat Sangkapreecha) and his vampire lover Lan (Kalaya Lertkasemsap). On her 17th birthday Lan is required to prove her vampiric identity to her family, but fails the test. After being hit by a truck, Lan loses her memory and is found by Ken. Ever the innocent optimist, Ken lets Lan stay with him, inviting her to watch his work as a film stunt performer. When Lan's vampire family eventually find her again, Lan is punished by her grandfather and, while Ken rushes to rescue her, Lan ultimately decides to destroy herself in the morning sunlight rather than being forever tortured by her unattainable love for Ken. When Ken is finally injured in a car accident, he meets Lan while unconscious, and although she pushes him back to the world of the living, Ken decides to die to be with her. In true Thai fashion, the two lovers are then finally reunited in the afterlife.

As a "vampire teen pic" the film touches upon familiar coming-of-age themes, most obviously the identity crisis of and familial restrictions placed upon teenagers. Lan is pushed to be a real vampire under pressure from her patriarchal family of her grandfather and many brothers, but seeks her own path in life. Likewise, Ken is pursuing his dream career and wants to be a leading film actor. For both characters, their innocence and optimism is quickly devastated as their romance and dreams are shattered by the violent and abusive world of adults. In the end, Ken refuses to live without Lan, and decides to die in order to be reunited with her in the afterlife, so escaping the world of adults forever.

As a teen pic, *A Couple in Two Worlds* was a star vehicle for the leading couple, who were at the forefront of the Thai entertainment industry in the 1990s. The film was singer Saharat Sangkapreecha's onscreen début while Kalaya Lertkasemsap was a successful model. The film was also well-received and won awards from the Bangkok Critics Assembly for Best Film, Best Director, Best Cinematography and Best Film Editing in

1994. Sangkapreecha also won the best actor award from the Federation of National Film Associations of Thailand (the Suphannahong Awards).

The film also inspired some other later paranormal romance productions, such as Prachya Pinkaew's *Dark Side Romance* (1995), and was adapted for television in 1997. Udomroj followed *A Couple in Two Worlds* with a number of romantic comedy films, including *Destiny Upside Down* (1997) and *As It Happens* (2009). The film underwent a small resurgence of interest when the director sadly passed away in 2011, though is not yet available with English subtitles.

Natthanai Prasannam

Title: *Muen and Rid / Amdaeng Muean Kap Nai Rit*
Director: Cherd Songsri
Studio: Cherdchai Films
Year: 1994

By the time Cherd Songsri made *Muen and Rid*, he was already well-known for producing intense romantic dramas, many of which were set against the verdant backdrop of the Thai countryside. With *Muen and Rid,* Songsri used his signature approach to tell the nineteenth-century love story of Amdaeng Muen and Nai Rid. The film is based on true events, in which Amdaeng Muen successfully petitioned King Mongkut in 1865 to allow her to marry based on love, rather than her father's mandate. The case resulted in the promulgation of a new law, which granted greater choice over marital partners to commoner women over the age of twenty (Loos, 2008, p. 8).

In a provocative opening, the film begins with Rid (Santisuk Promsiri) as a monk, sitting at the edge of a river as a storm blows through. Seeing someone in trouble, he swims to save them but as he pulls the person on land, he discovers a topless Muen (Chintara Sukapatana). After this encounter Rid struggles to erase the image from his mind and the two fall deeply in love. Unfortunately, Muen's father gives her to Nai Phu (Ron Rittichai), a wealthy producer of Buddha statues, to settle a gambling debt, and Muen's mother, who observes traditional subservience to men, will not help her. Phu forcefully takes Muen to his compound, which resembles a fiery hell complete with the statues as furnaces, where Phu's main wife reigns cruelly over Phu's many minor wives and children. After Muen escapes, Phu sues her as an adulterer, claiming that she was married to him through the consent of her father. Muen is finally saved by Rid, after which the two flee to the jungle, which, for the lovers, is both freeing and punishing. Muen determines to write a petition about her case to King Mongkut, and as a result, Muen's relationship with Rid is validated and a new law on marital choice is passed. As with the opening, the film ends with Amdaeng Muen and Nai Rid together in the rain, this time in a loving embrace.

The film was released during a period when television had bypassed film as the most popular form of entertainment, and the Thai film industry was primarily dominated by teen films (Ingawanij, 2006). Yet Songsri's meticulous attention to recreating nineteenth-century Siam, as well as the folk songs and Pali chanting which provide the soundtrack to fairs, dancing, and temple life proved a success, with the film earning significant domestic revenue and praise at international film festivals. What is more, the nostalgic style, evocative depictions of the Thai landscape, and emphasis on international artistic authenticity ensure that *Muen and Rid* can be regarded as a significant predecessor of the post-1997 heritage films (Ingawanij, 2007).

Rebecca Townsend

Title: *Red Bike Story / Chakkrayan Si Daeng*
Director: Euthana Mukdasanit
Studio: GMM Pictures
Year: 1997

Red Bike Story is an iconic Thai teen movie of the late 1990s directed by the well-established Euthana Mukdasanit. Mukdasanit was known for making social problem films in the 1970s and 1980s but shifted his genre style to address teen comedy following the blockbuster success of *A Little Bit Gloomy, a Lot More Slick* in 1985. Subsequently, *Red Bike Story* went on to break all Thai box office records in 1997.

Reflecting the dominance and desirability of American popular culture in Thailand in the 1990s, Mukdasanit combined the source text of a local novel (set in Kasetsart University, where bicycles are the students' main mode of transportation) with the iconography of a typical American college movie. Eastern University in *Red Bike Story* is a fully Americanized campus, with students on rollerblades, cheerleaders in miniskirts, rich kids with cars, and a pocket of nerdy and eccentric freshmen. The film's two female stars Champagne X and Tata Young were part of a generation of Thai transmedia stars who also embodied this international outlook. As an award-winning Thai-American pop singer, Tata Young's persona is very much incorporated into the film, while model Champagne X is depicted as a college femme fatale with many suitors, one who even makes her entrance to the soundtrack of Peter Andre's international pop music hit "Mysterious Girl."

The story begins as Watee (Moss Patiparn Pataweekarn) walks into campus and is nearly run over by a convertible. Though he manages to avoid the car, Watee crashes into Khom (Amita Tata Young) who is riding her bike. The two accidentally swap suitcases, an incident that brings them together again on module registration day. Later on, Watee is distracted by the arrival of Priew (Champagne X), a hot rich girl who causes a commotion on campus, and so must ask Khom for help to enrol in a class. The main story then revolves around Watee's attempts to get Priew's attention, much of which gets him into trouble with senior students, and Khom's enduring kindness towards and romantic interest in Watee. Finally, after she becomes fed up with Watee's lack of interest in her, Khom unveils a radical new look and performs a solo concert at the university freshmen party. When Priew then leaves the university to continue her study in Boston, Watee reconciles with Khom as she tries to help him pass the course for which she enrolled him.

While *Red Bike Story* ends happily, the genre of teen comedy combined with American pop culture virtually disappeared in Thai film after the Asian economic crisis of 1997. The Thai studio system instead turned to nationalistic heritage films, while new technology brought about the rise of independent cinema and regional co-productions. *Red Bike Story* was re-released on DVD as part of GMM Grammy's *Memory Collection* in 2009 and a retrospective examination of this film outlines the successful convergence of the music and film industries by GMM Grammy during this period. The film text also demonstrates the durability of American soft power in Thailand long after the end of the Cold War, and perhaps offers a reflection on the Thai university systems' notorious hazing rituals, which continue to be the subject of public debate today.

Wikanda Promkhuntong

3

New Thai Cinema

Defining a corpus of films as "New Thai Cinema" is not an easy task, since despite the enormous boom in filmmaking at this period, there is no sudden and clear-cut "new Thai cinema" movement at this moment (Chaiworaporn and Knee, 2006, p. 60). Yet certainly, with regards to *mise-en-scène*, cinematography and the general increased budget of Thai films, we can recognize substantial changes that Thai filmmaking underwent in the late 1990s and early 2000s. There was not only an increase in filmmaking quality from a budgetary perspective during this period, but for possibly the first time since the 1970s, filmmakers began to insert much more complex and subjective examinations of Thai society, many connected to the problematic economic context of the late 1990s. The return of several new and significant directors from film schools abroad also helped to kick start this new body of films, as did the emergence of a cinephile culture which likewise fed into the increased awareness of international film culture and a desire to begin exhibiting Thai film at international festivals.

Indeed, these significant films are clustered around the early to mid-2000s, before the main studios of the Thai industry were fully conglomerated, when filmmakers could still enjoy and explore the new opportunities and attention that this boom period of filmmaking allowed. Such films explore the complex forces enacting upon the individual with many, such as *Transistor Love Story* (Pen-Ek Ratanaruang, 2001) and *6ixtynin9* (Pen-Ek Ratanaruang, 1999), addressing the difficult and unequal relationship between urban and rural Thailand. Overwhelmingly we see a focus upon struggling individuals and the often unfair yet dreamlike world they inhabit. Indeed, directors such as Wisit Sasanatieng, Yuthlert Sippapak, and Nonzee Nimibutr do not glorify or romanticize Thailand and Thai people, and such examinations are very different to the "Heritage" films which offer a retreat from the difficulties of the present through a romanticized (and often nationalistic) construction of the past.

Yet, as May Adadol Ingawanij (2006) notes, despite these substantial thematic and budgetary changes, there was no significant industrial change to Thai filmmaking with regards to the overall organization of the industry itself. The network of urban based cinemas that was to host and open up Thai cinema to a much more discerning and cinematically savvy urban consumer with an increased disposal income for such leisure activities as film-going, was already established during the late 1980s thanks to the bevvy of teen movies which kept the industry afloat during this period. Likewise, while such films are social critically, both thematically and formally, the texts never quite drift into the non-narrative filmmaking of the substantial Thai avant-garde, which developed much later in the 2000s and was spurred on by the later international success of Apichatpong Weerasethakul. Indeed, while defining such films is difficult, identifying such characteristics today is even rarer. Within studio conglomeration comes a more fixed definition of filmmaking, and a now clear corpus of avant-garde films and directors means that such experimentation now has its own clearly marked "space" alongside the mainstream Thai industry.

If these late 1990s films are to form a loose corpus, then such films must not be seen as a clear set of characteristics, but rather part of the process by which contemporary Thai cinema and its film industry morphed into a much more internationally savvy industry catering for a new bourgeois urban spectator, one apart from the teen or provincial (up-country) niche audiences addressed in decades before. This brief period then becomes integral to understanding Thai cinema today, indeed it is from such inventive films and such early experimentation that the internationally savvy and big-budget contemporary Thai cinema of the present day takes its origins.

Mary J. Ainslie

Title:	*Fun Bar Karaoke / Fan Ba Karaoke*
Director:	Pen-Ek Ratanaruang
Studio:	Five Star Production, The Film Factory
Year:	1997

Fun Bar Karaoke marked a significant point in Thai cinema as the first local production selected for world premiere at the Berlin International Film Festival. While Thailand and many East Asian countries entered a period of economic crisis in 1997, the New Thai cinema scene in Bangkok had just begun. Some of the first contributors to start experimenting with stylized feature films were directors of TV commercials, among them Pen-Ek Ratanaruang and Wisit Sasanatieng who had both been working for The Film Factory advertising agency. Although *Fun Bar Karaoke* ultimately did not break into the global cult canon, the positive festival receptions marked Ratanaruang as a significant director in the New Thai industry and sparked the late 1990s surge of Thai filmmaking.

The story of *Fun Bar Karaoke* revolves around Pu (Fay Atsawet) who begins to dream of her dead mother building a model house. As the house develops in subsequent dreams, Pu's karaoke-loving father (Phaibunkiat Khiaogao) descends deeper into the underworld of the Bangkok mafia, and, after refusing to engage with a mistress of the mafia boss, is beaten and marked to be killed. Concerned with the dreams and her father's absence, Pu seeks Thai-style spiritual resolutions including donating a coffin in her father's name. Eventually, her father's life is spared by Noi (Ray MacDonald), a secret hitman who shares a mutual crush with Pu.

Through this story and themes, the film marks a backlash against the fast-growing capitalist city, highlighting Pu's lack of a mother figure and her search for human intimacy, both needs that cannot be fulfilled in a nightclub or a franchise convenience store. A better future can instead be achieved, the film implies, by seeking such dreams alone (as in Noi's case) or by returning home to the family (as represented in Pu and her father), and director Ratanaruang revisited such themes in subsequent films.

Beyond the textual level, the film is situated in the 1990s juncture of the Thai entertainment industry, the Hollywood indie, and Hong Kong cinema, targeting a wide range of Thai audiences through well-known transmedia stars including the middle-aged romantic singer Khiaogao, the half-Thai teen idol TV host MacDonald, and the sexy model Champagne X at the height of her career. Reflecting the director's transnational influences, the musical torture scene of Pu's father is reminiscent of Quentin Tarantino's debut *Reservoir Dogs* (1992) while the *mise-en-scène* of Thai hoodlums and seedy bars recalls Hong Kong crime films. At the same time, the contemplating character of Pu and her apartment evoke the cinematic universe of Wong Kar-wai, whose film *Chungking Express* (1997) came out in the same year. This Wong Kar-wai association is also further established as his long-time cinematographer, Christopher Doyle, was to join Ratanaruang for the pan-Asian co-productions *Last Life in the Universe* (2003) and *Invisible Waves* (2006).

Wikanda Promkhuntong

Title: *6ixtynin9 / Rueang Talok 69*
Director: Pen-Ek Ratanaruang
Studio: Five Star Production, The Film Factory
Year: 1999

6ixtynin9 continues Pen-Ek Ratanaruang's exploration of Bangkok life during the 1990s economic crisis. The film positions itself as a dark comedy with mysterious twists, reflected in the Thai title *Ruaeng Talok 69* – "a funny story about numbers six and nine."

The film's mystery begins with a large sum of money delivered in an instant noodle box in front of the wrong apartment room. The metal signage on the room number six keeps falling down, causing the deliverers to mistake the room for number nine. Desperate to keep the money after having been fired the previous day, the room's occupant Tum (Lalita Panyopas) accidentally murders two men who come back to retrieve the box and hides their bodies in her room. Within 24 hours, a series of killings is carried out

Figure 3 A confused and unnerved Tum after mistakenly receiving a noodle box full of money in *6ixtynin9* (1999).

by two parties who attempt to uncover the truth behind the disappearance of the money. After everyone involved is killed in an episodic gun fight, Tum returns to her room only to find more dead bodies, one of which is the boss who fired her. Abandoning her plan to start a new life in the UK, Tum eventually destroys the money and returns to her hometown in the South of Thailand.

Similar to other post-1997 Bangkok-based melancholic dramas, the protagonist roams around transit spaces, from an apartment to a tour agent's office, trying to find direction in her life. Marked by Ratanaruang's directorial style, in which unfortunate circumstances force protagonists to break societal rules, Tum plunges deeper into the chaotic situation, with the only possible resolution being to begin afresh in provincial Thailand.

Yet while this core story is similar to the director's other work, *6ixtynin9* is a much more complex story told through various agents, each with their own individual missions. For fans of East Asian crime films these excessive side-line stories can seem to disrupt the thrill of the event in Tum's room, yet it is this mishmash of events and characters that ultimately enables

Ratanaruang to create his own universe of intertextual connections. These include a reference to Phaibunkiat Khiaogao (who played a lead role in Ratanaruang's *Fun Bar Karaoke*, 1997) through a romantic song, which also serves to suggest a possible love interest between Tum and the policeman who enters her room attempting to catch a drug dealer next door. Lalita Panyopas, who breaks away from her memorable roles in romantic TV dramas for the first time in this film, also returns again as a former TV star in Ratanaruang's *Ploy* (2007).

Now widely available in DVD and streaming sites after being purchased for the US distribution and remake rights, the international promotion of the film drew associations with Western stylized cult hits of the 1990s, most notably Quentin Tarantino's *Pulp Fiction* (1994), and various festival recognitions from Berlin, Brooklyn and Hong Kong followed. While a remake or sequel has yet to be made, Ratanaruang went on to make a series of movies that both revisit and extend the strands of melancholic drama, thriller and comedy, all of which began in *6ixtynin9*.

Wikanda Promkhuntong

Title:	*Tears of the Black Tiger / Fa Thalai Chon*
Director:	Wisit Sasanatieng
Studio:	Film Bangkok, Five Star Production
Year:	2000

One of the pioneers of New Thai Cinema in the late 1990s, Wisit Sasanatieng was deeply embedded within this corpus of directors, working for the same agency as Pen-Ek Ratanaruang and writing the script for Nonzee Nimibutr's *Nang Nak* (1999). His 2000 production *Tears of the Black Tiger* became the first Thai film in the Cannes film festival's official selection.

Tears of the Black Tiger is based upon an old narrative associated with Thai drama, telling a story of class differences and forbidden love between Rampoei (Stella Malucchi), the daughter of a governor, and Dam (Chartchai Ngamsan), her childhood friend from a farmer's family who later becomes a bandit. When Rampoei tries to run away from her engagement to be with Dam, the bandit is so occupied with a killing job that he misses their appointment. Rampoei's fiancé is later caught by Dam's gangsters and Dam releases him out of sympathy for Rampoei, a deadly betrayal of the gangsters which leads to a final shoot-out at Rampoei's wedding party.

The film is a postmodern spectacle and a simulation of the past which offers visual homage to previous eras of Thai filmmaking. Aesthetically, *Tears of the Black Tiger* pays tribute to Thai action movies from the post-World War II era, with Thai cowboy-lookalikes, exact quotes, clichés and exaggerated scenes. These various mountain shootouts, huts in flames, bodily scars, oaths, double-crossing and even the heroine's handkerchief are all familiar motifs to Thais born before 1970. Indeed, several scenes include direct quotes from popular scenes in TV and movies: the sequence of Rampoei carrying her suitcase and walking back to her home is reminiscent of the Thai popular melodrama *Golden Sand House* (1980). Likewise, the macho hero Dam is very similar to the top Thai actor from previous decades, Chana Sri-Ubon. Yet Sasanatieng also blends this older action style with arthouse cinema, a technique that offers particular homage and parody to famous Thai director Ratana Pestonji's experimental style of filmmaking. For instance, while Dam is an American cowboy figure similar to 1960s Thai heroes, he is also an existentialist loner and a melancholic, firstly due to his class status and secondly as result of the nature of his career.

Despite its fame and significance in the New Thai industry, *Tears of the Black Tiger* flopped at the local box office. After its rewards at Cannes however, the film became very successful overseas and Miramax reportedly paid half a million dollars to buy the film.

Anchalee Chaiworaporn

Title: *Transistor Love Story / Monrak Transistor*
Director: **Pen-Ek Ratanaruang**
Studio: **Cinemasia**
Year: **2001**

Premiering in the wake of Thailand's great economic crisis, *Transistor Love Story* is a key film of what came to be known as New Thai Cinema. The film ironically critiques the era's zeitgeist: the vigorous celebration of a "back to basics" Thai-ness and a retro-imagined "Thai way of life." This reliable set of "native" values was often realized in the sturdy image of the hardworking rural Thai peasant, a discourse that could now supposedly sustain the country, its wellbeing and identity after the crisis of "Western" capitalism.

Transistor Love Story tells the story of Paen (Supakorn Kitsuwon), a young country boy, whose naïve charm and talent for singing make him a born entertainer. He falls in love with and soon marries Sadao (Siriyakorn Pukkavesh) amid an idyllic country village setting, and the film's happy ending appears obvious. However, Paen soon has to leave his wife in order to serve in the military. In a thoughtless moment, he deserts the army and runs away to Bangkok to follow his dream of becoming a singer. Lured by false promises, he is soon led astray, and it is only after long years of suffering, broken dreams and a prison sentence that Paen finally and ruefully returns home to his village and his wife, begging her forgiveness.

The plot is built around the dual rural and urban spheres, idealizing country life and characterizing the city as a hostile place. The contrasting spaces signify the traditional and the modern – namely, Westernized – ways of life, clearly attributing moral values to each. The divide between

Figure 4 Paen and Sadao's idyllic country romance in the early parts of *Transistor Love Story* (2001).

Bangkok and the rural is a recurrent theme in Thai intellectual, literary and artistic traditions, especially in a movement known as *sinlapa phuea chiwit* (art for life), which is highly concerned with social realist ideals and aesthetics, appreciation of folk art, and a commitment to the political liberation of the masses. However, *Transistor Love Story* does not simply indulge in nostalgia. Instead, by treating discursive elements of Thai-ness as pastiche or, at times, in an ironic way, the film comments on the constructedness of national identity and on the retro-idealization of a "native" way of life. In the end, the sad fate of Paen and Sadao highlights the unfairness and inequality of contemporary Thai society.

The film is based on a novel by Wat Wanglayangkoon and features Ratanaruang's high-concept visual style, with saturated colours and a film style influenced by 1990s pop music videos and advertising aesthetics. As Paen's fate worsens, the pop culture fantasy evolves into social realism, with a grittier, grainier look and darker colours. The high production values are indicative of the financial and technical upswing in Thai cinema at the time, brought about by foreign-trained directors with transnational careers that also allowed the industry easier access to foreign festivals and markets. Indeed, *Transistor Love Story* was produced by influential Thai director Nonzee Nimibutr's semi-independent company Cinemasia, and was screened at various foreign festivals, including at Cannes.

Natalie Boehler

Title: *Mekhong Full Moon Party / Sip Ha Kham Duean Sip Et*
Director: Jira Maligool
Studio: GTH
Year: 2002

After writing the script of the successful comedy *The Iron Ladies* (2000), Jira Maligool directed his first film, *Mekhong Full Moon Party* two years later. Maligool already had extensive experience directing music videos and TV commercials and was also a co-founder of "Hub-ho-hin," an advertising production house and a former partner of the GTH film studio, where he had been a key player until the studio's dissolution in 2015.

Mekhong Full Moon Party is a comedy-drama based on the real-life unresolved Northeastern myth of the Naga fireballs (*bangfai phayanak*). In this phenomenon, dozens to hundreds of glowing fireballs allegedly rise naturally from the Mekong river in Phonphisai District, Nong Khai province at the end of the Buddhist Lent in late October. According to Thai-Lao beliefs, the Naga fireballs are produced by the Naga king, a giant serpent, to worship the Lord Buddha. The film deploys this disputable phenomenon as a means to portray the clash between rational modernity and indigenous superstition in modern Thailand.

The film depicts the story of Khan (Anuchit Sapanpong), a temple boy who helps Luang Por Lo (the temple's abbot who organizes the phenomenon, played by Noppadol Duangporn) to produce and plant the fireballs at the bottom of the Mekong river. After going to the university in Bangkok, Khan hesitates and refuses to do his usual job to perpetuate the hoax, which he now disapproves of and thinks makes people credulous. Luang Por Lo, who believes that the fireballs help strengthen people's faith in Buddhism, is upset by Khan's newly rationalized rebellion. The situation is then complicated by the arrival of doctors, scientists and news reporters attempting to explain the phenomenon with various hypotheses.

In *Mekhong Full Moon Party*, Maligool deliberately portrays the phenomenon as an encounter of contesting social discourses. The film thereby reflects the "crisis of modernity" in Thailand after the tempestuous decade of 1990s, when the country was swept up in economic boom and bust amidst the arrival of globalization. Nevertheless the film still seems to conclude that faith remains the answer to crisis, as reflected in the film's punch line "Do what you believe and believe in what you do." Such serious conflict is also countered by the many ubiquitous jokes which play around with local belief, making a potentially serious subject optimistically light-hearted. Despite its nuanced portrayal, the production initially faced controversy when it was first released, and was criticized as being disrespectful of local beliefs. Yet after its first screening, the film was quickly well-received, earning 55 million baht and winning nine awards at the Thailand National Film Awards, including Best Picture, Best Director and Best Screenplay.

Chanokporn Chutikamoltham

Title: *Last Life in the Universe / Rueang Rak Noi Nit Mahasan*
Director: Pen-Ek Ratanaruang
Studio: Cinemasia
Year: 2003

Last Life in the Universe, a Thai-European co-production, had a Thai cast and crew, yet also included renowned Australian director of photography Christopher Doyle, and Tadanobu Asano, a Japanese movie star. The film was symptomatic of the changes taking place in the Thai industry at the time, as together with its higher production values, the film's transnational mode of co-production and distribution was a key characteristic of post-97 New Thai Cinema.

The story focuses on Kanji (Tadanobu Asano), an introverted Japanese man living in Bangkok, and outspoken Thai bar girl Noi (Sinitta Boonyasak). They meet by chance, both having just endured major upheaval in their lives. Noi takes Kanji to her house in a small seaside town, where they spend a few idle days together before Noi leaves for Japan. During this time, they grapple with their opposing characters and each confronts their difficult past. Their growing friendship then enables each character to overcome their own loneliness and move on into their respective future lives, while an open ending suggests they may meet again.

Transnational communication is a major theme throughout the film. After initial difficulties and misunderstandings, Noi and Kanji begin to form a friendly bond with the help of three languages: Thai, Japanese and English, so transgressing geographical, linguistic and cultural borders. The friendship also develops within a kind of "no man's land": Noi's unkempt, derelict house that becomes a welcome getaway from the challenges of outside life. This strange haven forms a dreamy atmosphere cut off from any outside context and offers refuge in a place where time seems to dissolve. This setting contrasts sharply with the typical tourist image of sunny, beautiful Thai beaches, instead depicting a scruffy, rather deserted seaside town and melancholic beach scenery with an overcast sky, scenery which corresponds to the off-centred characters and their unlikely connection.

An internationally oriented auteur-inflected production, *Last Life in the Universe* was aimed more towards festival audiences than local cinemas. Christopher Doyle's lyrically shot, carefully framed images and brightly coloured signature style echo Wong Kar-Wai's style of film making, but also recall Pen-Ek Ratanaruang's background in advertising and music videos. The film was not commercially successful at the Thai box office, but was screened at various international festivals, among them the newly created and short-lived Bangkok International Film Festival, where it won the Fipresci prize.

Natalie Boehler

Title: *Citizen Dog / Ma Nakhon*
Director: Wisit Sasanatieng
Studio: Five Star Production, The Film Factory
Year: 2004

After building his reputation as a scriptwriter for the late 1990s hits *Dang Bireley's and Young Gangsters* (1997) and *Nang Nak* (1999), Wisit Sasanatieng went on to direct his own works starting with *Tears of the Black Tiger* (2000), later followed by *Citizen Dog* (2004). Unlike Sasanatieng's first feature, which became a cult title through its association with kitsch aesthetics and Western genre traditions, *Citizen Dog* is much more grounded in Thai popular culture.

Adapted from a Thai novel written by the director's wife, the story follows a chapter structure narrated by a voice-over from Sasanatieng's director colleague, Pen-Ek Ratanaruang. The film begins as Pod (Mahasamut Boonyaruk) travels to Bangkok in search of a job opportunity, despite his grandmother's warning that he may grow a tail like all people in the city. After a period of working in a canned fish factory where he loses his index finger, Pod becomes a security guard at one of the city's high-rises where he meets Jin (Saengthong Gate-Uthong) who works there as a cleaner. Unlike Pod and others, Jin aspires to have a middle-class life. She develops rashes when using public buses and always pretends to read a foreign-language book that fell from the sky. This causes her to decline Pod's marriage proposal, reasoning that their child would still be a tail-less person. The distraught Pod attempts to kill himself when he is visited by

Figure 5 A disillusioned Pod contemplates life as a factory worker in *Citizen Dog* (2004).

his dead grandmother in the form of a gecko with a human face. Losing all motivation, Pod visits his hometown and then becomes an instant star upon his return to Bangkok, as he is the only remaining person without a tail. While stardom does not ultimately lead to a better life, Pod eventually reunites with Jin.

The film depicts the disillusionment of Bangkok citizens (especially the provincial working class and foreign visitors) with the modernized city and the futile dreams it promises. Characters are reduced to scraping a living out of leftovers, represented in the visually iconic mountain of plastic bottles that Jin collects. The Thai name of the film is also a play on words, with the literal translation of "great city" (*Maha Nakhon*) instead becoming *Ma Nakhon* – "city of dogs" – when said quickly. While "dog" is often used derogatively in Thai slang, in this film the term refers to people who have become modernized. This also references the film's theme tune by the Thai rock band "Modern Dog," whose lead singer is also called Pod. This mix of musical and aesthetic traditions in the film (including a rap music video, which offers a backstory to the grandmother's reincarnations into a gecko) also highlights the strange mashup of contemporary Thai culture itself. Yet while *Citizen Dog*'s social commentary may be specific to the local context, the film's audio-visual aesthetics have been interpreted as a wider innovative style of urban surrealism, one which added much diversity and richness to the growth in Thai Cinema during the 2000s.

Wikanda Promkhuntong

Title: *Invisible Waves / Khamphiphaksa Khong Mahasamut*
Director: Pen-Ek Ratanaruang
Studio: Fortissimo Films, Dedicate, Focus Film, CJ Entertainment
Year: 2006

Invisible Waves is a mesmerizingly contemplative and oddly humorous crime thriller. Like Ratanaruang's previous production *Last Life in the Universe* (2003), the film is an international coproduction, and is shot on location in Hong Kong, Macau, and Phuket. Yet Ratanaruang and his Australian-Hong Kong cinematographer Christopher Doyle withhold the familiar tourist iconography expected from these sites: the Hong Kong skyline, momentarily glimpsed from the harbour, appears enshrouded in a gloomy daytime fog. There are no glamorous casino lights depicted in Macau, which is instead represented through gritty, forlorn alleyways and construction sites. Rather than pristine beaches, scenes of Phuket include a pier and two unremarkable hotels. Besides reprising Japanese actor Tadanobu Asano in the lead role of Kyoji Hamamura, *Invisible Waves* features a trans-Asian cast with hazily detailed character backstories: Korean actress Kang Hye-jung plays Noi; Macanese singer-actress Maria Cordero plays Kyoji's Macau landlord; Hong Kong action-comedy star Eric Tsang plays an alcohol-drinking and arms-dealing Buddhist pseudo-monk; and Thai actor Toon Hiranyasap plays Wiwat, a Hong Kong-based chef.

The film's visual aestheticism overshadows its narrative incoherence, indeed the storyline merely serves an existential and metaphysical reflection upon the characters and their situation. Kyoji works for Wiwat in his Hong Kong restaurant, but runs afoul of his boss by having an affair with Wiwat's Japanese wife, Seiko (Tomono Kuga). Wiwat hires Kyoji to murder Seiko, whereupon he orders Kyoji into hiding by paying for his illicit passage to Phuket on a decrepit, outdated ocean cruise liner. At sea, Kyoji meets Noi (Wiwat's mistress), a negligent young mother who repeatedly entrusts her baby to her new acquaintance so she can go swimming. The bizarre cruise ship, with its oddly reversed bathroom appliances and hallway screens, is the film's most provocative protagonist: engendering seasickness, the ship tinges misery with humour. This quality is epitomized by the film's understated climactic stunt in Phuket when Kyoji, climbing down bamboo poles placed between the exterior hotel walls for window-cleaning, slips and falls, knocking against each pole until he lands in the back of a construction vehicle hauling sand.

The Thai National Film Association initially announced *Invisible Waves* as Thailand's submission for Best Foreign Language Film at the 2006 American Academy Awards, but then rescinded its nomination. This decision was likely related to the Association's earlier opposition that year to *Invisible Waves* as the opening film at the Bangkok International Film Festival on the grounds that the film's minority Thai cast, crew, and script (most of the dialogue is in English and Japanese, with minimal Cantonese and Thai) did not qualify it as a "Thai" film. Beyond pushing the boundaries that define Thai national cinema, the film's self-conscious metafiction, with characters overtly wondering "what the end will be like," cleverly reflects its context of production and circulation in the regional film festival circuit as a sea-traversing artistic showpiece between East and Southeast Asia.

Brian Bernards

Title: *Ploy*
Director: Pen-Ek Ratanaruang
Studio: Fortissimo Films, Dedicate, Focus Film, CJ Entertainment
Year: 2007

Ploy is a mind-bending suspense drama that proceeds at a languid pace, with tense, sexually charged, and violent undertones. With a hallucinatory style and partially revealed backstory from dialogue snippets between questionable characters, *Ploy* stylistically follows new wave auteur Pen-Ek Ratanaruang's two preceding features, *Last Life in the Universe* (2003) and *Invisible Waves* (2006), but reverts to an exclusively Thai setting and cast, with Lalita Panyopas of *6ixtynin9* (1999) again in a lead role.

Most of *Ploy*'s action occurs in a literal grey area: a drab, mostly vacant Bangkok hotel with monochromatic grey interiors. This unremarkable yet provocative *mise-en-scène*, mottled with areas awash in blinding sunrays or shadowed behind drawn curtains, engenders the limited visibility, liminal anonymity, ethical ambiguity, and transgressive temptation that define the onscreen encounters between the characters. This setting also magnifies the clouded judgement of the main protagonists, whose decision-making faculties are critically impaired by a potentially lethal combination of jetlag, sleep deprivation, nicotine, caffeine, alcohol, sedatives, prescription drugs (including pills treating erectile dysfunction), and pent-up resentments.

Embodying the hotel's grey-area liminality, the eponymous Ploy (an androgynous child, hinting of womanhood, portrayed by Apinya Sakuljaroensuk) is a precocious teenager whose entrance illuminates the crumbling seven-year marriage between Daeng (Lalita Panyopas), a former movie star, and Wit (Pornwut Sarasin), an émigré restaurateur living in the United States. In Thai, *ploy* denotes jewellery, yet her name (in Romanized lettering on her gold necklace) alludes to its English meaning as a cleverly contrived foil.

Arriving in Bangkok to attend a funeral, Wit and Daeng check into their hotel room at sunrise, too tired to sleep but too sleepy to stay awake. Retreating alone to the lobby bar, Wit meets Ploy, who is ostensibly waiting for her mother's arrival. Without exchanging names or consulting Daeng, Wit invites Ploy to their room to wash up and take a nap. A jealous Daeng eventually departs in anger, leaving Wit and Ploy in a nebulous space charged with latent sexuality. This relational ambiguity is further highlighted by a series of interspersed cutaways to a sexual tryst between the hotel's bartender and maid in an uncannily identical room. Garbed for anonymous role-play, he in a suit that his lover has stolen from dry-cleaning, the couple (never uttering a word to each other) enjoy the taboo nature of their encounter. Their passionate chemistry provides a stark counterpoint to the strained and bickering Daeng and Wit, who no longer "hug, kiss, or have sex," as Ploy prescribes.

Thailand's Censorship Board forced eight cuts to *Ploy*'s graphic sex scenes for its domestic release. While not detracting from the plot, the cuts diminish the potency of the film's montage aesthetic, excising rare cinematic sequences that focus primarily on female bodily pleasure. Nevertheless, the film compels audiences to uncomfortably reconcile the prevalence of rape, marital infidelity, underage prostitution, and woman's overly accommodating attitudes toward men who prey on them. Gliding between this juxtaposition of implicit and explicit, the film does not seek to define social mores or taboos, but rather serves as a litmus test for its viewers.

Brian Bernards and Lalita Singhasri

4

Heritage / Nostalgia

The movement of what Ingawanij (2006) refers to as "Heritage films," arguably began with the success of Nonzee Nimibutr's 1950s-set gangster tale *Dang Bireley's and Young Gangsters* (1997), a film which highlighted the cultural resonance of nostalgia during this late 1990s period. Such an aesthetic can be recognized in the *mise-en-scène* and themes of the new Thai Heritage films in the 2000s, a corpus of films which grew quickly in the new big budget Thai industry. Many productions consist of traditional stories or reference true people and events interspersed with intertextual references specific to Thai culture, history and people as a means to reinforce an identity based upon nationalism. Each film also takes place in a setting that is able to foreground landscape, settings, costumes and props of historical Thailand, presenting an idyllic vision of the nation and the unique traits of Thai-ness in a luscious and exotic portrayal that is attractive to both international and national audiences.

Yet, such a depiction is also problematic. Andrew Higson (2003) defines "Heritage" productions as a model of film that constructs an idyllic but inaccurate distortion of the past in order to retreat from the turmoil of the present. Rather than a critical examination or political analysis of the past therefore, Heritage is an inaccurate distortion and restructuring of historical actuality to suit the present point in time. Higson links the traumatic context of uncertainty and anxiety to such a response as it offers compensation for the destabilisation of society, one to be found in the sense of "identity" and "belonging" that the heritage industry and its corresponding ideology offers. The deployment of Heritage discourses in film is therefore interpreted as a cinematic response to social upheaval, one which promotes a unifying and nationalistic construction of the nation yet which does not attempt to heal or fix the inequality that caused such upheaval.

Certainly, the post-crisis Thai audiences of the late 1990s and early 2000s had much to retreat from, with economic instability resulting in the loss of personal fortunes overnight, all part of a major economic downturn which hurt the poor and impoverished rural and urban Thais the hardest. While such films may therefore contain a very beautiful and quintessentially Thai portrayal of history and culture, this attractive aesthetic should not eclipse the unfair systems and internal turmoil these texts seek to both erase and even condone. Such a corpus operates to uphold the nationalist agenda of Thai elites in the contemporary era and, notably, tended to become far less prominent in the context of growing rural affluence after the 2010s.

Mary J. Ainslie

Title: *Dang Bireley's and Young Gangsters / 2499 Anthaphan Khrong Mueang*
Director: Nonzee Nimibutr
Studio: Tai Entertainment
Year: 1997

A landmark film in the creation of the New Thai industry, *Dang Bireley's and Young Gangsters* first proved that Thai film could be viable as a blockbuster industry, and that a wider audience was accessible through the use of high quality aesthetics presenting an older, somewhat more exoticized version of Thailand and Thai-ness. *Dang Bireley's* was arguably the first Thai film to truly bridge the gap between the teen audiences addressed in the previous decades and the more respectable Bangkokian crowd who now frequented new urban-based luxury cinemas. As such, the post-crisis

Heritage / Nostalgia

New Thai industry owes much to this often overlooked yet highly profitable venture.

This 1950s-set gangster tale positioned itself as both an action number, a teen film and a nostalgic diversion into living memory through its depiction of teenagers in the 1950s and a real-life young gangster who was killed at the time (Ingawanij, 2006). The film follows the young gangster Dang, the son of a prostitute who has been involved in murder and violent crime from a young age. Pressured by his love interest and his mother to leave his life of crime, Dang instead becomes caught up in a circle of violence and is unable to quit the gangster lifestyle. Nostalgia is evoked through both the story itself and the retro spectacle *mise-en-scène* of teen dance halls, a "rockabilly" *mise-en-scène*, Elvis-style haircuts and the carefree yet ultimately self-destructive James Dean-esque attitudes of the young post-war Thai gangsters. Indeed, an epilogue reveals that like James Dean, lead character Dang was ultimately killed in a car accident aged 24.

The success of *Dang Bireley's* indicated that nostalgia had a particular cultural resonance at this moment in Thai history, when the country was suffering the effects of economic crisis. After *Dang Bireley's*, post-1997 Thai Cinema continued to construct depictions that placed emphasis upon nostalgia and the representation of an authentic Thai-ness. However, such depictions largely sought to create an idyllic previous era, and the violence and flaws represented in *Dang Bireley's* were undoubtedly lost in favour of a somewhat sanitized and nationalistic portrayal of Thai-ness, seen in the later development of Thai heritage films.

Mary J. Ainslie

Title: *Bang Rajan: The Legend of the Village Warriors / Bang Rajan*
Director: Tanit Jitnukul
Studio: Film Bangkok
Year: 2000

Tanit Jitnukul is a long-serving veteran of the Thai film industry. He debuted as a co-director of the popular teen flick *Happy Go Lucky* (1985) with Adirek Wattaleela and has continued to work in various positions (director, producer, screen writer and even actor) spreading his work across many different genres. *Bang Rajan* is Jitnukul's best known work thus far, earning him the best director honours at the 2000 Thailand National Film Awards.

Based on a famous historical nationalist tale, *Bang Rajan* tells the story of the central Thai village of the same name, whose inhabitants are forced to fight to the death against the powerful Burmese army in the Siamese-Burmese war. This very notable historical conflict led to the fall of the pre-modern Ayutthaya kingdom during the eighteenth century, so changing the cultural and geographical state of this region. When the villagers' leader Nai Taen is injured in battle, the Bang Rajan villagers invite Nai Chan Nuad Kheo (Jaran Ngamdee), an independent warrior to be their new leader. With limited manpower and resources, the group attempt to fight back against the much more powerful and brutal Burmese invaders who threaten their village. When the Ayutthaya capital refuses their request for a canon, they melt down all available metal objects to construct their own. This ultimately turns out to be unusable, so partly causing the ending tragic defeat ending of the village and the deaths of all its inhabitants.

Bang Rajan became a huge hit for Thai cinema, earning more than 150 million baht at the box office and also enjoyed a limited screening in the US in 2004 thanks to interest from Oliver Stone. Released in the aftermath of the 1997 economic crisis, the film also performed an important nationalistic function during a period when Thai national pride was severely dented. Antagonism towards the contemporary enemy of foreign funds and the IMF are channelled into intense nationalistic sentiments towards the ancient Burmese enemy. The film revolves around themes of unity and sacrifice, the most poignant of which is male protection of the family. Nai In protects his pregnant wife, Nai Mueang safeguards his lover and Nai Thongmen seeks revenge for his dead family. Indeed, *Bang Rajan* was a pioneering text in this depiction of Thai masculine heroic protection towards various symbolic representatives of the nation and Thai-ness. Such a theme continued in later hits such as *Muay Thai Nai Khanom Tom* (2003), *Ong-Bak* (2003) and *The Protector* (2005), all of which reflect a desire to reclaim patriotic heroism in order to restore the nation's image and overcome economic struggle (Kitiarsa, 2007). A far less successful sequel *Bang Rajan 2* was released in 2010 during the height of political unrest.

Chanokporn Chutikamoltham

Title: *Behind the Painting / Khanglang Phap*
Director: Cherd Songsri
Studio: Sahamongkol Film
Year: 2001

Behind the Painting is the eighteenth and the last film of veteran Thai filmmaker Cherd Songsri, who spent the last four years of his life battling cancer and passed away in 2006. As a Western-trained director, Songsri was best known for making period films. His success culminated in the 1970s, when he made what is considered to be his masterwork, *The Scar*, in 1977.

Behind the Painting is a film adaptation of the 1937 highly acclaimed novel of the same name, written by Siburapha (Kulap Saipradit), a newspaper editor and a prolific writer whose works focus on themes of social injustice, particularly social class. Songsri's 2001 production is the second film version of this novel, which was adapted by Piak Poster in 1985. Adapting the novel had been a long term ambition for Songsri, who initially planned to make the film after *The Scar* (having already bought the licence and finished the script). However the project was abandoned after he could not find anybody suitable to play the role of the heroine Keerati.

Behind the Painting narrates the story of Mom Rajawongse Keerati (Kara Polasit), a perfect woman from an aristocratic family who was raised in an elite world away from the rest of society and desperate to get married. In her mid-thirties, Keerati agrees to marry an elderly bureaucrat, Phraya Athikanbodi. To entertain his young wife, Phraya Athikanbodi takes Keerati on a trip to Japan where he asks the student Nopporn (Theeradej Wongpuapan), the son of his friend, to be her tour guide. Nopporn and Keerati find themselves growing closer throughout the experience and finally fall in love. While on a picnic at Mitake mountain, Nopporn professes his love to Keerati, who indirectly reciprocates. Yet Nopporn fails to fully comprehend Keerati's true feelings and situation, which leads to a lovelorn and tragic ending.

Taking place against the backdrop of the 1932 Siamese revolution which overthrew the absolute monarchy, *Behind the Painting* subtly reflects the changes enacted upon class status in Thai society. The tragic Keerati represents the diminishing elite class imprisoned in an oppressive older world, while the young Nopporn represents the rise of the commoners who are beginning to prosper enough to overcome the old elite. Songsri skillfully visualizes this very significant Thai novel, with intricately composed *mise-en-scène* and a subtle narrative pace which portrays the tragic love life of Keerati in a very classical and old-fashioned manner. The script quotes dialogue directly from the novel, making the film poetic and dreamlike rather than realistic. However, the film was not a huge success at the Thai box office, seeming somewhat old-fashioned compared to the faster paced New Thai films of the contemporary industry. Despite this, the film remains a dignified and very beautiful ending to Songsri's impressive oeuvre.

Chanokporn Chutikamoltham

Title: ***Jan Dara***
Director: **Nonzee Nimibutr**
Studio: **Applause Pictures**
Year: **2001**

Following his success as one of the spearheads of the New Thai Cinema movement with *Dang Bireley's and Young Gangsters* (1997) and *Nang Nak* (1999), Nonzee Nimibutr went on to direct his third feature film *Jan Dara*, an erotic period drama film. The film premiered at the 2001 Toronto International Film Festival and was screened in Thailand and elsewhere in Asia. However, due to its sexually explicit content, some of the more erotic scenes had to be removed from the version released in Thailand.

Jan Dara is a film adaptation of a 1964 Thai modern classic erotic novel *The Story of Jan Dara* written by Utsana Phloengtham. Set in 1930s Bangkok, the film depicts the life story of Jan, the son of a wealthy minor bureaucrat known by his title as "Khun Luang." As his mother died while giving birth to him, Jan's father condemns him as a jinx who brings bad luck to the family. Jan is raised by Aunt Waad, his mother's cousin who is also a wife of the highly promiscuous Khun Luang. Growing up in the household with openly excessive sexual activities, Jan adopts Khun Luang's promiscuity, having affairs with maids and even Khun Bunlueang, Khun Luang's lover. Jan is subsequently expelled from the household and returns some years later to enact his revenge, in which history intriguingly repeats itself and Jan finally discovers the shocking truth about his origins.

Jan Dara can be interpreted through a psychoanalytic Freudian lens, with many scenes depicting themes of Oedipal desire and forbidden lust. Jan's earliest memory is of Khun Luang having sex with his "mother" Aunt Waad. Longing for a mother's love, Jan asks Aunt Waad for permission to kiss her breast, where for the first time he experiences climactic sexual pleasure. Despite these numerous explicit scenes however, the Buddhist subtext clearly condemns such excessive desire with severe consequences.

With a budget of 2 million USD, *Jan Dara* was the first contemporary Thai film to be funded wholly by foreign money. Funding came from Applause Pictures, a Hong Kong based company that sought to push pan-Asian cinema on the world stage. The film also co-starred famous Hong Kong actress Christy Chung as Khun Bunlueang, to help attract a pan-Asian audience. Even though the domestic reception of *Jan Dara* was not as good as Nonzee's previous films, the film did mark an important step in the New Thai film industry as arguably the first Thai film to be made purposely for international consumption.

Chanokporn Chutikamoltham

Title: **The Legend of Suriyothai / Suriyothai**
Director: **Chatrichalerm Yukol**
Studio: **Prommitr Film**
Year: **2001**

Prince Chatrichalerm Yukol was an important figure in Thai filmmaking during the 1970s, making noted social-critique films, such as *Citizen* (1977), *Gunman* (1983), and *The Elephant Keeper* (1987). Even when the Thai film industry focused largely upon teen flicks, Yukol still continued to make films such as *Daughter* (1994) and *Daughter 2* (1996), both of which reflect teenage problems and concerns around issues such as HIV in a society that was changing rapidly. *Suriyothai* marked his first shift from the depiction of the poor and commoners to engage in royalty and propaganda, followed later by six episodes of *King Naresuan* from 2007 to 2015.

The film traces the (largely legendary) life of the young princess Suriyothai who, after being married to a prince who later became one of Ayutthaya's kings, was involved with royal politics and battles for the throne in sixteenth-century Thailand. The film tells the story of a fratricidal war between brothers and brothers, as well as old and new dynasties, all of which involve adultery and murder. This royal conflict ends with the coming of the invading Burmese forces, when Queen Suriyothai rides into battle on an elephant armed with a slingblade to defend her city and her culture – and to lose her life.

Suriyothai is rigidly structured into a storyline which follows five dynasty periods. This strictly chronological narrative can be attributed to the director's declaration that "In Thailand, there are few history lessons and the aim of this film, therefore, is to tell our people about our history." Due to its long and at times convoluted narrative, most cuts come far too quickly for any emotional build-up, which was the director's signature attribute in his earlier films. Veteran actors and actresses also have little screen time, and are largely overlooked in favour of the protagonist, who is played by real-life high-class lady and royal descent Piyapas Bhirombhakdi. However, in pursuit of historical accuracy the depiction of the Burmese is also somewhat softened, perhaps by the involvement of Burmese specialist Sunait Chutintaranond.

Nevertheless, Yukol's true originality and signature can be seen through the empowerment of women and suggestions of hidden lesbianism in the court's private life. The three main female characters are juxtaposed to show the different ways women interact with this masculine power game. An ordinary peasant Phra Akkarachaya (Wannasa Thongviset) exercises her sexuality and then brings about the downfall of a dynasty while the "bad" woman Srisudachan (Mai Charoenpura) betrays her husband to restore her own dynasty. In the end, the "good" woman Queen Suriyothai, highly intelligent, brave and dedicated to the kingdom and her husband, succeeds, sacrificing herself in the process.

These female role models confirm the old Thai proverb that "women are the rear end of elephants," a.k.a. pillars of strength. Yet at the same time, female sexuality is devious and must be controlled, and lesbianism is portrayed as "evil" through the depiction of Srisudachan and her private servants and soldiers.

Suriyothai was supported by Thailand's Queen Sirikit and was intended to function as a very public history lesson. The film was first proposed in 1998, a year after the 1997 economic crisis and was funded by 100 million USD from the then Thaksin government. The project was first released in 2001 under the slogan "The Movie of the Siamese Nation" and quickly became the highest grossing Thai film ever made, taking around 200 million USD.

Anchalee Chaiworaporn

Title: *My Girl / Faen Chan*
Directors: Vitcha Gojiew, Songyos Sugmakanan, Nithiwat Tharatorn, Witthaya Thongyooyong, Adisorn Trisirikasem, Komgrit Triwimol
Studio: GTH
Year: 2003

My Girl is the directorial debut of the "365 film" group, which consists of six film school classmates who graduated from Chulalongkorn University several years prior. A huge surprise hit, the film marked the first major success for the newly created film studio GTH (GMM Tai Hub) and the six young directors would go on to become the driving forces behind the studio's prominence. The film helped set up high profile careers for all members of the group and the phrase "from one of the directors of *My Girl*" was used as a mark of quality to promote subsequent individual works of the members for years.

Based on a short story written by Witthaya Thongyooyong (one of the directors) *My Girl* tells the nostalgia-driven story of Jeab (played by Charlie Trairat, with the adult role performed by Charwin Jitsomboon), a man who is invited to the wedding of his childhood sweetheart Noi Na (Focus Jirakul). While making the trip home to his provincial town, Jeab

Figure 6 The gang of boys in 1980s provincial Thailand in *My Girl* (2003).

recalls his happy childhood in 1980s rural Thailand when he enjoyed playing with his friends around the neighbourhood. As a feel-good coming-of-age film, the conflict emerges when the young Jeab, entering adolescence, would rather join the gang of local boys than play with Noi Na and her female friends. Required by the boys to prove his masculinity, Jeab becomes estranged from Noi Na and immediately regrets his actions when she moves away from the village before he can apologize and make amends.

Released in 2003, *My Girl* was part of a nostalgic trend in New Thai cinema during the aftermath of 1997 economic crisis, depicting the "good old days" during a period when Thailand had not yet fully recovered financially. The film evokes an intensive collective memory of 1980s Thailand, one shared by the young adult viewers who grew up during this period. There is significant deployment of various nostalgic elements such as 1980s pop music, retro objects, traditional children's games, and clips from TV shows, even casting 1980s idols and pop singers as Jeab and Noi Na's parents. The film's success therefore typifies this use of fantasy images from the past during an uncertain contemporary period. Yet while the film may romanticize recent history, it does not attempt to bring this back, and instead marks a shift amongst the younger Thai generation, for whom the past is a memory to be kept and temporarily recalled but not revived

Figure 7 Close friends Jeab and Noi Na, the young protagonists of *My Girl* (2003).

(Chaiworaporn, 2006, p. 121). A runaway hit, the film earned over 140 million baht and was the most popular domestic film of 2003, even outgrossing *Ong-Bak* (2003), which remains the more internationally successful and well-known film.

Chanokporn Chutikamoltham

Title: *The Overture / Hom Rong*
Director: Ittisoontorn Vichailak
Studio: Sahamongkol Film, Prommitr Film, Filmhanza, Gimmick Film
Year: 2004

The Overture is, so far, the best known work of veteran Thai film director Ittisoontorn Vichailak. Vichailak began as a member of *Sumo Sam-ang*, a group of Architectural graduates from Chulalongkorn University who ran a popular comedy TV show during the 1980s. After the break-up of the group, he continued to work as a television producer and script writer debuting as a film director in 1993 with the critically acclaimed comedy-drama *Luk Ba Thiao Lasut*.

Considered a flop when it was first released, *The Overture* was pulled from many cinemas after a disastrous first weekend, yet later turned out to be a surprise success. Due to word of mouth, especially on the popular Thai internet forum pantip.com, the film was brought back and quickly became a box office success. The music-drama film is based on the biographical story of Luang Pradit Phairoh (Sorn Silapabanleng), one of the most influential classical Thai music masters. It depicts the life of Sorn, a talented young boy who plays the *ranat-ek* (Thai xylophone). The nonlinear narration jumps between the contrasting lives of arrogant young Sorn and mellow old Sorn, with the protagonists' life paralleled by the story of classical Thai music; from its golden era as a court patronized music troupe during the reign of king Chulalongkorn (Rama V) to its decline in the 1940s, when classical Thai music was banned and labelled as uncivilized by the Phibunsongkram government's modernization efforts.

Like its filmic counterparts also made in the aftermath of 1997 economic crisis, *The Overture* stresses the yearning for the "good old days" and authentic Thai cultural roots. The film's message can be summed up in a conversation between the old Sorn and the government officer who comes to arrest one of Sorn's disciples who breaks the prohibition of playing classical Thai music in public: Sorn likens the Thai nation to a tree which could never survive a storm without its strong cultural roots. Certainly, the film beautifully romanticizes premodern Thai life as one unpolluted by Western influences. This is in stark contrast to the later gloomy wartime period when Thailand was struggling to be "civilized" by imitating the West, with the film's *mise-en-scène* and colour palette designed to reflect such a comparison. The music in the film is also significant; the film employed classical Thai music masters as advisors and even cast a professional musician to play Khun In, Sorn's rival.

The Overture earned over 50 million baht and won many national film awards, creating a brief craze for Thai classical music. The film was also Thailand's official selection for Best Foreign Language Film for the 77th Academy Awards. Its legacy was such, that the film was remade into a TV series in 2004 and a musical play in 2015.

Chanokporn Chutikamoltham

Heritage / Nostalgia

Title: *The Siam Renaissance / Thawi Phop*
Director: Surapong Pinijkhar
Studio: Film Bangkok, Tai Entertainment
Year: 2004

Surapong Pinijkhar's earlier works, such as *Atsacheri* (1976) and *Chinatown Montage* (1982), defined him as a documentarian. Inspired by Russian directors of the 1920s and after teaching film in universities, he became known as a film scholar as well as a director. Such a description is well deserved given his outstanding docudrama *The Silk Knots*, an enigmatic biography of the late silk entrepreneur Jim Thompson, which was shot on film and televised in 2001.

Pinijkhar's historical interests are again manifested in *The Siam Renaissance*, an adaptation of Wimon Siriphaibun's 1987 popular novel *Two Worlds*. The book has been reproduced in popular media many times before, with a 1990 film version, a television series in 1994 and 2011 and several musical adaptations staged in 2005, 2006 and 2011. However, Pinijkhar's was a unique reinterpretation which attracted significant criticism due to its deviation from the source text and other adaptations.

The film tells the story of Maneechan (Florence Faivre), the daughter of a historian who grows up and is educated in France, later working as an officer at the Thai consul bureau in Paris. After taking part in a press conference about the discovery of *Le Voyageur*, Maneechan is brought back to Thailand where she finds an enigmatic time warp to nineteenth-century Siam. Journeying into the past, she meets Luang Akharadhep Warakorn (Rangsiroj Panpeng) who interrogates Maneechan about modern Thailand. Maneechan continues to commute between the two worlds, while the romance between her and Warakorn flourishes. She finally becomes stuck in the past after witnessing the death of her lover in the Franco-Siamese War of 1893.

In this adaptation, Pinijkhar notably shifts the setting from the Reign of King Chulalongkorn (1868–1910) in the novel to that of King Mongkut (1851–1868), so offering a new notion of the "renaissance" and countering the general ignoring of Siam in Eurocentric global history. The film depicts several historical figures involved in both the modernization and colonization of the region, such as King Mongkut, Chaophraya Srisuriyawongse, Dan Beach Bradley, Gabriel Aubaret, and Sir John Bowring. The film also aimed to counter depictions of Siam from *The King and I* franchise, although these scenes were finally removed to avoid any potential controversy.

Given its release in the aftermath of the 1997 economic crisis, the film can be interpreted as another royal-nationalistic and nostalgic depiction of New Thai Cinema. Praised by the Ministry of Culture, the film criticizes present-day society and Maneechan, with her hybrid Eurasian looks, becomes a representation of Thai people who are supposedly leaving their cultural roots behind. This new age of globalization worries Pinijkhar, who has expressed concern about what he sees as the decline of Thai identity. The threats from the British and French colonizers in the film certainly function as an allegory of cultural imperialism in the new millennium. When studied through a postcolonial lens therefore, *The Siam Renaissance* is not simply a historical film but an important commentary upon post-crisis Thailand.

Natthanai Prasannam

5

Nang Phi / Nang Sayong Khwan / Horror

Horror has always been a staple part of Thai cinematic repertoire, although most Thai horror films, steeped in local folklore, history and modes of narrative, have relatively little in common with the genre as defined by major Western productions. While in English horror derives its name from the emotion it is meant to evoke, in Thai it is the content that gives the films their name. Since most Thai horror films follow strictly supernatural plots built around a variety of beings described collectively as *phi* (ghosts, spirits, deities, and demons), they are commonly known as *nang phi*, a term often translated as "ghost films," although the category also includes cautionary tales about the disastrous consequences of abusing black magic. The golden age of *nang phi* lasted from the 1950s to 1970s, a direct result of Thai filmmakers' move to 16mm production. Set in the countryside and infused with supernatural elements, these films wooed rural audiences in a bid to compete with the Hollywood imports that dominated Bangkok's expensive air-conditioned cinemas. More recently, cinematic experiments with non-supernatural horror films have led to the introduction of another category, *nang sayong khwan*, which simply translated as "scary films," although the term has began to be replaced by a foreign-sounding "thriller."

Alongside comedies, Thai horror films are amongst the most profitable Thai commercial productions and they have contributed greatly to the modernization of the Thai film industry. Seen as relatively low-risk investment by film studios and producers alike, they have launched the careers of many talented filmmakers and actors, introduced new production and post-production technologies to the industry, challenged local narrative strategies, and proved that fear is truly a universal (and highly profitable) emotion. It is also not an exaggeration to state that horror films have been largely responsible for introducing Thai cinema to international audiences. Indeed, the history of Thai cinematic achievements is to a large extent the history of Thai horror. In 1999, *Nang Nak* (Nonzee Nimibutr) became the first ever Thai film that found a foreign distributor. In 2004, *Shutter* (Banjong Pisanthanakun and Parkpoom Wongpoom) made history as the first ever Thai film that got a Hollywood remake (Masayuki Ochiai, 2008). In 2013, *Pee Mak* (Banjong Pisanthanakun) broke all records as the highest-grossing Thai film ever and became an international sensation, particularly within Asia. Each of the three should not only be seen as a horror film but also a milestone in Thai cinema. Even the critically acclaimed *Uncle Boonmee Who Can Recall His Past Lives* (Apichatpong Weerasethakul, 2010), the winner of Palme d'Or at Cannes, is in effect a ghost story.

Today Thai horror has its fair share of Thai and international followers. To reach this global level of popularity, however, the genre had to redefine itself quite drastically. Thai horror films are often separated into "early" (pre-1999) and "modern" (post-1999) productions. The said "modernization" of the genre is commonly attributed to Nimibutr's *Nang Nak*, which returned to the classic story of the Thai most beloved ghost-wife Mae Nak to engage with the symbolic narrative of "Thai-ness" and evoke nostalgic sentiments for the idealized national past that played well with the contemporary audiences recovering from the aftermath of the Asian Crisis. While the pre-1999 movies were preoccupied with the Thai village, since the rural periphery with its prevailing animistic belief system was commonly seen as prone to superstition and also a likely site of supernatural manifestation, the post-1999 films have taken the action to the city and have been refashioned to suit the tastes of the middle-class urban audiences. Influenced, to a certain extent, by the horror trends promoted in Japanese and Korean movies, and largely devoted to telling gripping stories of vengeful spirits spiced with graphic imagery of bodily destruction, these films have succeeded in blending supernatural and body horror into one attractive and highly marketable package.

Katarzyna Ancuta

Title: *Nang Nak*
Director: Nonzee Nimibutr
Studio: Tai Entertainment
Year: 1999

Nonzee Nimibutr's 1999 rendition of the oft-remade supernatural tale of the legendary Mae Nak – a woman who dies in childbirth while her husband is away serving in the army and who then dutifully awaits his return – is considered to be a landmark in Thai cinema on a number of levels. Most importantly, its success was crucial in helping revive what was at that time a fairly moribund Thai film industry and raise international awareness of the existence of Thai cinema. Originally developing his production skills in the advertising industry, Nonzee already had a domestic commercial hit with his 1997 debut period crime feature *Dang Bireley's and Young Gangsters*. However his 1999 production of *Nang Nak* not only broke domestic box office records of the time, but proved a hit on the international film festival circuit as well, something almost unheard of for a Thai film at that time.

The repercussions of this success were significant, inspiring would-be producers and filmmakers to put more focus on local feature production. *Nang Nak* thus helped spur the return of a modestly active local film industry by the early 2000s while also creating (in the perceptions of audiences) a strong association between Thai film and the horror genre. Indeed, not surprisingly, a good deal of this local production was in the horror genre (given further momentum by the contemporaneous trend in Asian horror in the wake of 1998's *The Ring*) and the film thereby contributed significantly to solidifying this as a key component of the modern Thai cinema "brand." *Nang Nak* can also be seen as central to the start of a trend of Thai productions made with a global audience in mind (with its emphasis on global-standard production values and clarity of narration) and also

Figure 8 A ferocious Nak lashes out at the tormentors who would send her back to the dead and away from her family in *Nang Nak* (1999).

of productions self-consciously preoccupied with questions of national historical legacies and cultural traditions (and thus, implicitly, of national identity).

While certain earlier versions of the Mae Nak tale (and, indeed, earlier traditions of Thai supernatural film more broadly) had been characterized by regular modulations in tone and shifts from the horrific into sequences of slapstick comedy, Nonzee's approach is much more consistent and even handed (again in keeping with global convention). Indeed, its fantastic subject matter notwithstanding, the film can be described as the singularly most realistic and historically accurate version of this narrative (for which the director expended great effort on period research). The film also emphasizes a heightened sense of pathos and sympathy for the Nak character, rendering the tale more one of a tragic love story than of abject horror. Likewise, there is also a strong focus on the theological (and implicitly political) contradictions of Nak's own assertion of her right to remain on earth as a spirit and to pursue her love in a patriarchal Buddhist context, one which insists upon self-denial and the relinquishing of earthly desires and connections.

Adam Knee

Nang Phi / Nang Sayong Khwan / Horror

Figure 9 A subdued Nak sits in her grave and says goodbye to her husband Mak under the watchful eye of the monk in *Nang Nak* (1999).

Title: *Buppha Ratri: Flower of the Night / Buppha Ratri*
Director: **Yuthlert Sippapak**
Studio: **Mahagan Films, Mangpong, Nakomthai Picture**
Year: **2003**

Mobilizing the ever-popular sub-genre of horror comedy, *Buppha Ratri* proves that despite the creation of a new commercially viable blockbuster industry and an infrastructure of urban multiplexes to support it, Thai film style remains indebted to the earlier eras of Thai cinema.

Buppha Ratri tells the story of the lower-class female student Buppha (Laila Boonyasak), who is seduced by a rich young playboy Ake (Krit Sripoomseth) for a bet. Abandoned by Ake, Buppha dies from a botched abortion while waiting to be evicted from her dingy Bangkok apartment. Like the much more successful *Shutter* released a year later, the film chooses a sprawling urban setting and, similarly to both *Nang Nak* (1999) and *Shutter* (2004), it also depicts the callous mistreatment of a young woman. Yet while the opening seduction, death, and ghostly return of Buppha appear to set up the familiar tragi-horror revenge narrative, the film quickly shifts to become a series of slapstick comedy, graphic horror and action numbers, as the story focuses on the terrified reactions of the building's other bizarre residents to their new ghost neighbour.

These include the obese ladyboys who own the hairdressing salon downstairs, a shop clerk with Down's syndrome with his sidekicks, a troupe of whiskey-swigging fake ghost busters and a room full of teenage wannabe rock stars (responsible for much of the film's soundtrack). The frustrated landlady, who is losing tenants due to the blood-curdling screams emitting from room 609, employs various means to remove Buppha's ghost, including a fake magician, a Catholic priest, and finally a genuine shaman, all of whom fail. The original tragic tale is lost in the chaotic antics of visual humour and extended comedy scenes in which the ghost terrorizes her would-be exorcisers, chasing them down corridors and appearing suddenly in elevators.

Buppha Ratri appears pulled between the visual excess of the earlier eras of Thai cinema and the globally recognizable horror style of J-horror and K-horror that *Shutter* so deliberately adopts. This is encapsulated within the very different marketing styles adapted to promote the film, with international editions adopting the more refined psychological horror traits associated with East Asia and the Thai edition depicting a blood and vomit splattered hacksaw-wielding figure of Buppha staring down menacingly from huge posters.

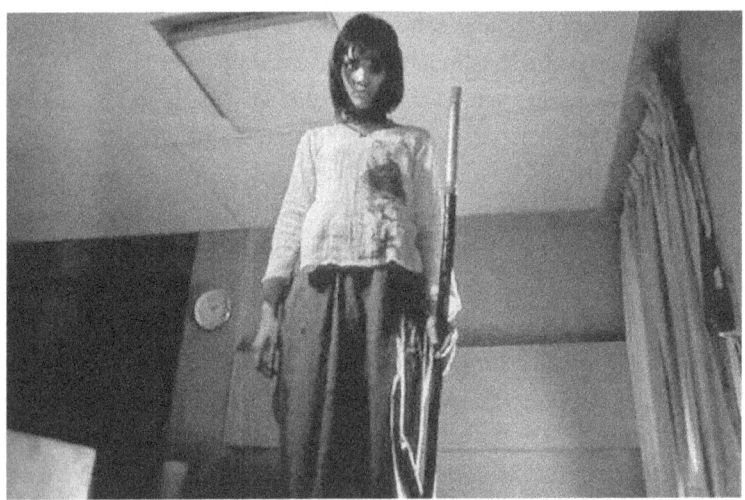

Figure 10 The dead Buppha stares down at her next victim in *Buppha Ratri: Flower of the Night* (2003).

This fusion pulls the film between different genre expectations and notably, while *Buppha Ratri* performed well in Thailand and was the third highest grossing film of 2003, its non-Thai reviewers appeared perplexed by the strange format when it appeared at the Toronto International Film Festival 2004. The high level of parody was regarded as unoriginal, and the mixing of visceral genre traits a "disaster." Yet the film's ending also elevates the film's significance as social commentary. A major twist ensures that the undead Buppha and her lover are stuck together for eternity in room 609, and in consequence the film refuses to offer any solution to the inequality and abuse of contemporary Thailand. Three more sequels were to follow.

Mary J. Ainslie

Title: *The Unborn / Hian*
Director: Bhandit Thongdee
Studio: Sahamongkol Film
Year: 2003

Director, writer, and producer Bhandit Thongdee builds upon his already eclectic generic corpus with *The Unborn*, a horror film, which joins Thongdee's previous genre hybrids *Hoedown Showdown* (2002) – comedy-musical, *Mercury Man* (2006) – superhero-martial arts-drama, *4 Romance* (2008) – romance, and *Pumpuang* (2011) – a biopic-musical. With its high production values, *The Unborn* draws from the aesthetics of previous New Thai horror films, with a *mise-en-scène* that is similar to such successes as *Nang Nak* (1999) and *The Eye* (2002). Indeed, in an intertextual nod to fans of Thai horror, central actress Inthira Charoenpura previously also portrayed Nak in *Nang Nak*.

The Unborn centres on Por (Inthira Charoenpura), a working class female protagonist who survives a near drowning at the hands of a violent drug dealer. The narrative follows her as she comes to terms with her unexpected pregnancy and subsequent haunting by the fearful spectral presence of Mai (Prangthong Changthom), who, the audience soon learns, was murdered and her foetus was then cut from her dead body. Both Por and Mai are linked through their pregnancies to the extent that Por feels the need to right the injustice perpetrated upon Mai and her unborn child.

Similarly to *The Eye*, the film depicts a horrific and sensuous tension between the various senses of hearing, taste, touch, and, most provocatively, smell, all attached to the experiences and subjectivity of the central protagonist. Thongdee evokes this sense of smell through hallucinations (or perhaps flashbacks) depicting Mai's tortured somatic memory, during which Mai's foetus is removed from her dead body. The scene draws attention to the desiccation and decay of flesh; the once vibrant red pulse of blood is now a viscous black and reaction shots from the characters are prominent, as they watch the undertaker reach into the womb to pull out the dead foetus. Gelatinous sounds and close ups of the witnesses' reactions hint at the rancid smell emanating from the putrid womb; some grimace, while others hold their noses at the gases emitted by the decayed body.

This complex tapestry of sounds, smells, tastes, tactility, and vision becomes a means to engage with the Thai pantheon of spirits or *phi*: the *phi tai hong* (spirits who have died a violent death), *phi tai thang klom* (the vengeful spirit of a dead pregnant woman) and the *kuman thong* (a foetus ripped from his mother's womb). The *kuman thong* in particular features prominently through sound; the poignant wails of the foetus and otherworldly laughter reverberate as a series of spectral echoes, and the story follows Por and her companion as they attempt to uncover the origin of this *kuman thong*. Clues lead the characters to a casino owned by a Taiwanese businessman, and they eventually discover the foetus encased in the casino wall, ostensibly to bring luck and prosperity. Por spends the rest of the film attempting to reunite mother and foetus in the hope that they can both rest in peace.

Sophia Siddique

Title:	*Sars Wars / Khun Krabi Phi Rabat*
Director:	Taweewat Wantha
Studio:	Chalermthai Studio
Year:	2004

Sars Wars is a fast-paced gore-infused Technicolor race-against-time set to a thumping pop soundtrack. The film begins when Bangkok is infected by a new virus from Africa. The virus turns the unwitting hosts into bloodthirsty zombies complete with fangs, exploding heads and psychotic foetuses that burst out of their mother's womb. Isolating the virus in a skyscraper, the beautiful Dr Diana (Lena Christensen) believes she can find a cure and reverse the infection before the authorities blow up the building. Also inside, however, young superhero champion Khun Krabi (Supakorn Kitsuwon) is setting out to rescue Liu (Phintusuda Tinphairao), the daughter of a diplomat, who has been kidnapped to ransom. When he is in need of assistance, his incompetent, overconfident and slightly sleazy mentor Thep (Suthep Po-ngam) arrives to save the day.

The zombie is not a character in Thai mythology. The dead are conscious and present when they return in Thailand, and notably the zombies of *Sars Wars* are able to make somewhat semi-conscious decisions. None of the familiar rules governing monstrous creatures, or even filmic logic of what can and can't happen are present, with characters able to stop the movie and speak to the audience at will. The Sars virus never actually appeared in Thailand, but it did have a significant impact upon the ever so crucial tourist industry and the Thai imagination. Bird Flu did follow with a few deaths, and the plot of a foreign disease infecting Thailand can certainly be attributed to these events, with some very stereotypical depictions of Africa opening the film.

With its many parodies and ridiculing of mainstream zombie movies coupled with slapstick humour, *Sars Wars* carved a name for itself on the festival circuit. A send-up of almost every convention known to film, it is certainly fun to spot the many intertextual filmic references present, as well as the veiled criticism of government corruption and hypocrisy: the minister charged with containing the break-out of the new virus bears a close resemblance to the Thai health minister at the time. The production also demonstrates the very successful and skilful insertion of physical comedy alongside graphic horror, as well as what is possibly the first use of manga-style animation in a Thai movie. *Sars Wars* also contains deliberate and heavy criticism of the Thai censorship code while demonstrating the ingenuity of young directors to grapple with its constraints (the use of Muay Thai boxing complete with noodles to simulate forbidden sex scenes is particularly inventive). The plot is loose, the jokes crude and the familiar cast of sexy scientists, cliché-ridden superheroes and obese transsexuals, all very familiar and staple figures in the world of slapstick Thai comedy, ensures that this is a movie to which you can truly attach the label "only in Thailand…"

Mary J. Ainslie

Title: *Shutter / Shutter Kot Tit Winyan*
Directors: Banjong Pisanthanakun, Parkpoom Wongpoom
Studio: GMM Pictures, Phenomena
Year: 2004

Still regarded as the "scariest Thai horror movie ever," *Shutter*'s success within the rapidly growing New Thai industry was remarkable. Of the 48 Thai films released in 2004, *Shutter* was the highest grossing and the 4th highest at the overall 2004 Thai box office, surpassing several Hollywood blockbusters. Billboards and posters for *Shutter* covered Thai shopping malls and the film arguably launched the high-profile careers of both the actor Ananda Everingham and director Banjong Pisanthanakun.

For such a remarkable film, the story of *Shutter* is relatively conventional. The film follows a young and fairly affluent Bangkok-based couple: Thun (Ananda Everingham), a photographer, and his student-girlfriend Jane (Natthaweeranuch Tongmee). When driving home one night from a friends' wedding, they accidentally hit a girl in the road. After driving off and leaving her, strange white blurs appear on Thun's photographs and Jane begins investigating the spirit she believes is haunting them. A prior story of abuse by Thun and his friends towards a shy upcountry girl Natre (Achita Sikamana) is slowly revealed as Natre's spirit intrudes into the couples' life.

The film's narrative is easily characterized as a revenge story in-keeping with Creed's familiar "monstrous feminine." The whoring, boozing "bromance" culture of Thai men is placed firmly under a critical spotlight and the consequences of using and abusing lower-class women as vessels for masculine bonding are suitably horrific. Several "twists" also cast doubt upon the viewer's own knowledge and identification with the protagonists. The cinematography is similarly complex and

Figure 11 Standing next to jars of preserved creatures in the university biology lab, Jane attempts to take a photograph of the ghost she believes is haunting her and her boyfriend Thun in *Shutter* (2004).

impressive: memorable scenes include a chase sequence as Thun and Jane drive through rural Thailand in search of the elusive Natre, while a scene in a cheap hotel involves a particularly frightening ghostly apparition at the end of a bed and sees the terrified Thun trapped in a never-ending stairwell.

Yet for its quintessentially Thai ghost plot the film resonates with a global audience. *Shutter* adopts the *mise-en-scène* of a prominent image of "Asian horror" with its Far East Asian aesthetic. The film's black-haired and white-skinned female ghost is remarkably *Ringu-esque* while Thun's dark, linear Bangkok apartment conjures up images of K-horror and J-horror while the narrative is altered to incorporate the question and answer suspense structures associated with globally successful horror films.

Such alterations arguably played a large part in moving *Shutter* beyond purely local audiences and the film has probably achieved much wider international distribution than any other Thai horror film before or since. Yet while *Shutter* can be found on DVD racks internationally, marketing often includes virtually no reference to its Thai origins, an indication perhaps of the continuing coagulated image of "Asia." While lauded as a

Figure 12 The ghostly Natre appears at the end of Thun's bed in *Shutter* (2004).

successful Thai film therefore, *Shutter* ironically erases many of the cultural and stylistic specificities seen in other post-1997 Thai horror films such as *Nang Nak* (1999) and *Buppha Ratri* (2003). This is perhaps most evident in the film's 2008 Hollywood remake, which was set in Japan and follows an American couple haunted by the ghost of a Japanese woman. The film remains highly significant as a work of Thai cinema however: few Thai films have surpassed *Shutter*'s legacy, and the film remains popular in Thailand and in countries where Thai popular culture is not otherwise prominent.

Mary J. Ainslie

Title: *Zee-Oui*
Director: Buranee Rachjaibun, Nida Suthat Na Ayutthaya
Studio: Matching Motion Pictures
Year: 2004

Given its historical subject matter, *Zee-Oui* fits within the corpus of Thai "heritage" films of the 2000s, albeit without the glossy idealized depiction of old Thailand. The film was the directorial debut for Thai sisters and cinematographers Nida Suthat Na Ayutthaya and Buranee Rachjaibun, and was the first feature film release for the newly formed Matching Motion Pictures Co. Ltd., a subsidiary company of the largest advertising production company in Thailand Matching Studio. Despite the studio's ambitious aspirations however, *Zee-Oui* became one of many underperforming productions from newly created companies hoping to join the boom of Thai cinema in the early 2000s.

The film is based upon the true story of the Chinese serial killer Li Hui (colloquially known as Zee-Oui in Thai) who entered Thailand in 1946 and was executed in 1959 for killing and cannibalizing eight Thai children. For their first production, the Matching Studio deliberately chose an old and well-known story which resonated well with its target audience, many of whom had grown up with the frightening tale of the Chinese foreigner who ate Thai children. Indeed, Zee-Oui himself has been portrayed in an earlier TV adaptation (Channel 5, 1984), and his preserved body remains on display in the Bangkok Siriraj museum of forensic medicine for all to view. The 2004 film follows the main protagonist (played, unusually, by a Chinese actor, Yihong Duan) as he arrives in Thailand from China, gets a job as a servant to a local Thai family, and then moves further around the country looking for work. During this time, Zee-Oui kills and eats the various Thai children before he is eventually caught by a local female journalist and the police.

The film suited the climate of heightened suspicion towards outsider influence generated by the post-1997 period of economic crisis in Thailand, which favoured a "localist" movement towards Thai self-sufficiency. Yet this initially xenophobic portrayal of outsider influence actually depicts the character in a very sympathetic light, showing the anti-Chinese racism Zee-Oui encounters within Thailand and the terrible conditions he is forced to live in. Eventually however, the film attributes Zee-Oui's cannibalistic qualities strongly to his Chinese heritage. Such scenes include a flashback to forced cannibalism by the Chinese army and a Chinese knife given to him by his mother that he uses to kill the children. The film even ends with a flashback scene set in China depicting the protagonist's peasant mother cutting out the heart of an executed criminal and feeding it to a young and sickly Zee-Oui in an attempt at curing his illness, a practice firmly situated as a Chinese custom.

Such xenophobia and paranoia is then continued into the ending credits, which depict closing scenes from Zee-Oui's trial. In prison the criminal is approached by a police officer who informs him that if he "confesses" to the murder of all eight children, he will be allowed to return to China (a goal that he has spent the second half of the film pursuing). However, the heroine journalist (Premsinee Ratanasopha) confides to her colleague that there is no possible means for Zee-Oui to be responsible for all deaths. The film therefore suggests that despite Zee-Oui's death, another threat remains internally but cannot be located and will continue to prey upon Thai citizens.

Mary J. Ainslie

Title: *Art of the Devil 2 / Long Khong*
Directors: Kongkiat Khomsiri, Art Thamthrakul, Yosapong Polsap, Putipong Saisikaew, Isara Nadee, Pasith Buranajan, Seree Phongnithi
Studio: Five Star Production
Year: 2005

This 2005 feast of gore was directed by a collective of seven directors who call themselves "the Ronin Team." Like Banjong Pisanthanakun and Parkpoom Wongpoom's popular *Shutter* (2004) the year before, the story of *Art of the Devil 2* revolves around the tale of a vengeful spirit. The film performed modestly domestically taking in just under 315,000 USD, with the bulk of its total gross (1 million+ USD) coming from international releases. While revenge and black magic are also themes of the original *Art of the Devil* (2004), *Art of the Devil 2* shares only a name, not characters or scenarios, with its predecessor. Since the two films were released in Thailand under unrelated titles, it is questionable whether *Art of the Devil 2* should be considered as a sequel at all. To add to the confusion, the Thai title, *Long Khong,* reappears in the prequel, released in 2008 as *Art of the Devil 3*, or *Long Khong 2*.

The story offers a cautionary tale about the dangers of consulting spiritualists or witch doctors for advice in fortune and love, a popular practice in Thailand. When teacher Ms Panor (Napakpapha Nakprasitte) is humiliated at school by students who publically broadcast a video of her adulterous encounter with a school coach, she seeks out a witch doctor to enact her gruesome revenge on the students. Through a series of flashbacks it is then revealed that Ms Panor has not been the only one to turn to black magic, and this dangerous use eventually causes suffering and death to everyone it touches, with the circle of friends enduring a series of horrors throughout the film.

The suffering body is the key spectacle of the film, with each student undergoing a different form of torture. Perhaps the most enigmatic image is of a man being torn apart by fishhooks that appear from within his own body. Other grotesque spectacles include cannibalism, geckos bursting out of a man's body and another young man being burned alive with boiling water and a blow torch. Similar to films such as *Ghost Game* (2006), the film also depicts witchcraft and black magic as strongly linked to Khmer culture, with curses traced back to Cambodia and Khmer characters carved into Ms Panor's arms.

The destructive consequences of sexual transgressions are also important. Ms Panor was previously married to one of the student's fathers while simultaneously carrying on an affair with both the school coach and another student. When the coach discovers that the friends had filmed his sexual encounter, he attacks and sexually assaults them. Likewise, in a final

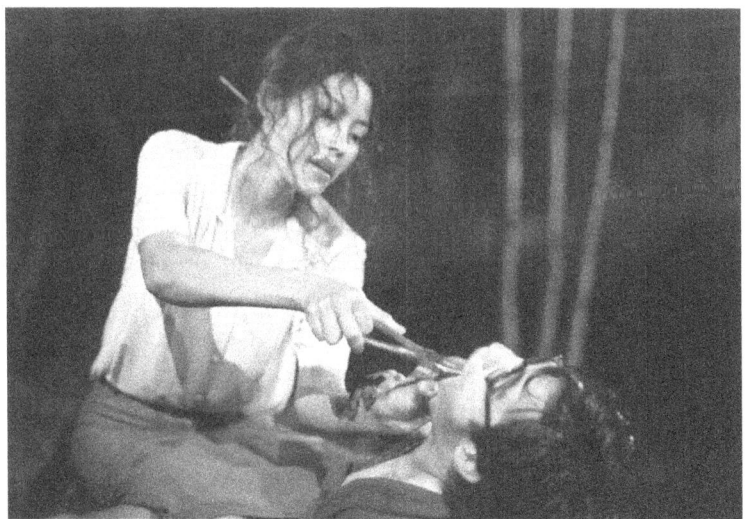

Figure 13 Miss Panor enacts her brutal revenge in *Art of the Devil 2* (2005).

surprise plot twist, we also learn that one of the students was actually a vengeful spirit who had orchestrated the events to ensure that his friends would suffer as he had before his death. The last surviving member of the group then eventually takes her own life in the final moments of the film. It is revealed that she too had turned to black magic to help earn his love and her death is presumably a final act to purify her transgression.

Raphael Raphael

Title:	*Scared / Rap Nong Sayong Khwan*
Director:	Pakphum Wongjinda
Studio:	Sahamongkol Film
Year:	2005

Scared is the second film of Pakhpum Wongjinda, who debuted in 2004 with *Formalin Man*, a lighthearted comedy about a country music star who continues to perform with his band despite the fact that he is dead and decomposing. Released a year later, *Scared* takes a more serious approach to horror, resulting in a rather effective Thai variation of a slasher movie with cute students being dispatched one after another by masked killers in spectacular fashion. The Thai title of the film refers to a controversial hazing ritual known as *rap nong*, performed as an initiation rite on groups of new students at Thai universities. Every year the Thai press reports on incidents bordering on abuse and torture intended to inspire blind obedience in the new generations of "freshies," as such students are commonly called in Thailand. The film portrays a bonding trip to the forest (organized as part of the *rap nong* events) that goes horribly wrong.

In the opening scenes the film provides us with the ultimate "money shot" which took a large part of the film's budget; a bus full of students plunges into a river from a collapsing rickety wooden bridge. A few survivors then attempt to find their way back to civilization only to be brutally killed one by one under mysterious circumstances. The first deaths look suspiciously supernatural, and the film suggests the students are killed as punishment for offending forest spirits. Yet it soon becomes obvious that they are being hunted by humans. While the identity of the killers is never revealed, we are asked to view this as part of some bigger intrigue that is ultimately never clearly explained. The resulting confusion can be partially attributed to the producers' unwillingness to embrace the director's originally proposed serial killer plot, since they worried this might alienate local audiences who expect Thai horror films to deal exclusively with ghosts and black magic. The film's young actors also did not help, with some insisting upon changing the ending as they did not want to die in their first film (Ngoenwichit, 2008, p. 130).

Despite such complications, *Scared* is remarkably effective as a slasher film and largely delivers the promised gory thrills. The first deaths, resulting from the bus crash, occur seventeen minutes into the movie and keep on coming. The complex death scenes are inspired by their locations, progressing from natural to more industrial settings. Wongjinda is known for his preference of working with inexperienced young actors, whose "rawness" he finds both fresh and natural. *Scared* is the first of his films to focus upon teenagers and young adults, addressing the dark side of growing up in Thailand, a topic to which he returned in *Video Clip* (2007) and *Who R U?* (2010).

Katarzyna Ancuta

Title: *13 Beloved / 13 Game Sayong*
Director: Chookiat Sakveerakul
Studio: Sahamongkol Film
Year: 2006

While heritage and nostalgia productions were a crucial part of revitalizing the New Thai Cinema industry, *13 Beloved* reminds us that this industry also emerged during a post-crisis atmosphere of frustration and powerlessness. The film follows a day in the life of struggling salesman Chit (Krissada Sukosol), who is shackled by debt and an oppressive, yet morally enforced, network of family obligations. One day, Chit receives a mysterious phone call inviting him to play a game for money which consists of a series of 13 tasks. These become increasingly depraved as Chit continues, yet completion offers cash prizes that he could otherwise never afford.

Chit's female friend Tawng (Achita Sikamana) attempts to investigate the purpose of the mysterious game and who is running it, and her ending war of words with the elusive game creators seems to articulate the questions and queries regarding life and freedom that the movie is grappling with. Mirroring the plight of Bangkok workers at the mercy of an elite that is rarely held to account, the organization behind the game seems purely focused upon humiliating Chit for the sport of unreachable and unknowable others. While Tawng begs the organizers to stop torturing her friend, screaming "How can you screw with people's lives?" she is met with the reply "People make their own choices," questioning how free people can be at the mercy of a global economy. In the ending, Chit makes what is possibly his only true choice, yet one which has tragic results.

The half-Western Chit also has significant financial obligations to his family, a situation shared by a great many Bangkok workers. Chit cannot refuse these requests for money, and has no control over their spending. Yet this dependence and obligation is also mirrored by the uncaring responses from an obviously richer Bangkokian family in the film, who have neglected their grandfather and in their obsession with video games, nail polish and the trimmings of a consumerist lifestyle haven't noticed that he's died.

The intriguing story is complemented with a healthy dose of slapstick comedy and action, which is potentially attributable to the film's origins as a graphic novel. The tale itself is taken from a short story episode of the *My Mania* Thai graphic novel series called "13th Quiz Show" and also had a promotional short film prequel *12 Begin* (2006) and a graphic novel sequel "14 Beyond" released in 2012 as the forerunner of an anticipated sequel. Director Chookiat Sakveerakul, who at 26 years old was the youngest professional filmmaker in Thailand at the time, also had *Ong-Bak* director Prachya Pinkaew as co-producer. Pinkaew's expertize in reaching international audiences creates exactly the right balance of Thai and global cinematic trends. A film that would perhaps have been a low budget production unlikely to reach beyond its national borders became an international festival hit and received the Asian Film Award at the Bucheon International film festival as well as two awards at the national Thai film awards, including best actor for Krissada Sukosol. The rights were sold and the film was remade in America as *13 Sins* (2014).

Mary J. Ainslie

Title: *Dorm / Dek Ho*
Director: Songyos Sugmanakan
Studio: GTH
Year: 2006

Dorm is an odd hybrid film: a straightforward ghost story but one which eschews the standard clichés of the genre, and instead aims at being something of a *Bildungsroman* about a young boy at the transitional age of 12/13 years old.

Young Ton (Charlie Trairat) is sent away to a boarding school by his father in the hope that a school with better standards will improve the boy's exam results. Ton hates his father for this, and instead thinks he's been "got rid of" because he saw his father *in flagrante delicto* with the maid. At this new school, Ton has a miserable time: trying to avoid, on the one hand, a gang of bullies, while also trying to avoid the headmistress, Miss Pranee (Chintara Sukapatana), who runs the establishment with Nurse Ratched-like efficiency. His only friend comes in the form of another lonely boy, Vichien (Sirachuch Chienthawon), who he quickly realizes is a ghost.

The age of the boys is significant; at ages 12/13 years old, boys are in a liminal state between childhood and adolescence, and folklore is full of narratives about this particular age group. While the leader of the bullies, Master Peng (Jirat Sukchaloen), looks like a proper teenager, others in the gang, like Pok (Pakasit Pantural) still have very babyish faces. Ghosts too are liminal, as they exist between two states, the living and the reincarnate, and as the focus for ghostly encounters as these two liminal states metaphysically bleed into one another. As *Dorm* focuses on these stages of liminality, the crumbling haunted school and the abandoned swimming pool (in which Vichien died) all create a Thai Gothic sensibility in which characters tend to be haunted by ghosts of living memory. In *Dorm* Pranee blames herself for Vichien's death, believing he committed suicide because she was hiding the truth about his father's arrest on corruption charges.

But it is the relationship between the two boys Ton and Vichien, both of whom are lonely, that really fuels *Dorm*. Every day, at 6pm sharp, Ton must watch helplessly as his friend re-experiences his death in the swimming pool. Eventually, it is Ton's love for Vichien that motivates him to try and find a way to help his friend over to the next side in order to be reborn, ideally without killing himself in the process. Unlike the Christian-centric Gothic narratives of the West, the Thai Gothic is grounded within these Buddhist principles; Ton wanting his friend to be reborn is the Thai equivalent of "going into the light," and for Ton this is the greatest gift he can give his friend. There is no maudlin sadness of loss; Vichien's passing over is a release and, once done, Ton is able to take control of his own life and return to the world as a studious young man.

Mikel J. Koven

Title: *Ghost Game / La-Tha-Phi*
Director: Sarawut Wichiensarn
Studio: NGR
Year: 2006

A highly problematic work of Thai cinema, *Ghost Game* tells the story of a group of urban middle-class Thai youths who meet their untimely ends as participants of a game show set in what is clearly a former Khmer Rouge prison. Condemned by the Cambodian culture minister Kong Kendara as a grave affront to the historic suffering of his people, the film is an unabashedly racist depiction of the supposed savagery of Cambodian culture. Such was the strain the film placed on diplomatic relations between the two countries, in fact, that producers were forced to apologize to the Cambodian ambassador in Bangkok. Perhaps apologies should also have been made for the film's pointless violence, its shallow characterization, pedestrian performances and entirely predictable storyline.

That said, *Ghost Game* is of some interest to horror film scholars. Participating in the recent stylistic tendency to embody technological innovations of the digital age in both style and content, the film competently deploys surveillance footage, 16mm film, stills, night vision footage and hand-held video sequences in a manner that adds a frisson of contemporaneity to the slasher-movie style deaths of the participants. This is not to argue, however, that such developments can bear witness to the suffering of the Cambodian people. For whilst the ghosts of the Khmer dead may attempt to warn the contestants of their immanent death, the viewing audience cannot see them. It is therefore impossible, it seems, for Thai audiences to witness the horror of the Cambodian past – participants and programme-makers alike being utterly indifferent to the mounds of skulls and implements of torture that litter the camp.

The adoption of the "game show" device is similarly problematic. This motif is a highly self-reflexive variant of the massacre or slasher movie in which contestants are picked off in a variety of gruesome ways until only one survives, all whilst a number of surveillance techniques are deployed to record the carnage. In American films from *The Running Man* (1987) to *The Hunger Games* (2012), such stylistics are typically underpinned by an affirmation of human altruism in the face of authoritarian ruthlessness. No such social critique or vision of social solidarity emerges from *Ghost Game*, however. The film remains a reactionary reaffirmation of Thai nationalism and the politically expedient racism that underscores it. Alongside the graphic depictions of the contestants being crushed, drowned and mutilated, the film emerges as a rankly exploitative re-enactment of the body in pain for the pleasure of a paying audience.

Linnie Blake

Title:	*Ghost of Valentine / Krasue Valentine*
Director:	Yuthlert Sippapak
Studio:	Sahamongkol Film
Year:	2006

Ghost of Valentine is the most recent cinematic incarnation of the popular *phi krasue* theme. The film is a tragic tale of guilt and the inevitability of karmic retribution. It tells the story of Sao (Ploy Jindachote) a shy nurse, who comes from the countryside to start a new job at a Bangkok hospital. The half-abandoned hospital is a creepy place in a state of constant deterioration. The many locked sections indicate dark secrets from bygone ages amid an atmosphere of melancholy and decay. However, Sao's arrival seems somewhat anticipated by Num (Pitisak Yaowananon) the hospital's partly disabled porter.

When spectres from the past begin to appear, the audience learns that Sao left her boyfriend because he accused her of being possessed by a ghost. These accusations soon turn out to be true: Sao changes into a *phi krasue* to feast on the hospital's hazardous wastes. However, the next morning Sao's human body rejects this putrescent food by vomiting blood and human flesh. This abjection of loathsome matter indicates the antagonism between the human and non-human elements that make up the protagonist's uncanny personality. Meanwhile Num is involved in an accident with the hospital's director and a flower-selling girl that leaves him paralyzed, so Sao starts to take care of him as the hospital's last patient.

Slowly the building begins to disclose some of its uncanny secrets; ultimately, it is Karmic debt that binds the protagonists to the hospital as the place where they committed inexcusable sins in a past life. Sao was as a nurse in the 1940s and Num a young soldier who fell in love with her. When he had to leave Bangkok he did not know that Sao was pregnant and thus he married the daughter of his superior. Sao waited in vain for her lover to return and finally decided to abort the unborn child. All protagonists played a crucial role in the killing of this unborn life and all are punished by the little flower-selling girl, who turns out to be the vengeful revenant.

Ghost of Valentine is marked by a high degree of intertextuality, a cross-reference between texts and genres that is not only characteristic for Thai horror in general but especially for Yuthlert Sippapak's artwork. However, *Ghost of Valentine* features not only these genre-mixes and cross-references to the director's earlier films, but is also an homage to the much earlier *Ghost of Guts Eater* (1973), the film that introduced *phi krasue's* ghostly image to modern Thai cinema. The female protagonist's name is significant in this regard, but it is the depiction of a woman's uncanny transformation as a form of karmic retribution for sins committed in a past life that really demonstrates the film's narrative indebtedness to *Ghost of Guts Eater*.

Benjamin Baumann

Title:	*The Unseeable / Pen Chu Kap Phi*
Director:	Wisit Sasanatieng
Studio:	Five Star Production, The Film Factory
Year:	2006

While Thai horror films can often seem overly dependent on shock-scares and clichés, *The Unseeable* is something different; a brilliantly executed ghost story which delivers the necessary creeps, even if its story can be somewhat predictable.

The plot begins with the heavily pregnant village girl Nualjan (Siraphan Wattanajinda) arriving at a seemingly derelict estate looking for a place to stay while she searches for her husband, Chob, who appears to have abandoned her. There Nualjan makes friends with Choy (Sombatsara Teerasaroch) a crude and mouthy maid who also lives on the premises. Choy teaches Nualjan the ways of the household, including telling her the many ghost stories attached to the place. The household itself is run by the Mrs Danvers-like matron, Miss Somjit (Tassawan Seneewongse) on behalf of the lady of the house, Madame Ranjuan (Suporntip Chaungrangsri), who has also been abandoned by her husband and keeps to her rooms in Miss Havisham-type isolation. Lurking in the overgrown gardens and dark creepy corridors of the house, ghostly apparitions appear in the corner of

Figure 14 The sinister Miss Somjit patrols the near-derelict mansion in the atmospheric *The Unseeable* (2006).

Nualjan's eye, including a mysterious hand that emerges from shrines, or under the bed, or out of large pots in the garden.

The Unseeable is, at its heart, a classic English-style Gothic melodrama, filled with adultery, betrayal, lost children, murder, old dark houses, abandoned women, mad women, icy women, and ghostly lovers. The haunting itself replays a series of tragic events focusing on the same four characters, yet Sasanatieng films the story with a timeless style that is simultaneously nostalgic and contemporary, evoking a 1950s Hollywood melodrama sensibility that balances East and West influences masterfully. Simultaneous to this Gothic sensibility is an equally strong sense of its own Thai-ness. Ghosts and vampires are more-or-less interchangeable: *Phi* are ghosts, but with strong vampire-like attributes, including eating babies' umbilical cords, and biting or scratching their victims.

Rather than relying on (now) clichéd J-horror imagery of long, lanky black hair covering the face of a ghost, Sasanatieng films his ghosts indistinctly. Some exist just out of focus in the background, or framed in such a way as to obstruct the character's face by a veil and at a distance, or glimpsed at a ¾ angle. The obviousness of these obstructed images only enhances the film's uncanny and creepy elements, calling attention to something odd which will clearly be important later in the film (which it indubitably is). While there are a few jump-scares, unlike most contemporary horror films *The Unseeable* relies on atmosphere and suspense. Despite limited release outside of Asia, renowned auteur Sasanatieng offers another masterpiece of Thai cinema and, in marked contrast to his other films, such as *Tears of the Black Tiger* (2000) and *Red Eagle* (2010), keeps the blood to a minimum, terrifying the audiences as opposed to simply horrifying them.

Mikel J. Koven

Title: *The Victim / Phi Khon Pen*
Director: Monthon Arayangkoon
Studio: RS Film
Year: 2006

Monthon Arayangkoon debuted in 2004 with *Garuda* – a *kaiju*-style monster movie set in Bangkok, but he fully realized his potential in his ghost stories. Released in 2006, *The Victim* brought much needed complexity to the genre, even if this occasionally came at the cost of clarity. The first part of the film focuses on the story of Ting (Pitchanart Sakakorn), an actress employed by the police to stage re-enactments of murder cases for the court and the press, and her apparent possession by the ghost of a murdered film star. As the film progresses, however, we learn that all of the above was in fact the plot of a new Thai horror film in production, a fragment of which we had just seen. Then comes the revelation that the film crew is haunted by a ghost, or, to be more precise, eliminated one after another by a vengeful spirit with serial killer-like precision. The final and rather rushed part of the story exposes the mysterious ghost as the grudge-bearing spirit of a non-related transsexual dancer who died as a result of a botched illegal plastic surgery that was supposed to make them look like the leading actress in the movie. The ghost attached itself to an old costume tiara used for traditional Thai dancing, and, together with this object, found its way on to the movie set.

Perhaps one of the most innovatory aspects of *The Victim* lies in its introduction of a new type of apparition. This is contrasted with the more traditionally rendered ghosts, which are also present in the movie. Thai cinematic ghosts have a long tradition of iconic and anthropomorphic representation and have mostly been portrayed by heavily made-up actors. Yet Arayangkoon makes a very clear distinction between the way his "cinematic" and "real" ghosts are portrayed. The ghosts of murder victims, which we encounter in the first part of the movie (the film within the film) are portrayed in a manner typical of most Thai ghost films, as blue-skinned, sunken-eyed, humanoid entities made to look more horrifying by retaining the physical marks of their deaths. Yet the "real" ghost haunting the film crew is presented as a shadowy, shape-shifting cloud of dust consisting of hundreds of minuscule particles, ready to take any form it desires, impossible to fight with and to capture, since it is always on the verge of disintegrating into thin air. This change in the way the spirit is represented goes against the established conventions of Thai cinema and can be seen as a nod towards the international audience that is more likely to measure the film against global rather than local examples of the genre. The film is a hybrid in this aspect, combining elements of the global and the local and so offering a subtext known only to locals (for instance the shot of a damaged Bangkok shrine which was believed to be a political omen at the time) while still embracing the affective character of global horror.

Katarzyna Ancuta

Title: *Alone / Faet*
Directors: Banjong Pisanthanakun, Parkpoom Wongpoom
Studio: GTH
Year: 2007

Alone was the follow up film to the remarkably successful *Shutter* (2004). The pressure on the two directors to produce another similarly high-grossing hit ensured that they took no chances for failure, enlisting *Shutter* co-screenwriter Sophon Sakdaphisit to contribute to the screenplay.

Alone is a fairly straightforward ghost story: Pim (Marsha Wattanapanich) is haunted by the ghost of her conjoined twin Ploy when she and her husband/partner Vee (Vittaya Wasukraipaisan) return to Bangkok to look after Pim's ailing mother after several years away. Pim needs to confront her own past, particularly around the death of her sister, while the agitated spirit wreaks havoc in her palatial family home.

The conjoined twin riff has strong echoes of Brian de Palma's *Sisters* (1973) and David Cronenberg's *Dead Ringers* (1988) in exploring the perverse extremes of identical twin inseparability (much of which comes from Chatchai Pongprapaphan's evocative score over the opening credits). In the representations of conjoined twins, *Alone* echoes *Sisters*' tag line: "what the devil has joined together let no man cut asunder," indicating that woe will betide those who desire to separate such twins. While this may be a hackneyed motif in itself, it is still effective. Throughout the film, Pisanthanakun and Wongpoom include echoes of conjoined doubling: images of the Queen of Spades in a deck of cards or the inkblots in a Rorschach test. Likewise, Pim's closet at home is filled with identical sets of clothes and her music box has two ballerinas dancing back-to-back. Even when we see Pim and Vee in bed together, they are back to back. Like most movies about twins, one sister is a good girl, while the other is evil. *Alone* goes out of its way to point out that the "bad sister,"

Ploy, wears glasses, as a symptom of her degenerate state; that Ploy is somehow "less perfect" than Pim (such a device is also useful in distinguishing between the two characters). Pisanthanakun and Wongpoom cast two other sets of identical twins to play Pim and Ploy at ages 7 and 15; in fact, the closeness of the girls in these flashbacks makes up the heart of the film; a heart that gets broken when 15 year-old Vee falls in love with Pim while convalescing at the same hospital, and Ploy is left out as a useless appendage.

The film's major twist is fairly obvious, and telegraphed very early on in the film, but it is the focus upon memories, of being haunted by one's past, on which the narrative turns. The haunting is based on a personal past and not a collective one. Pim must answer for her deeds, as Thun had to in *Shutter*. Individuals not only have responsibility for their actions, they must also be responsible to the spiritual realm because of those actions.

Mikel J. Koven

Title: *Body #19 / Body Sop 19*
Director: Paween Purikitpanya
Studio: Avant
Year: 2007

The release of *Body #19*, the directorial debut of Paween Purikitpanya, catapulted the director to instant fame, landing him a place among the most influential Thai horror filmmakers of the decade and securing him a spot within the two highly profitable GTH horror collections that followed – *Phobia* (2008) and *Phobia 2* (2009). The film itself was nominated for nine National Film Association awards and won for Best Special Effects. Indeed, *Body #19* utilized computer-generated effects on an unprecedented scale. More importantly however, it was perhaps the first mainstream Thai ghost film to question the supernatural premise of the genre.

Set in the less-than-glamorous world of medical professionals, the film toys with both mental illness (schizophrenia) and hypnosis, building upon cultural beliefs that have long attributed mental illness to the effects of spiritual possession. The protagonist, Chon (Arak Amornsupasiri), is a young medical student living with his sister Ae (Ornjira Lamwilai).

Plagued by recurring nightmares and unexplained periods of spatial and temporal confusion, Chon is referred to a psychologist for treatment. Reluctant at first, doctor Usa (Kritteera Inpornwijit) eventually accepts him as her patient. Their sessions/investigations uncover an affair between Usa's husband (Ae's mentor) and another doctor, who has recently gone missing. The closer we get to the truth the more people end up dead, killed by the same mysterious ghost that haunts Chon in his dreams. Finally, it is revealed that the man who we think is Chon is in fact Usa's husband, his missing/dead lover is an older version of Ae, and the youthful face he sees in the mirror – the face the viewers see – belongs to Ae's dead brother, killed in an unrelated accident, whose body has been kept in the hospital morgue for years.

The success of *Body #19* may be attributed to its embracing of culturally fostered pluralistic beliefs around mental illness. Such plurality allows for multiple interpretations and so the film can thus cater for a much wider and more versatile audience. The dual (spiritual/medical) nature of mental illness in Thai popular imagination also allows filmmakers to create a film that can be seen as simultaneously repeating and breaking the established Thai horror formulas. While, akin to other similar productions, the film features an angry and vindictive spirit, its ghost can also be read as a post-hypnotic suggestion, a guilt-induced hallucination, or a schizophrenic delusion, and the fact that the ghost in question is a 3D-animated computer image only makes it easier to believe that it is not quite there. By directing our attention to the notion of disease and the Thai understanding of disease, the film also offers a metaphorical representation of the disintegration of traditional hierarchical Thai society and its values, as criticism is aimed at entitled elites who often escape legal judgment. Oscillating between a familiar story of karmic retribution, psychoanalytical symbolism, hypnotism, possession, and a modernist metaphor for disease, the film is an ambitious reconfiguration of familiar Thai horror tropes and a much welcome addition to the genre.

Katarzyna Ancuta

Title: *The House / Ban Phi Sing*
Director: Monthon Arayangkoon
Studio: Avant
Year: 2007

Released a year after *The Victim* (2006), *The House* catered specifically to the needs of a Thai audience hungry for ghost-related urban legends based on real-life criminal cases. In Thailand, marketing made much of the film's recollecting three notorious murder cases from the last half-century: the 1959 murder of a nurse, Nualchawee Petchrung, the 1998 murder of Jenjira Ployangunsri, and the 2001 murder of Phassaporn Boonkasemsanti. All the women were killed by their partners who happened to be doctors or medical students, a common denominator for the filmmakers who linked the cases together. Much effort was made to recreate the well-publicized details of the cases – the film's killers closely resemble the murderers, Wisut Boonkasemsanti and Serm Sakhonrat, and the ghost of Nuanchavee bears an uncanny similarity to the old photographs of the dead nurse, whose actual clothes, displayed at the Siriraj Forensic Medicine Museum in Bangkok as "evidence from a murder case," also made it into the film.

The plot of *The House* focuses on the story of Chalinee (Inthira Charoenpura, an actress very familiar to Thai horror fans, celebrated for her portrayal of Nang Nak), a female television reporter investigating a possible connection between three gruesome murders that all took place in the same house within the last 50 years. Plagued by unexpected appearances of the ghosts of murder victims, Chalinee discovers that the house itself is the source of evil responsible for poisoning the minds of three loving husbands and turning them against their spouses. As a result of this discovery, Chalinee begins to fear her own husband and rather unexpectedly ends up as a murderer herself.

The success of the film with local audiences owes much to its apparent realism. Thai horror films generally display a high degree of intertextuality in their construction of cinematic ghosts which are often connected to broader social discourses, cultural beliefs and media forms. As a result of this there is very little distinction between the production of ghost stories as entertainment and wider interactions with the world of spirits, both of which begin to blend together. The film's reputation outside of Thailand also owes much to its excellent cinematography and convincing scares.

Similarly to *The Victim*, *The House* presents us with two different varieties of spirits: the conventional sunken-eyed mournful ghosts of the victims and the boundless dark energy resident at the house capable of forming a variety of shapes. These secondary spirits escape the typical classifications derived from Thai folklore and popular beliefs. Neither house spirits, nor vengeful ghosts, these gigantic, grotesque alien-like entities are formed out of smoke and particles of dirt. Such a depiction is in fact easier to accept as a visual representation of rot and corruption affecting generations and causing any type of evil that man is capable of. While it remains uncertain whether these spirits can exist independently of humans or are born out of human greed and anger, they certainly prove more than capable of spreading the disease they epitomize further.

Katarzyna Ancuta

Title: *Coming Soon / Program Na Winyan Akhat*
Director: Sophon Sakdaphisit
Studio: GTH
Year: 2008

Coming Soon marked the directorial debut of screenwriter Sophon Sakdaphisit, who co-wrote *Shutter* (2004) and *Alone* (2007). While Sakdaphisit went on to direct the better known *Ladda Land* (2011) and *The Swimmers* (2014), *Coming Soon* demonstrates the emergence of a solid filmmaker as well as a writer.

From the very start of *Coming Soon*, we are thrown *in medias res*: Shomba (Oraphan Arjsamat) is an evil witch who has kidnapped local children, mutilating them into substitutes for her own children lost in a house fire. The villagers have hunted Shomba down to her cabin, confronting the witch, rescuing the children and then hanging the crazed lady. This dramatic opening is revealed as a scene from a much anticipated new horror film "Evil Spirit," apparently based on a true story, and the real setting for the film is a modern Bangkok multiplex. "Evil Spirit" is being screened in advance in order for one of the projectionists to illegally video the film for the pirate market. But at the crucial scene when Shomba is hung, something happens to the projectionist that is only partially glimpsed on the video; he seems to have disappeared. For Chen (Chantavit Dhanasevi), a fellow projectionist, "Evil Spirit" is a haunted film and Shomba will come for anyone who watches her death scene. Chen enlists the help of his ex-wife Som (Vorakarn Rajjanavatchra) to find out what happened to Shomba as a means to try and put her spirit to rest before the film opens and the "Evil Spirit" is released.

The opening credits sequence depicts loops of film dripping down like blood; this clever visual motif illustrates the kind of self-awareness and playfulness that *Coming Soon* engages with. The milieu of modern young metropolitan Thais, working at and patronizing local multiplexes, queuing up for a new horror movie, just like (it is assumed) we are doing in watching *Coming Soon* is teasingly self-reflexive. The film also plays with well-worn conventions with which, it is anticipated, we are familiar: an evil witch who kidnaps children is familiar from fairy tales, a ghost haunting anyone who watches a movie references *The Ring* (1998), and the investigation into the death of a local urban legend is similar to *Shutter*. All of these are familiar tropes, and yet, Sukdaphisit still manages to breathe new life into them.

Likewise, while the theme of film piracy is recurrent, it is treated more as an inevitable evil; young folks are offered good money to supply the criminal underworld with the latest films. *Coming Soon* offers a kind of meta-textual discourse regarding the intricate mechanisms film production companies demand in order to prevent film piracy, though the ultimate moral message regarding this practice is unclear.

Mikel J. Koven

Title: *Phobia / Si Phraeng*
Directors: Banjong Pisanthanakun, Paween Purikitpanya, Yongyoot Thongkongtoon, Parkpoom Wongpoom
Studio: GTH
Year: 2008

Phobia is an anthology consisting of four horror films which last between 20 and 25 minutes each. Prior to this collaboration, the four directors were nationally recognized film-makers: Banjong Pisanthanakun and Parkpoom

Wongpoom both co-directed and wrote the box-office hit *Shutter* (2004); Paween Purikitpanya directed the horror-thriller *Body #19* (2007); while Yongyoot Thongkongtoon was known for popular queer comedies such as *The Iron Ladies* (2000), *The Iron Ladies 2* (2003), and *Metrosexual* (2006). In *Phobia* each of the four stories revolve around the violation of social norms through violence, terror, and fear, with unrelated yet thematically connected plots. By focusing on transgressions of social and religio-cultural norms, the stories comment on the dilemmas and anxieties of modern Thai society.

In the first episode *Happiness*, a young woman Pin (Maneerat Khamuan) is confined to her apartment after breaking her leg in a car accident. The taxi Pin was riding in overturned after hitting a young man, and the trapped Pin was forced to stare into the man's eyes as the life drained out of him. Sitting lonely and bored in her apartment after the accident, Pin starts to exchange text messages, beginning a virtual flirt after receiving a message from an unknown man. This finally results in the ghostly crash victim visiting her, who attacks Pin, leading to her falling from her high-rise apartment building and dying. Pin's failure was glancing into the eyes of a dying person, a taboo that was violated involuntarily, but nevertheless punished by the ghost of the deceased.

Tit for Tat is a revenge tale. A group of violent kids who were kicked out of school abduct their former classmate Ngid (Nattapol Pohphay), whom they blame for their expulsion. They brutally beat Ngid, and accidentally cause his death. The bullied boy then returns as a spectre, using black magic to take his revenge through the cursed pages of an old book which causes its readers to suffer a violent death.

In *In the Middle* a group of young men set out for a jungle camping trip. In the evening, ghost stories circulate. Excited by the tales, one of the boys, Aey (Kantapat Permpoonpatcharasuk), jokingly boasts that if he were dead, he would haunt his friends, starting with the boy sleeping in the middle of the tent. The next day the kayak capsizes, Aey gets lost, and in the coming night no one dares to sleep in the middle. All are relieved when Aey shows up the following day, apparently safe and sound. However, this impression is deceptive, and the boys soon realize that challenging the supernatural has disastrous consequences.

The last episode *Last Fright* is about an attractive air steward Pim (Laila Boonyasak). In the past, she had often attended a wealthy prince, with whom she had an affair. This time she had to accompany the prince's new wife alone. Due to a food allergy, the sadistic and hostile princess suffers an accidental death. Pim is assigned to guard the cloth-wrapped corpse on the return flight, falling victim to the attacks of the infuriated ghost punishing her extra-marital sin.

Peter Braeunlein

Title: *The Screen at Kamchanod / Phi Chang Nang*
Director: Songsak Mongkolthong
Studio: Five Star Production
Year: 2008

With *The Screen at Kamchanod* Songsak Mongkolthong, assistant director on the Pang Brothers' *Bangkok Dangerous* (2000), makes his debut as an author-director with a noteworthy Thai ghost movie, later going on to direct the romantic comedy *My Valentine* (2010).

The film is reputedly based on "true events" from 1987, in which, according to a newspaper report, four projectionists were hired by an anonymous client to screen a film in the Kamchanod forest in Udon Thani province. Much to the projectionists' astonishment, no audience arrived for the screening until the end, when a group of people emerged out of the darkness and lined up in front of the screen, before disappearing without trace. Eighteen years later, young doctor Yut (Achita Pramoj Na Ayudhya), who is obsessed with the mystery behind the screening, locates the very same film reels and identifies the exact location of the screening. Yut, his nurse girlfriend Aon (Pakkaramai Potranan), two journalist friends, and Roj (Namo Tongkumnerd), a homeless boy who dotes on Aon, set out to the remote forest to re-enact the screening. Yut aims to draw out the ghosts again and unveil the truth behind the spooky event. In the wilderness of Udon Thani, the Bangkokians are exposed to a never ending series of terrifying encounters with ghosts, finally resulting in homicide and suicide. Despite the macabre turn of events and the casualties caused by his obsessive quest, Yut remains determined to go on. In the end, Yut realizes that the ghostly audience he was looking for are, in fact, him and his companions. During the flickery screening in the forest, their images merge with those of the projected film, which eventually rips. To recall the famous line from Shakespeare's *The Tempest*, the actors become "spirits, and are melted into air, into thin air." This is, however, only one possible interpretation, as Mongkolthong offers the audience no clear or explicit answers.

The Screen was released during the boom period of Thai horror. The film uses typical genre techniques, primarily lots of scary scenes, to create an intense atmosphere of dreadful horror. The skillful employment of sound effects, camera angles, and editing make it a useful example in film courses to demonstrate how dread and horror can be generated. The plot is less convincing; while the basic idea of film as a bridge to the realm of the deceased has its potential, the narrative and the inner life of the characters are poorly realized. Until the end, both Yut's obsessiveness and Aon's odd behavior remain unexplained. As with the motivations of the protagonists, the many twists in the story remain enigmatic and illogical. To resume the plot coherently and in detail is almost impossible and the finale is likewise vague, leaving the viewer with more questions than satisfactory answers.

Peter Braeunlein

Title:	*Meat Grinder / Chueat Kon Chim*
Director:	Tiwa Moeithaisong
Studio:	Phranakorn Film
Year:	2009

With its premise of a killer/chef serving dishes made from human flesh in a restaurant, *Meat Grinder* draws immediate comparisons with the Hong Kong classic, *The Untold Story* (1993). Indeed, just like Anthony Wong, Mai Charoenpura (who plays the lead character, Buss) is a veteran of the genre, and both films engage with serious social critique while managing to remain graphic and exploitative at the same time. Director Tiwa Moeithaisong is no stranger to the horror genre, debuting in 2003 with a ghost comedy *Ghost Delivery* but making a name for himself with *The Sisters* (2004), a horror film about a ghost haunting an airconditioning unit. *Meat Grinder*, which he wrote, directed, shot and edited is undoubtedly his most ambitious film to date.

The film follows a non-linear narrative oscillating between different timelines, each retrospective scene revealing more back story of the main character, which is where the true horror is contained. Buss is an unassuming beef noodle soup vendor who runs a small riverside shop and pushes her noodle cart around a quiet neighbourhood. She shares the house with her disabled daughter who, as we later find out is actually the ghost or memory of a child she lost a few years back. Caught in a military crackdown on student protesters, Buss is forced to abandon her cart in the street. When she recovers it, she realizes that it contains the body of a dead student. Undisturbed by this discovery, she takes a pragmatic approach and serves his flesh to her customers the next day.

We soon realize that this was neither the first nor the last time Buss took to human butchery. Indeed, the restaurant business seems to be an ideal cover up for the unsavoury means by which she solves her problems. The film abounds in visual clues that hint at Buss's disturbed mental state and perhaps even prolonged mental illness. Shaky camera movements, double exposure, blurry images, rapid changes of focus, or bizarre colouration of some shots contribute to the creation of multiple parallel universes in which the worlds of memory and fantasy take over reality.

Buss's condition, we learn, was caused by continuous domestic abuse culminating in rape committed by her father and brother. Her idea of culinary retribution was also something she picked up at home. The film ends with a direct appeal to the audience not to ignore acts of violence against women, warning that every bullied girl may in turn grow up to become a monster herself. Interestingly, the inclusion of the shots of the military assaulting student protesters, reminiscent of the 1976 Thammasat University Massacre, draws parallels with a different kind of trauma. As discourses on political unrest are censored by the Thai government in the interest of "promoting national harmony," such events can be interpreted as "wounds" that fester and continue to haunt the Thai collective imagination through films such as this.

Katarzyna Ancuta

Title: *Slice / Chuean*
Director: Kongkiat Khomsiri
Studio: Five Star Production
Year: 2009

Despite its apparent lack of popularity with domestic audiences (the film made only 190,000 USD at the Thai box office), *Slice* remains one of the most interesting Thai horror films to date. This is not to say that the film was completely unappreciated on home ground, in 2010 it received three National Film Association Awards, including the Best Director, and was nominated in eleven more categories. With its dark plot focusing on a serial killer set to expose the corruption of Thai society, *Slice* is a rare example of Thai non-supernatural horror, or *nang sayong khwan*, although it was marketed locally as a thriller.

The film opens with the gruesome discovery of a bright red suitcase containing a dismembered body, the work of a serial killer who begins to leave similar packages all around Thailand. Tai (Arak Amornsupasiri), a rookie cop framed by his corrupt colleagues to take the fall for an ill-executed drug heist, is given a chance for redemption when he reveals that he may know the identity of the killer. His quest takes him back to his hometown and the trip brings back memories of dark deeds from the past.

Discussing *Slice*, with its portrayal of police corruption and socially accepted paedophilia and child prostitution, is akin to opening a proverbial can of worms. The film's kaleidoscope of violence includes a debased, drug-abusing police captain (Chatchai Plengpanich) who sacrifices the lives of his men for personal gain and forces them to commit murder on his behalf; a father raping his 10-year-old son as a "replacement" for the absent mother; schoolboys penetrating the same boy with toys because his epilepsy attacks are interpreted as a sign of "gayness"; a primary school teacher forcing students to perform oral sex as punishment; ladyboy gangs abducting and selling street kids to sex tourists; small-town beauty queens becoming prostitutes to make ends meet; and politicians engaging in orgies and debauchery. Although these acts have a firm grounding in reality, such topics rarely feature in Thai films, whose typical portrayal of the country and its people is more idealistic, and propagated upon an idealized trio of nation, religion and monarchy.

Director Khomsiri's own fascination with horror is evident in the graphic displays of brutality and violence. Cinematic influences of film noir, classic American cop movies, violent Korean thrillers and gangster films, and the excessive works of Takashi Miike are also abundant, although the film remains firmly embedded within local reality. Through its aestheticization of violence and glorification of suffering, *Slice* also engages with the Gothic on the visual and narrative level, obsessing over disease, corruption, deformity, disability, and transgression. Indeed, Khomsiri's social criticism is overt and *Slice* drives its message a little too close to home, perhaps explaining why it was ultimately rejected by the Thai audience. Despite that, *Slice* is a remarkable film, adding a much welcome touch of Gothic to Thai horror.

Katarzyna Ancuta

Title: *Ladda Land*
Director: Sophon Sakdaphisit
Studio: GTH
Year: 2011

Sakdaphisit broke into the industry as one of the co-writers of *Shutter* (2004) and the writer of *Alone* (2007), and secured his position among Thai horror greats with his directorial debut, *Coming Soon* (2008). Barring the phenomenally successful horror comedy, *Pee Mak* (2013), Sakdapisit's second film, *Ladda Land* remains the highest grossing Thai horror production, with box office figures reaching almost 4 million US dollars in Thailand alone.

The narrative follows a Thai middle-class man, Thee (Saharat Sangkapreecha), who moves his family into a new home in a picture-perfect suburban gated community called Ladda Land, where their life quickly descends into a nightmare. As the rumours of a haunting wreak havoc on the neighbourhood and turn the bustling community into a wasteland, and Thee's best laid plans of successful professional and domestic life go to ruin,

Ladda Land delivers a poignant message that a blind race to keep up with the materialistic middle-class lifestyle models and social aspirations that seem to dominate contemporary Thai society tend to come at a price.

Ladda Land is a perfect example of newer Thai horror films' adaptation to accommodate the needs of the global market. The film follows a coherent script, and the clean visual aesthetics it employs, reminiscent of commercial videography used in advertising, expresses the desire of its makers to appeal to a broader audience. All the scenes involving the supernatural seem to follow the patterns popularized by successful pan-Asian Horror productions and the construction of the film's ghosts allows for a multiplicity of literal and metaphorical readings relating the film to the local folkloric tradition and making it relevant for its contemporary urban audience.

With its reconfiguration of the typical Thai ghost story formula, *Ladda Land* brings horror closer to home for its middle-class audience and does so by shifting the attention from its usual medley of vengeful spirits to the more realistic threats exposed by the film's socio-economic contexts. The novelty of the film lies in its introduction of a new figure of fear – the failed modern man unable to stay afloat in the modern world despite his education and relative social privilege. Indeed, the film's suburban spaces are haunted not so much by the earth-bound revenants seeking to reconcile the past, but rather by ghosts of the present, ghosts of global desires.

The success of *Ladda Land* as a distinctly middle-class-situated film is indicative of Thai horror's movement to cater to the middle classes and the film's ability to engage with real issues in contemporary Thailand. At a time when Thai household debt continues to grow at an alarming rate, the film delivers a powerful warning: caught in the never-ending process of confirming their identity through the accumulation of material artefacts, the Thai middle-classes risk becoming living ghosts, trapped within the temporality of a dream of social mobility and economic success that is far more terrifying than the more familiar monstrosities that continue to populate Thai films.

Katarzyna Ancuta

Title: *Pee Mak / Phi Mak Phra Khanong*
Director: Banjong Pisanthanakun
Studio: GTH
Year: 2013

Pee Mak was arguably a watershed in contemporary Thai film history in definitively establishing the earning potential of a clearly Thai-identified production across the region. Working from a locally well-known Thai-specific narrative and generic elements, the film not only broke all-time domestic box office records, but also had successful theatrical runs across Asia, followed by broad international DVD distribution. The film leveraged upon the continuing regional success of a number of genres for which Thailand had been gaining "brand recognition," specifically horror and romantic comedy. No less important was the regional draw of its Thai-German star, Mario Maurer, who was mobbed by adoring fans when the cast joined publicity events in the region.

The title of the film and the narrative elements in the advertising materials (not to mention the advanced publicity) alert local audiences from the start to expect a variation on the oft-remade supernatural tale of the legendary Mae Nak. Indeed, *Pee Mak* quickly shifts narratively and generically from the standard period plotting of this tale and focuses upon a group of four friends – fellow soldiers – with whom Nak's husband Mak returns home. The comical interactions, slapstick pratfalls, and witty wordplay of the four men (often involving anachronistic contemporary references) as Nak's non-living status is gradually revealed to them, constitutes at least as much of the narrative focus as the central relationship between Nak and Mak. That relationship itself is commensurately addressed in terms that are more comic and romantic than horrific and tragic and the aggregate effect is to render *Pee Mak* much more a romantic comedy than a period horror film.

Referencing Mak rather than Nak in the film's title signals another dimension of the film's revisionism. Most iterations of the tale do have a substantial focus upon Nak's husband, but Maurer's specific portrayal of Mak is designed to substantially undermine the traditional ideals of heroic masculinity that usually apply to this character. This particular Mak is "soft," even effeminate – fearful of ghosts, unable to ride a merry-go-round without vomiting – and he is also highly emotional, weeping openly when first reunited with his wife, admitting his thoughts in battle were not for the nation but for Nak. This emotional link to Nak also proves to be his strength: Mak is able to set aside his mortal fear for the sake of being with his spirit-wife (whom, it is eventually revealed, he knew fully well to be dead from early on in the plot) and, in a still more radical departure from earlier iterations of the tale, chooses to remain with her at the film's close. Whatever the practical difficulties of cohabiting with a partner from another realm might be, Mak's love now triumphs over the pressure to adhere to societal judgments about appropriate mates.

Adam Knee

6

Muay Thai / Action

Although currently rather overshadowed by horror and comedy, action films make up a significant portion of Thai cinematic production. In their most popular format, known as *nang bu* (action films), often telling stories of cops and gangsters, or mercenaries scouring the jungle in search of missing treasure, they have been a particular favourite with many post-war 16mm era directors and spurred the cinematic careers of several actors. Among the latter, one must mention the giants of the Golden Age of Thai filmmaking, Mitr Chaibancha and Sombat Metanee, who have starred in hundreds of films, many of them falling into the *nang bu* category. Some of the best known action roles of Chaibancha include *Operation Bangkok* (1966), a relatively grand 35mm production funded by Hong Kong's Cathay Studios and shot in Bangkok and Hong Kong that saw him in the role of an undercover agent trying to bring down the drug ring, and *Golden Eagle* (1970), the film featuring the masked avenger Insi Daeng, that cost Chaibancha his life when he fell to the ground during a helicopter stunt. Sombat Metanee, who boasts of over 600 film roles and 2,000 screen appearances and still remains active on occasions, has starred in some of the action classics including *Tarutao, Devil's Island* (1970), *Magnum Killers* (1976), *Operation Black Panther* (1977), *Golden Triangle*

(1980), or *Gold Riders* (1982). Metanee was also the star of *Thong* (1973) directed by Chalong Pakdeevijit, the movie that wowed its audience with the most explosive special effects to date. The title of the film, which means "gold," refers to the familiar plot which sees a group of mercenaries sent to the jungle to retrieve the missing gold. The film was later dubbed and recut for international distribution as *S.T.A.B.* (1976) with more focus on its Hollywood hero, portrayed by Greg Morris known chiefly from his TV role in *Mission Impossible*.

While *nang bu* movies may mostly be a thing of the past, contemporary Thai action cinema has seen a resurgence in the recent years. This can be attributed to the influence of director Prachya Pinkaew and his Ba-Ram-Ewe studio which was formed chiefly with the mind to promote a previously non-existent category of Muay Thai movies, the local answer (and potential challenge) to Hong Kong *kung-fu* movies. While this may have seemed a far-fetched idea at first, after *Ong-Bak* (2003) took the world by storm, Muay Thai films began to make a name for themselves in the world of martial arts films. *Ong-Bak* was swiftly followed by *The Protector* (2005), a more international re-telling of basically the same story of the countryside underdog with amazing Muay Thai skills, in both cases portrayed by the rising star Tony Jaa, quickly hailed to be "the next Bruce Lee." Both films played on the long association of Muay Thai with the Thai cultural concept of strong masculinity and national pride (according to the legend Muay Thai was first used by a Thai soldier Nai Khanom Tom who used it to singlehandedly combat and defeat over 20 Burmese opponents). They were later followed by a number of sequels, with *Ong-Bak 2* (2008) and *Ong-Bak 3* (2010) directed by Tony Jaa and Panna Rittikrai and *The Protector 2* (2013) being shot in 3D by Pinkaew himself. Muay Thai cinema also saw the emergence of other martial arts stars, most notably Dan Chupong, known for *Born to Fight* (2004) and *Dynamite Warrior* (2006), and the actress Jeeja Yanin, the heroine of *Chocolate* (2008), *Raging Phoenix* (2009), and *The Kick* (2011).

Not all contemporary Thai action films, however, are martial arts productions. Like with most Thai films, genre boundaries can be rather fluid for action as well. There are action comedies like *Killer Tattoo* (2001), slow-paced action dramas like *Muay Thai Chaiya* (2007), Korean-style gangster movies like *The Gangster* (2012), and superhero movies like *Red Eagle* (2010). Similarly to horror, action films are among the best known Thai productions on international market and can boast a steady following of fans. They are also likely to attract a healthy audience in local cinemas and get good returns at the box office.

Katarzyna Ancuta

Title: *Killer Tattoo / Mue Puen Lok Phra Chan*
Director: Yuthlert Sippapak
Studio: Avant
Year: 2001

Killer Tattoo, a commercially successful offbeat action film, is notable for marking the beginnings of several film careers: it was the debut of director Yuthlert Sippapak, who later made hit horror film *Buppha Ratri* (2003), as well as comedians Petchtai Wongkamlao, Pongsak Pongsuwan, and Suthep Po-ngam.

The film is noteworthy for its skilful mixing of action clichés with quirkier elements, as well as its strong sense of morality. There are two central narratives. The first is an assassination gone wrong in which a colourful assortment of hired guns are supposed to murder a senior policeman. The attempt goes awry and the hunters quickly become the hunted. The second involves the film's protagonist, Kit Silencer (Somchai Kemglad), seeking vengeance for the murder of his mother by a mysterious killer whose inner wrist has a trident tattoo. Alongside these two narratives is a background story for each of the hired guns, mostly told through flashbacks.

These various narrative threads are tied together by a karmic motif which bookends and recurs throughout the film: a Buddhist monk teaches that "nightmares come from the mind, therefore need to be extinguished in the mind. They can't be [extinguished] through the taking of another life." The morality of this statement is contrasted by the violence and death surrounding each of the central characters' lives, all of whom are depicted as having suffered a tragedy of their own doing for which they are now struggling with the karmic consequences. Significantly, the final scene portrays

Kit Silencer eventually coming to terms with his past actions and making a life changing decision.

The seriousness of this theme and the sorrow of the characters' lives is given levity by the idiosyncrasies of the characters and running jokes about speaking English as a second language. Indeed, the film is set in a futuristic Thailand inundated by white Westerners, several of whom play the villains. Characters also have humorous names (Buffalo Gun, Dog Badbomb, Kit Silencer, Ghost Rifle) and one suffers from amnesia, now believing he is Elvis Presley. This well-worn cliché is given a redemptive playful Thai spin in that the Thai Elvis must accordingly only speak English, a language at which he and those around him are very poor.

Due to *Killer Tattoo*'s apparently low budget it appears similar to a stereotypically shallow B level action film, yet this appearance is misleading given its intelligent and uniquely Thai blend of karma, Buddhism, goofy humour and action. The film is also able to cross cultural boundaries and appeal to Western and Asian audiences alike due to its exotic blend of Thai Buddhism and action sequences. As such, a contemporary remake seems overdue.

Jesse Sessoms

Title: *Beautiful Boxer*
Director: Ekachai Uekrongtham
Studio: GMM Pictures
Year: 2003

This 2003 biopic based on the life of famed transgender Muay Thai champion, Parinya Charoenphol, or "Nong Toom" (played by Asanee Suwan), was one of a wave of *kathoei*-themed films that emerged during the Thai film revival of the late 1990s and early 2000s. Indeed, so many films with *kathoei* characters were released in these years that they effectively laid the grounds for what has become an established format of contemporary Thai cinema, *nang kathoei*, a comic sub-genre of enormous popularity at home and considerable curiosity abroad.

Like *The Iron Ladies* (2000) before it – one of the earliest and most commercially successful of the *nang kathoei* and, thus, something of a genre-defining prototype – *Beautiful Boxer* uses a real-life source story about a transgender sports figure to forge an uplifting narrative of triumphant survivalism. Unfolding as a series of biographical flashbacks narrated by the adult Nong Toom on the eve of her gender reassignment surgery, the film chronicles her journey from impoverished rural childhood through the ranks of the Muay Thai circuit to international championship, drawing parallels between her sporting battles and her struggle to embrace her identity as a transwoman.

Unlike most *kathoei* films, however, *Beautiful Boxer* is not a comedy. In fact, the film studiously avoids any hint of comic levity – Thai popular culture's default register for representations of *kathoei* – to forward an earnestly dignified and aesthetically lyrical portrayal of transgenderism. Director Ekachai Uekrongtham came to the film from a principal background in international theatre and visual arts and brought a decidedly refined sensibility to proceedings. Sporting ultra-professional production values, elegant visuals, and a masterfully understated performance from Muay Thai boxer turned acting newcomer, Asanee Suwan, *Beautiful Boxer* is more akin to the cultured cosmopolitanism of international art cinema than the populist excess of *nang kathoei*.

A strong international orientation is equally manifest within the film's internal textual structure. Framed by an intra-diegetic narrational device wherein Nong Toom recounts her life story to a visiting Western journalist, in English no less, the narrative of *Beautiful Boxer* is literally coded from the outset as a text addressed to a foreign audience. In this way, *Beautiful Boxer* shares the transnational aspirations – popularly dubbed *"go inter"* in Thai – widely associated with the Thai film revival. Critical commentary routinely interprets the Thai revival as subtended by a collective cultural fantasy of international conquest that is linked to the sociohistorical trauma of the 1997 Asian financial crisis and Thailand's desire to reprove itself on the global stage.

Though not perhaps quite achieving a fully fledged fantasy of international conquest, *Beautiful Boxer* proved a definite winner in overseas markets. On its release, the film earned widespread praise from international critics and picked up a number of awards. Back home, however, the film failed to find much traction. Despite editing the Thai theatrical release to make the film shorter and lighter in tone, domestic audiences were put off by its sober aesthetics and, for the most part, stayed away.

Brett Farmer

Title: *Ong-Bak: The Thai Warrior / Ong-Bak*
Director: Prachya Pinkaew
Studio: Baa-Ram-Ewe
Year: 2003

Ong-Bak is the film responsible for invigorating global interest in Thai martial arts cinema, and for establishing the brief transnational stardom of leading actor Tony Jaa. The film's release was well-timed, and the brutal realism of its spectacular fight scenes represented an appealing alternative to action films from Hong Kong and Hollywood, most of which rely on wire-work and computer-generated effects.

The film's plot has the pared-down simplicity of a typical heroic quest: an honourable but inexperienced young man must leave his familiar village and journey to a dangerous metropolis to recover a sacred Buddhist statue. Motivated by religious devotion and loyalty to his community, Ting (Tony Jaa) is an uncomplicated figure, a paragon of virtue and a symbol of national pride. He's also an expert, if reluctant, martial artist, capable of incredible feats of violence thanks to his training in Muay Thai kickboxing.

Authenticity is the central concept informing the film's numerous action set-pieces. The film thrives within its budgetary constraints, celebrating the artistry of the stunt performer and the martial artist. Fight scenes are shot with a sparse realism, with few sound effects and minimal cuts, showcasing the simple effectiveness of Jaa's ability to run, jump, punch and kick. The central character is far from invincible, however, with a vulnerability that serves to make his triumphs more engaging. Although Tony Jaa was frequently promoted as the "next" Bruce Lee, his ethos of action has much more in common with Jackie Chan, who likewise performed his own stunts and emphasized his scrappy imperfections.

Figure 15 The stoical Ting reclaims Thai masculinity and virtue in *Ong-Bak: The Thai Warrior* (2003).

Ong-Bak self-consciously functions to establish Thai cinema as a new challenger to the long-dominant Hong Kong model. Indeed, Ting's unwilling but victorious participation in an illegal fight club which earns him applause from an all-foreign audience reflects the film's global ambitions and, ultimately, its warm international reception. Thai nationalism pervades virtually every scene, typically with little subtlety; one scene features Jaa defending two innocent Thai citizens from a beating by a bullish Westerner spouting racist rhetoric. Ting's most vicious opponent, meanwhile, is a Burmese boxer, recalling the nationalist sentiment that made films such as Tanit Jitnukul's historical epic *Bang Rajan* a smash hit in the domestic market in 2000.

This theme is also embodied in the morally conflicted George (Petchtai Wongkamlao), a character who changed his name and bleached his hair blonde to reject both his Thai identity the associations of his hometown village. The character is a foil for Ting in several ways, not least in his sharp contrast to Ting's pride in his own relative primitivism. Likewise, the village is coded as peaceful and pure, while the city is depicted as a corrupt and corrupting influence. The rejection of modernity personified by Ting functions as a metatextual affirmation and, once again, of the power of "authentic" martial arts over effects-driven action.

Daniel Martin

Title: *Born To Fight / Koet Ma Lui*
Director: Panna Rittikrai
Studio: Sahamongkol Film
Year: 2004

Director Panna Rittikrai was not well-known in Thai filmmaking until after the release of the internationally successful Thai martial arts movie *Ong-Bak* in 2003. Before then, Rittikrai had been a B-grade actor-cum-director whose films were released only in suburban and Northeastern second-run theatres or outdoor screenings. The mentor of the famous Thai martial artist Tony Jaa, Rittikrai kept a low profile as a choreographer under the directorship of Prachya Pinkaew. While directing very few movies, one success was *Born To Fight,* a remake in name only of his previous 1986 production. The film was intended to catapult Thai martial artist Dan Chupong to stardom, in a similar way to that of Tony Jaa in *Ong-Bak* (2003).

Born to Fight follows a group of national athletes at a charity event sponsored by the country's Sports Authority. The athletes are distributing relief goods to a village near the Thai-Burmese border. Undercover cop Deaw (Dan Chupong) accompanies his sister who is a taekwondo champion and a guest at the event. Deaw is also recovering from the loss of his friend who was captured by a drug lord. However when the tour group reaches the village, they find that an armed militia has already taken the villagers hostage in return for the release of a drug lord and is threatening to launch a nuclear missile in the south of Bangkok. Daew and the athletes must join forces and use their skills as a weapon to save their people and country.

Similar to *Ong-Bak,* Rittikrai and his producer Prachya Pinkaew employ both nationalism and authentic "no strings attached" choreography in *Born to Fight*. However, while *Ong-Bak* only engaged with Muay Thai boxing, *Born to Fight* depicts Western boxing, football, rugby, gymnastics, taekwondo, cycling, motor-cycling and even indigenous sports like *sepak takraw* (a sport involving a woven rattan ball). Thai national athletes represent their sports to save the nation – Olympic boxing champion Somrak Khamsing, world motorbike-racer Chakhrit Rungsuwan, football star Piyaphong Pew-on and various gymnastic stars all simultaneously made the film the most expensive Thai action film of the time, with a 1,250,000 USD budget.

Nationalism is again used as the motivation for all protagonists to take action. This time, however, it is inclusive of both men and women. Nationalism is now associated with the skills performed by national athletes, regardless of gender, and a focus upon masculinity (as represented by Dan Chupong) is kept to a minimum. Together with this emphasis upon "authenticity," the film's location and reference to the drug lord Khun Sa also signifies Thailand's long standing enemy Burma, marking another familiar nationalist portrayal reinforced though a very typical "other."

Anchalee Chaiworaporn

Title: *The Bodyguard / Bodyguard Na Liam*
Directors: Panna Rittikrai, Petchtai Wongkamlao
Studio: Sahamongkol Film
Year: 2004

This 2004 action comedy was directed by fight/stunt choreographer Panna Rittikrai and comedian Petchai Wongkamlao (known in Thailand under his stage name Mum Jokmok), who also co-wrote the screenplay and stars as the titular lead, the bodyguard Wongkom. The film emerged on the back of the huge success of *Ong-Bak* (2003), again fight-choreographed by Rittikrai and staring Wongkamlao as the comic relief. Tony Jaa (Japanom Yeerum), star of *Ong-Bak*, featured heavily in *The Bodyguard*'s promotional materials though he only makes one appearance, in a memorable fight scene when he insists on calling Wongkom by his character name from *Ong-Bak*.

The film opens with Wongkom protecting billionaire businessman Chot Petchpantakarn. When bumbling gangsters attack, Wongkom retaliates with over-the-top wire-choreographed gunplay. The sequence culminates in a spectacular tongue-in-cheek four-car aerial collision, and despite

Wongkom's efforts, Petchpantakarn dies. Petchpantakarn's son, Chaichol, is then kidnapped by the same gangsters and escapes to hide in a slum where he is taken in by Mae Jam, a spunky den mother played by singer/actress Apaporn Nakornsawan (who would win Best Supporting Actress at the Thailand National Film Awards for the role). Such sequences emphasize some of the struggles of disenfranchised Thais, and eventually Chaichol falls in love with Mae Jam's daughter Pok and helps finance a school for her village.

The exaggerated fight sequences with their postmodern comic book violence spoof the Hong Kong action cinema of auteurs such as John Woo. There are also nods to the excesses of Thai action films from the 1960s, with geysers of garishly coloured blood, cartoonish characterizations and colloquial dialogue complete with the usual vulgarities and irony. When Chaichol is recaptured, Wongkom faces down and defeats the gangsters in a finale which humorously shuffles through a variety of fighting styles as the film switches from the rules of one cinematic universe to another. One fight is with a gangster played by renowned Thai kickboxer Samart Payakarun. Wongkom defeats him with a comedic variation on the ploy from *Yojimbo* (1961), loading his suit with metal so the kickboxer injures himself as he strikes. Similarly, in a fight with a wire-fu artist, Wongkom comically improvises his own stylized fighting technique based on Ramwong (a popular folk dance).

Yet unlike the Hong Kong action comedies it references, which often feature a central character(s) engaging in slapstick action amongst a cast of mostly straight men, *The Bodyguard* creates comedy through an ensemble cast of incidental characters, many of whom are played by beloved character actors from Thai television and film. With few exceptions, comedian Wongkamlao arguably plays one of the straightest characters in the film, consistent with its theme of comic inversion. Such a formula appears to have been successful; *The Bodyguard* was the second highest grossing domestic film in Thailand of 2004, at 1,806,80 USD and was followed by a prequel, *The Bodyguard 2* in 2007.

Kom Kunyosying

Title: *The Protector / Tom Yum Kung*
Director: Prachya Pinkaew
Studio: Baa-Ram-Ewe, Sahamongkol Film
Year: 2005

The legacy of *Ong-Bak*'s (2003) international success lives on in *The Protector* which was similarly framed to appeal to global audiences. In Thailand, the film grossed 183,350 million baht, justifying the continuation of this franchise. In this film, Tony Jaa's performance remains "without slings, without stand-ins" in what is marketed as the exotic Thai martial art of *muai khotchasan* (elephant fists).

Kham (Tony Jaa), the film's protagonist, lives in a village of mahouts (elephant trainers) and is raised alongside an elephant family. One day a group of hunters led by a local politician kidnap Kham's elephants Phor Yai (Big Daddy) and Khon and murder Kham's father. Kham tracks his elephants to Sydney in Australia where he meets Mark (Petchai Wongkamlao), his new Thai friend, and comes across a Thai restaurant which also functions as a hub of human trafficking and illegal wildlife trade, led by the antagonists Madame Rose (Xing Jin) and Johnny (Johnny Nguyen). Kham fights against three fighters sent to destroy a Thai temple and eventually finds Khon tortured while Phor Yai is killed, the elephant's skeleton deployed as *feng shui*. Finally Kham defeats Madame Rose and her gangster entourage, unmasking their network of organized crime and bringing Khon, whom he loves as his brother, home.

Transnationalism is key to understanding *The Protector*. Alongside the protagonist's own transnational journey and the antagonist's transnational crime organization, the globality of the film is evident in the influences of Hong Kong martial arts films. There are significant references to Bruce Lee and Jackie Chan, the legacy of whom not only inspired Tony Jaa himself but also Panna Rittikrai's fight choreography. Such intertextual references are evident in fight scenes throughout the film: the fight on the stairs at the restaurant, the fight against international fighters with various martial arts and weapons, and the fight against a large gang of villains prior to defeating Madame Rose.

Yet alongside such a globalized outlook, *The Protector* seeks to represent a strong and definitive version of Thai-ness, one represented through both the exoticism and royal-nationalistic consciousness popularized in and by Thai film during the post-1997 era. *Muay gajasan* is given a historical and spiritualized connection to *chatulangkhabat*, Siamese warriors who protect the legs of royal war elephants. The unique boxing styles are also accompanied by the mythical setting of a remote Northeastern Thai village where (similar to *Ong-Bak*) folk belief and human-animal relationships remain dominant. In this way, the film integrates vernacular and diasporic Thai-ness into mainstream Thai-ness, fabricating an imagined community among Thais and those who are voluntarily Thaified (such as a *farang* – white person – monk in Sydney) while at the same time criticizing the supposed moral decadence of foreigners and foreign nations.

Natthanai Prasannam

Title: *Dynamite Warrior / Khon Fai Bin*
Director: **Chalerm Wongpim**
Studio: **Sahamongkol Film**
Year: **2006**

Produced by *Ong-Bak* (2003) director Prachya Pinkaew, *Dynamite Warrior* is set in Northeastern Siam in the late nineteenth/early twentieth century, and proves that not all superheroes of the New Thai industry adhere to the conservative ideological position of *Ong-Bak*. Mobilizing older and more local Thai cinematic traits such as slapstick comedy and toilet humour that were toned down in the internationalized *Ong-Bak*, the film offers a much more complex relationship between the superhero figure and the often nationalist and elitist discourses of New Thai Heritage cinema.

In *Dynamite Warrior*, the central character Siang (Dan Chupong) is a Robin Hood-type figure in the Northeast. Siang protects the rural farmers from local elites who try to kill their buffalos in order to force them to buy tractors. Siang embodies the detached, stoical and traumatized persona of so many contemporary superheroes; he is searching for a mysterious tattooed man who killed his parents. Yet while Siang is arguably again protecting the Northeastern villagers from "progress" and exploitation caused

Figure 16 Hero Siang rides to the rescue on top of a rocket in *Dynamite Warrior* (2006).

by an increasingly modern and urbanized Thailand, unlike *Ong-Bak*'s Ting, Siang's celebration of and situation within the myths, legends and cultural practices of the Northeastern Thai region (known as Isan) becomes an engagement from within this dynamic community and context rather than an outside depiction of its supposed passive purity and innocent spirituality. The masked Siang rides to the rescue on homemade rockets and fights amongst the silk looms of Isan, mobilizing a *mise-en-scène* familiar to the marginalized Northeast and its cultural festivals and myths. Likewise, the many slapstick sequences coupled with evil wizards and the hero impossibly flying to the attack ensure that this film and its central figure begins to have much in common with the visceral nature of films enjoyed by lower class Thai viewers in previous decades.

Such attributes make the film possibly the most socially progressive of the New Thai superhero incarnations, as rather than seeking to uphold the unfair and unequal status-quo, *Dynamite Warrior* appear to celebrate this lower-class context and even rejoice in the chaotic diversity the country now finds itself in. Filmed on location in Isan and starring Isan native and former stuntman Chupong Changprung (also known internationally as Dan Chupong), *Dynamite Warrior* suggests that the Thai superhero is a figure who can potentially cross the various ethnic, linguistic and economic divisions with which the nation grapples, and offer an inclusive and celebratory portrayal of these many Thai facets. The film achieved a limited distribution at international festivals and on DVD. It was nominated for six awards, winning best director at the Thai national film awards for Chalerm Wongpim, whose repertoire remains almost completely within the Muay Thai genre.

Mary J. Ainslie

Title: *Muay Thai Chaiya / Chaiya*
Director: **Kongkiat Khomsiri**
Studio: **Five Star Production**
Year: **2007**

Kongkiat Khomsiri's involvement with the cinema began with his work on Tanit Jitnukul's war epic *Bang Rajan* (2000). He made waves as co-director of a highly successful ultra-violent black-magic horror movie *Art of the Devil 2* (2005) and its sequel, and as a writer of several more or less noteworthy Thai horror films. In 2007, he debuted as a director with *Muay Thai Chaiya*, a dark period piece set in the world of professional Muay Thai boxing and the crime syndicates that control it.

Chaiya tells the story of three friends, Pao (Thawatchai Phanpakdee), Piak (Akara Amarttayakul) and Samor (Sonthaya Chitmanee), who leave the idyllic Thai South to seek fame and fortune in Bangkok, hoping to make a name for themselves as professional Muay Thai boxers. Pao, the best fighter of the three, gradually begins to realize this dream unaware that his success in the ring has less to do with his rigorous training than with the "invisible" protection he receives from his two friends who have joined the gang for that very purpose. The film's depiction of the Thai underworld, portrayed as the last refuge of Thai working-class male culture (and that is often marginalized in local productions in favour of its glossier middle-class metrosexual counterpart), may be seen as overly depressing, or fatalistic. Predictably, the story ends on a tragic note with Piak and Samor sacrificing their lives in the name of friendship.

Although Thai boxers are meant to epitomize the ideal of Thai masculinity, and the sport is typically constructed as the embodiment of nationalistic propaganda, *Chaiya* takes a more naturalistic approach, instead portraying a world where boxing is unequivocally related to poverty. Boxers are pawns in a game played by crime syndicates and their invisible wealthy sponsors, exploited to the limits of their endurance and disposed of when no longer useful. Ironically it is the outcasts and gangsters who seem to demonstrate "the honour of men," an old-fashioned cultural value that once served as the foundation for the Thai masculine ideology. When Pao eventually returns to his hometown he does so not as a national hero but rather a survivor, while the boxing business continues as corrupt as ever.

Khomsiri's protagonists are relics of the pre-metrosexual past, glorified through their nostalgic portrayals of Thai retro-masculinity. They accept their inevitable downfall with an unnerving degree of fatalistic resignation. But they are also portrayed as monstrous, not only because they exhibit a violent streak and engage in crime, but also through their poverty, lack of education, their effective unemployability, and their feeling of anger and resentment towards the society they perceive as unjust.

Despite critical acclaim *Chaiya* did not fare well with local audiences, grossing only slightly over 311,000 USD. The film's rejection by the Thai predominantly middle-class audience may be attributed to its sympathetic portrayal of the underdog social class, with whom the audience does not necessarily want to identify, and its strong criticism of social inequality – an uncomfortable issue seldom discussed in Thai media.

Katarzyna Ancuta

Title: *Chocolate*
Director: **Prachya Pinkaew**
Studio: **Ba-Ram-Ewe**
Year: **2008**

Chocolate serves as a spiritual sequel to the influential action film *Ong-Bak* (2003), with director Prachya Pinkaew returning to employ a similarly authentic, bare-bones celebration of Muay Thai kickboxing and likewise achieving significant international visibility as a result. While *Chocolate* failed to attain quite the same level of success as its predecessor, it is in many ways a more interesting film, with vastly more engaging characters and more complex, inventive fight sequences.

The protagonist of *Chocolate* is Zen (Jeeja Yanin Vismitananda), a half-Japanese teenager raised by her Thai mother, a former member of a criminal syndicate who has been ostracized as a consequence of her tragic romance with a *yakuza* enforcer from a rival gang. Zen is autistic, a quiet and reclusive girl for whom social integration is too great a challenge; she is also a martial arts savant, having mastered Muay Thai with incredible proficiency by observing the training routine at the gym next door and her obsessive repeat viewings of Tony Jaa movies. When Zen's mother falls ill and needs money for medical treatment, Zen embarks on a violent quest to collect a series of unpaid underworld debts.

Chocolate thus foregrounds not just gender issues, showcasing "girl power" wildly effectively by spending the vast majority of its runtime depicting a petit woman battling burly men, but also the increasingly urgent and woefully overlooked theme of disability. A brief sequence of stylish, experimental animation depicts Zen's perspective on the world, illuminating her endearingly cheerful attitude to violence. Zen's autism is ultimately presented as both the source of her strength and the cause of her difficulties, but the narrative never suggests this is a problem she needs to overcome: rather, it is an intrinsic part of her character and Jeeja Yanin's performance is both convincing and dignified.

The influence of *Ong-Bak* is evident not just in the film's aesthetic and fight choreography, but also literalized in the nature of Zen's skills: she is trained by Tony Jaa's mediated form, a disciple at the school of *Ong-Bak*. She masters her abilities by imitating the earlier film's fight scenes, thus offering a metatextual commentary on the inspirational influence of *Ong-Bak* on martial arts cinema, and on martial artists themselves. *Chocolate* also recycles *Ong-Bak*'s obvious nationalism, with a final confrontation that pits Zen's Muay Thai against a foreign opponent's Brazilian *capoeira*. Ultimately however, the film reflects a broader range of inter-Asian influence, appropriating the iconography of films such as *Kill Bill, Vol. 1* (2003) in a Japanese gangster sword-fight melee and containing an obvious nod to Bruce Lee's Hong Kong action debut *The Big Boss* (1971) in an ice factory fracas.

The unprecedented level of international interest in *Ong-Bak* led to a brief cycle of Thai action and martial arts films seeking wider global distribution. *Chocolate* has proven to be one of the most memorable of these, and its critical reception in the UK was largely positive. Indeed, the film deserves to be remembered as one of the best female-led martial arts films of its generation.

Daniel Martin

Title: *Raging Phoenix / Jeeja Due Suai Du*
Director: **Rashane Limtrakul**
Studio: **Baa-Ram-Ewe**
Year: **2009**

Released one year after Prachya Pinkaew's *Chocolate* (2008), which was also edited by director Limtrakul, *Raging Phoenix* showcases the same martial arts star, Yanin Vismistananda, popularly known as Jeeja Yanin. Indeed, the Thai title, *Jeeja Due Suai Du* even directly references the actress.

Yanin plays Deu, a young girl who joins a small group of vigilantes intent on tracking down the headquarters of the human trafficking gang "Jaguar." The group is intent on avenging their loved ones who were killed by the Jaguar gangsters, and practises a secret martial art they call "*meyraiyuth*" (a name derived from the Thai words meaning "drunk fighting") which requires fighters to utilize the raw energy obtained from drinking large quantities of alcohol. This fighting style, invented for the purpose of the movie, could best be described as a mix of Muay Thai, capoeira, and breakdancing. Deu is rescued from potential kidnappers by the group's leader Sanim (Kazu Patrick Tang), and insists on being trained as a *meyraiyuth* fighter and joining their cause. She begins falling in love with Sanim, albeit while knowing that he continues to search for his fiance, who was kidnapped on the day of their wedding.

The martial arts of *Raging Phoenix* are a joy to watch. The fights have been beautifully choreographed by veteran action choreographers Weerapon Poomatfon and Panna Rittikrai, both known for their collaboration on such films as *Ong-Bak* (2003), *Chocolate*, and *The Kick* (2011). However, while the hybrid quality of the martial arts technique and the showmanship of Jeeja and her crew are remarkable, other artistic decisions of the director are more questionable. Perhaps most disappointing is the overall simplicity of the plot which, coupled with characters' general lack of depth, turns the film into an overlong music video depicting fighting skills and costumes.

Yet unlike other productions from Prachya Pinkaew's Baa-Ram-Ewe action team, *Raging Phoenix* refuses to promote martial arts as a conduit for nationalistic propaganda. Instead the film prefers a more abstract approach: while the outcast heroes may speak Thai they otherwise appear as nationless drifters united by their pain-fuelled rage against global evil. Locations of the movie refuse to give off even a hint of Thai-ness, replacing local landscapes with fragmentary deconstructed sets instead. If anything, the obtrusive inclusion of Christian symbols (crosses, churches, and Catholic graveyards) seem to suggest that the action takes place in Latin America, although this may also be an influence from the Western, as suggested by the final shot of the heroes walking into the sunset. Such stylistic hybridity evidently proved the film's undoing. Seen as too experimental, *Raging Phoenix* did not fare well with Thai audiences, making only 600,000 USD at the box office.

Katarzyna Ancuta

Title:	*Red Eagle / Insi Daeng*
Director:	Wisit Sasanatieng
Studio:	Five Star Production, Local Color Films
Year:	2010

As a contemporary resurrection of the famous 1960s crime-fighting hero and the first film for four years from a director whose films helped kickstart the twenty-first-century New Thai industry, *Red Eagle* was one of the most anticipated Thai films of the decade. The choice of Wisit Sasanatieng to return to this major franchise of post-war Thai films was bold and inventive and publicity was correspondingly impressive.

The film tells the story of the vigilante former soldier Rom who disguises himself as a figure known as Insi Daeng or Red Eagle (Ananda Everingham) to kill crime lords and corrupt politicians in Bangkok. The story begins in 2010 with a party leader and NGO activist standing for election by campaigning against corruption and against the building of a nuclear power plant in Chumphon province. The film then moves forward to the near-future of 2013; the now-elected Prime Minister has gone back on his promises and a huge power station stands on the beach.

The film is in keeping with director Wisit Sasanatieng's unique abstract and high-concept style. Sasanatieng's 2013 Bangkok is a Gotham-inspired, dystopian neo-noir metallic cityscape of violent crime, corruption, drug deals, murders, police sirens screaming down streets and heavy chiaroscuro, all of which is controlled by a mysterious masked order of gangsters and politicians known as the Matulee. Instead of the idyllic beaches and luscious paddy fields that pepper both internal and external representations of Thailand, the film has an almost monochromatic grey palette with unattractive mobile low-angle shots that depict faceless skyscrapers and office blocks beneath overcast clouds. Insi Daeng himself is an excessively violent masked crime-fighter with an impressive array of weapons, a formidable motorbike, unmatched prowess with a sword and a violent past that constantly returns to torture him both mentally and physically. The film's action sequences are deliberately excessive to the extent that they quickly drift into the fantastical realm and become a deliberate homage to the histrionic film style of earlier eras of Thai cinema.

Such a depiction seems to deliberately reflect the chaos and upheaval of contemporary Thai politics, offering a damning indictment of Thai elites through exposing the damage caused by corrupt authority figures. Yet the film does not posit any solution for the rebuilding or reforming of Thailand, rather its damaged hero seems to call for the complete destruction of this fragmented and bleak dystopia that hardly seems worth defending. There is therefore much to laud about the text as a welcome break from the dominant conservative discourses of contemporary Thai cinema, and indeed this appears to echo the left-wing politics of its director. Yet the film proved a commercial failure upon its release and was widely panned by critics and audiences alike. This promptly put an end to the intended franchise from the re-launch of this superhero.

Mary J. Ainslie

Title:	*The Gangster / Anthaphan*
Director:	Kongkiat Khomsiri
Studio:	Sahamongkol Film
Year:	2012

Before its release in 2012, *The Gangster* was rumoured to be a remake of Nonzee Nimibutr's acclaimed *Dang Bireley's and Young Gangsters* (1997) and to tell "the real story" of its legendary hero. The film ultimately proved to be neither, but Khomsiri once again demonstrated his prowess in contemporary Thai filmmaking.

The Gangster returns to the world of 1950s Thai mafia, rock'n'roll and the iconic characters of *Dang Bireley's*. This time, however, the plot focuses on two generations of gangsters whose lives seem to follow a similar pattern. For Thong (Sakarin Suthamsamai) and Piak (Krisada Supapprom), working as film projectionists in a Bangkok cinema, the real world of Thai gangs and Hollywood seem equally alluring, and their personal heroes, Jod (Krissada Sukosol) and Dang (Somchai Kemglad), are easily reminiscent of Elvis and James Dean. This sentiment is reflected in the way the movie is put together, blending video inserts of "authentic" Bangkokians reminiscing the past, mock-documentary reconstructions of archival

Figure 17 The complex noir-esque protagonists of *The Gangster* (2012).

Figure 18 The recreated 1950s Thai cinema in *The Gangster* (2012).

footage, and explosive action cut to blaring rock'n'roll music to offset the graphic imagery of violence.

Jod, the central character in the movie, is the personification of the "honourable outlaw" trope characteristic of East Asian action films depicting Hong Kong triads, Japanese yakuza and Korean gangs, but also known from American Westerns and gangster movies. Indeed, critics were quick to point out the influences of Martin Scorsese and Johnny To, or look for references to *The Godfather* (1972), *Goodfellas* (1990), or *Butch Cassidy and the Sundance Kid* (1969). Jod is no stranger to violence. He is capable of killing a man with the claw of a crab and yet he loves his mother, will not tolerate violence against women and protects innocents. He can bond with his opponent over a ball game and a bottle of Coke and fight him to the death a moment later to settle a territorial dispute. In this, like many of Khomsiri's characters, Jod is the embodiment of *saksi luk puchai* ("the honour of men"), an old-fashioned cultural value that once served as the ideological foundation for Thai masculinity. This value is obviously lacking in the villains, who are beyond redemption and, typically of Khomsiri, represent the faulty system, here specifically the military regime of Field Marshal Sarit, exemplified by the psychotic butterfly-torturing Captain Kamnueng (Wasu Sangsingkaew).

Similarly to *Muay Thai Chaiya* (2007), and *Slice* (2009), the Thai underworld in *The Gangster* becomes the last refuge of Thai working-class masculinity, a culture marginalized in most local film productions in favour of its glossier urban metrosexual counterpart. As expected of Khomsiri, the film ends on a tragic, if at the same time heroic note. The historical setting suggests that abiding by the rules of the old code is a thing of the past. Crucially, the protagonists seem to understand this, accepting their inevitable downfall with an unnerving degree of Buddhist stoicism and resignation.

Katarzyna Ancuta

7

Comedy / Romantic Comedy

Such is the international prominence of Thai cinema in the contemporary era that it is not unusual or surprising to find Thai film as the only Southeast Asian industry on Western DVD racks alongside the more globally well-known East Asian industries of China, Japan, Hong Kong and South Korea. However, undoubtedly, this selection will be limited to a smattering of *Muay Thai* films, historical Heritage films, *Kathoei* films and the usual Horror numbers, all of which have come to characterize Thai cinema internationally. This is surprising, as within the country itself, while these genres are undoubtedly popular, it is Comedy and its subgenre Romantic Comedy that draws the largest crowds nationally and the biggest box office takings.

Not surprisingly, many of such films as *I Fine... Thank You... Love You* (2014), *Hello Stranger* (2010), *Bangkok Traffic Love Story* (2009), *30+ Single On Sale* (2011) focus upon clumsy yet well-meaning single female protagonists, following a Cinderella-esque story in which a beautiful and chaste, yet also aging and slighted, woman will eventually be united with her true love. Within such storylines, coincidence plays a large role, and such unions are often attributed to fate, manifested through Buddhist karma. Such universal themes of female desire and the difficulty of finding one's mate, are therefore given a specific Thai incarnation, one largely set in a competitive urban Bangkokian environment that owes much to the East Asian rom-coms that have grown popular across Southeast Asia over the last decade. Most notably, many of these films have also been particularly successful in other Southeast Asian countries, suggesting that an aethestic originally traced to an East Asian influence, may have been most effectively regionalized by Thailand.

Other more slapstick films concern themselves with the awkward divisions within Thailand, be they rural and urban or ethnic and religious. These "fish out of water" protagonists experience significant culture shock in their new environments, a strong source of physical comedy, as seen in *M.A.I.D: Mission Almost Impossible Done* (2004), *The Holy Man* (2005) and *OK Baytong* (2003). While such films may therefore be light-hearted and frivolous in terms of narratives and protagonists, the settings speak to and make safe modern anxieties around the status of women, gender relations and the complex divisions of contemporary Thailand, so performing an important overarching social function as well as remaining a popular form of communal entertainment.

Yet despite this highly popular nature and integral position in the Thai film industry, Thai comedy films remain underexplored on both a popular and academic level. This is indicative of the continued universal denigration of comedy, melodrama and "women's films," a perspective originally noted by film theorists in the 1970s and 1980s. This lack of attention is both disappointing and detrimental. Indeed theorists understand that national and regional studies of specific genres can add much to our understanding of these filmic categories, the prominence of many studies of "Asian horror" being a case in point. Yet it appears that while the study of horror may have been enriched by such national case studies, the same cannot yet be said for comedy, a genre that remains just as (if not more) popular in East and Southeast Asia. It is such a gap that this section is hopefully a step towards filling.

Mary J. Ainslie

Comedy / Romantic Comedy

Title: *OK Baytong*
Director: Nonzee Nimibutr
Studio: Sahamongkol Film
Year: 2003

OK Baytong is the fourth film directed by Nonzee Nimibutr, but in contrast to his previous lavish and exotic hits *Nang Nak* (1999) and *Jan Dara* (2001), *OK Baytong* is a low key, tragi-comic reflection on interethnic relations in Thailand's Muslim-majority "deep South" and the role of Buddhist values in contemporary Thai society. The story follows Tham (literally, "Dhamma," the teachings of the Buddha, played by Phoovarit Phumpuang), who has been a Buddhist monk since he was a young boy. Learning that his sister has been killed in a terrorist bombing at a Southern railway station, he travels from his forest monastery in the Northeast to his sister's home in Betong (Baytong), Thailand's southernmost city on the Malaysian border. There he is introduced to his young niece, Maria. With her mother dead and Malaysian father living in his own country, Maria is essentially orphaned. Unable even to hug her due to the monastic prohibition of touching females, Tham decides to disrobe in order to care for his niece and help run his sister's beauty salon.

The film follows the naïve Tham as he struggles to adjust to the life of a layman. He must learn how to wear trousers (he has a nasty accident with his fly), to use a mobile phone and to ride a bicycle. He is tempted by alcohol and sex in Betong's karaoke bars and later develops a romantic attraction to Lin (Jeeranan Manojam), a Sino-Thai Buddhist who runs a neighbouring travel agency and helps to look after Maria. However Lin is already in a relationship with Farook, a Muslim. To make matters worse, Farook is accused of plotting the bomb attack that killed Tham's sister. More bad news comes when Maria's father announces that she should move to Malaysia to live with him.

Given that Tham's name is synonymous with Buddha's teachings, the film can be read as an allegory of the ongoing relevance of the Dhamma in contemporary Thai society. In various ways Tham is forced to confront his attachments: his attraction to Lin, his affection for Maria, his desire for revenge against Farook, and his hankering for his former life as a monk. In each case he is gradually able to come to terms with and let go of the emotions that torment him. Ironically therefore, it is not in the monastery but in Betong that Tham learns important lessons about the Buddhist goal of non-attachment.

OK Baytong also strikes a hopeful note with regard to interethnic relations in the far South of Thailand. Released in 2003, at a time when there were signs that conflict was brewing again but before the major and sustained outbreak of violence in 2004, the film speaks directly to anxieties within Thailand about the future of the South. Although framed by a terrorist bombing, the film draws attention to the long-standing interconnections, and intermarriages, between Buddhists and Muslims in the South and emphasizes the possibility of overcoming distrust and hatred.

Jovan Maud

Title: *Sayew*
Directors: Kongdej Jaturanrasamee, Kiat Songsanant
Studio: Sahamongkol Film, Ba-Ram-Ewe
Year: 2003

Sayew follows one girl's struggle to navigate the moral economy of Bangkok during the 1992 backdrop of patriarchal military rule. The protagonist, Tao (Pimpaporn Leenutapong), is a young comparative literature student at a prominent Bangkok university writing her thesis on romance novels. Alongside her studies, Tao works as an unlikely intern for her Uncle's underground erotica column and delivers food part-time for her aunt's street-side restaurant.

Tao is new to the city and (similar to Thailand itself at this time), things are not going well: her baggy clothes seem unladylike and unfashionable, while her thesis committee believes her project fails to reflect Thai literature's relation to Thai society (a theme inspired by the social realist "for life" politics of the 1970s). Tao herself gravitates between masculine and feminine extremes, displaying a tomboy-ish fascination with a famous male police officer known as "the black hand" and enjoying an imagined sexual liaison with a female classmate at her university. Meanwhile, the political sensationalism of parliamentary infighting and soap operas that sanction Thai patriarchy is ever present, and to make matters worse, John, Tao's next-door neighbor of similar age, wants to be more than friends.

Amidst this confusion, Tao's uncle refuses to publish her columns, believing his niece lacks worldly experience and is unable to accurately capture the minds of the male readership. Seeking access to the male audiences of the magazine's erotica column, and therefore job security, Tao seeks out the masculine expertise of the magazine's "hit" writer, known as the Young Stallion. The Young Stallion brags of his latest acquisition, a "cutting edge" videotape in an analogue of the market of bootlegged videos that captured military violence in May 1992. Later in the film, Tao watches the shocking video footage, which the soundtrack reveals to be a dehumanizing snuff film assembled around cries for help, chainsaws, and a whimpering dog. Tao's disillusionment then extends into a scene in which she and John accidentally witness the "black hand" being unable to "finish" his own sexual encounters due to injuries sustained during war. Tao's own inability to cross-over into the world of the male fantasy is also symbolized in several scenes where she can only type "ญ," the first letter of "girl" in Thai language.

Ultimately the film focuses upon Tao's overall relationship to dominant media, a "reproductive" mode in which identity and so-called "reality" collide against the backdrop of military brutality. This rawness cuts abrasively against the film's final scene in which Tao is framed as a happy housewife and author of best-selling romance novels. Such an unlikely ending highlights how Thai politics and the rigid boundaries of gender leave only a very simple choice: to confront or retreat.

Noah Viernes

Title: *M.A.I.D.: Mission Almost Impossible Done / Chaeo*
Director: Yongyoot Thongkongtoon
Studio: GTH
Year: 2004

In *M.A.I.D.*, director Yongyoot Thongkongtoon uses slapstick action-comedy, a staple Thai film genre, to explore substantive Thai political and cultural issues. The film tells the story of two sisters in their 20s, Waew

(Pornchita Na Songkhla) and Jim (Jarupus Pattamasiri), who have come from the Northeastern region of Thailand to work as maids in Bangkok. Through a fortuitous turn of events, these two poorly educated countryside women are recruited as governmental spies to work on an undercover special investigation centred on a dishonest businessman who is attempting to bribe a politician in order to legalize gambling in Thailand. Resident in the mansion of the ultra-wealthy businessman, the sisters form a team with two other incumbent maids and seek to gather evidence about their employer's activities, with hilarious results.

Through this story the film addresses three central, underlying concerns: corruption, inequality (particularly in the Thai Northeast), and the oppression of women in patriarchal Thai culture. Indeed, the film is explicit in its empowerment of these impoverished Northeastern women. Despite their hilarious escapades, Waew and Jim are consistently portrayed as proactive and strong people who are able to think critically, thereby refuting the prevalent stereotype of the naïve, dumb, passive rural villager. Certainly the sisters are recruited as spies due to the skills they possess (their observational skills), rather than for their beauty or complaisance toward men. Another maid on their team, Ae (Panalak Na Lumpang), cannot keep any maid job, because she refuses to allow herself to be sexually harassed by any of her male employers. This determination and empowerment is deliberately enacted and symbolized by the use of household items as weapons by the maids, specifically items that are strongly associated with the traditional, stereotypical views of a woman's role (staying in the home, cooking and cleaning); in the promotional poster the four maids are shown holding a broom, a pestle, a soup ladle-sieve, and a toilet plunger. Through such a portrayal the film is thus elevated above the usual light-hearted and shallow action-comedy fare, while still retaining the charm and humour of the genre.

While *M.A.I.D.* works well as a comedy, with fun but simplistic slapstick action scenes, and does offer commentary on important issues in Thai politics and culture, its convoluted plot twists obscure any clear political and social message. Indeed the film is unfortunately undermined by plot twists in the story's second half which, ironically, contradict *M.A.I.D.*'s intended themes.

Jesse Sessoms

Title: *The Holy Man / Luang Phi Teng*
Director: Note Chern-Yim
Studio: Phranakorn Film
Year: 2005

That *The Holy Man* was even a hit was surprising; that it was a domestic box office smash, being the only Thai film of 2005 to earn 141 million baht domestically, was astounding. *The Holy Man* currently ranks as 13th for the top earning Thai films and has generated two sequels, the second of which was the top domestic film of 2008. Starring popular comedian Pongsak Pongsuwan, the film's success gleefully contradicted the marketing zeitgeist of the contemporary New Thai film industry at the time, which held that for a production to be successful it had to cater for the Thai middle classes and urbanites. Rather, *The Holy Man* demonstrated that the poorer, lower classes had significant box office purchasing power and should not be neglected.

A religious comedy, *The Holy Man* tells the story of a village in Northeastern Thailand (Isan) whose inhabitants have lost the spirit of Buddhism and have instead begun to seek quick fixes via charms and magic offered by con-artists posing as a spiritualist group. The local Buddhist temple is inactive as no monk has been able to successfully run it. In these circumstances the next monk Luang Phi Teng arrives, who inevitably (and humorously) enables the villagers to rediscover the genuine spirit of Buddhism.

As an "upcountry" film *The Holy Man* is set entirely in the Northeastern village and its characters are all, and only, villagers. Focusing upon themes of harmony and cooperation within the community and exemplifying long-term, genuine solutions (represented through Buddhist teachings) versus quick fixes (the "magic" of the con-artists), the film tackles serious social themes in a light-hearted manner. Despite its raucous gags and predictable happy ending, *The Holy Man* offers a serious mediation upon the merits of faith, but does so in a non-condescending manner while unequivocally and refreshingly devoting itself to the "upcountry" market.

Jesse Sessoms

Title: *Metrosexual / Kaeng Chani Kap I Aep*
Director: Yongyoot Thongkongtoon
Studio: GTH
Year: 2006

Metrosexual is a romantic comedy from Yongyoot Thongkongtoon also known for the *kathoei* comedy *The Iron Ladies* (2000). The Thai title *Kaeng Chani Kap I-Aep* literally translates as "The Gang of Girls and the Closet Case." This title is a pun on various Thai slang: "*chani*" (gibbon) is gay slang for a woman (based on the similarity between gibbon calls and the Thai word for husband "*phua*") while "*i-aep*" also refers to a gay man who hides his identity. The film follows a group of five female friends Fai (Pimolwan Suphayang), Nim (Orpreeya Hunsat), Pat (Kulnadda Pachimsawat), Pom (Patcharasri Benjamas) and Pang (Meesuk Jaengmeesuk), who are also co-hosts of a popular daytime talk show. Pom mistakenly believes that she previously witnessed Pang's fiancé Kong (Thienchai Jayasvasti Jr) embracing a male model at a fashion show she was covering for a magazine. Believing that Pang is about to unknowingly marry a gay man, the gang set out to prove to Pang that her fiancé is not metrosexual but is actually gay.

Kong is handsome, well-groomed, and knowledgeable about cooking, cosmetics, and fashion. He is meticulous, colour-coding his shirts in the closet and folding the ends of his toilet paper like in a hotel. For Pang's friends, Kong is obviously too perfect to be straight. Pat thus consults her gay flight attendant brother, Bee (Michael Shaowanasai), to find out how to identify a gay man. Bee contrasts older stereotypes of gay men (e.g. holding the pinky finger out when drinking tea or wearing an earring) with characteristics that supposedly are more likely to be true gauges of gayness (e.g. looking back rather than forward to check if something is stuck to the shoes or looking at fingernails palms out rather than palms in). He provides a list of indicators that the gang investigates to verify that Kong is gay.

In the meantime, each of the women has their own love interests and problems. For example, Pat is being wooed by an older Japanese man who appears to be as old as her father. Throughout this comedy of errors, nothing verifies that Kong is gay, although clues suggest that he did have a male lover in high school. Then, on their wedding day, Pang is confronted with the reality that Kong did, and perhaps still does, love other men. This film therefore confirms what many Thais already believe: that "metrosexual" has come to mean "closeted gay" in Thailand. That is, metrosexuals are not "gay acting" straight men in Thailand, but rather gay men who say they are straight.

Dredge Kang

Title: *Noo Hin: The Movie*
Director: **Komgrit Triwimol**
Studio: GTH
Year: 2006

Building up his career from "feel-good movies" produced by GTH and the success of *My Girl* in 2003, Komgrit Triwimol was well known for making comedic films and television series throughout the 2000s. In 2006, Triwimol adapted *Noo Hin Inter*, one of the most popular Thai comic books for the big screen. Written by Phadung Kraisri under his penname "O," more than 200 volumes of the *Noo Hin Inter* comic series have been published since 1995. With a strong fan base around this source material in both Bangkok and rural areas, it was not surprising that *Noo Hin: The Movie* was highly anticipated amongst film institutions and moviegoers.

The film features the story of Noo Hin (Rungrawan Tonahongsa), a troublemaker and a dreamer from None Hin Hae village in Ubon Ratchathani province in Isan, Northeastern Thailand. Leaving her village for Bangkok, Noo Hin is soon hired by Milk (Kochakorn Suppakarnkitjakul) as a housemaid (or a "house manager" in Noo Hin's terminology). Happily working, Noo Him quickly develops a crush on Thong (Adisorn Insee), the youngest son of Milk's neighbour. An attentive consumer of pop culture, Noo Hin also pushes Milk and her friend Som O (Panisa Buacharoen) into competing in a model contest organized by Sonia, a malicious Thai supermodel. When Milk is approached by a French designer to perform in his finale show, Sonia has Milk and Som O kidnapped while also throwing Noo Hin into a factory whose workers are supplied by a human trafficking movement. Ever the heroine, Noo Hin manages to emancipate all the female slave labourers while Milk finally fulfils her role in the finale, and Sonia is ultimately punished.

Noo Hin: The Movie stays very close to its original comic book version, with Noo Hin herself retaining cartoon-like actions and mannerisms. The use of animation and special effects, coupled with a strong female leading role and memorable theme song also earned significant praise from Thai film critics and institutions. Yet beneath its comic cover, the film also mobilizes some very notable cultural and political discourses. The source text *Noo Hin Inter* was launched during the age of "newly industrialized" Thailand of the 1990s, when there was a large migration influx from the Northeast to Bangkok. Migration literature and the music industry targeting such displaced rural audiences and texts such as *Noo Hin Inter* have remained popular ever since. Wittily, the film captures this so-called "atmosphere of the age," evident in scenes such as Noo Hin singing a Thai country song to empower the female slave labourers to emancipate themselves.

The film also criticizes contemporary superficial emphasis upon female beauty: Som O is obsessed with her body while Sonia uses a pair of fake breasts in order to get ahead. Ironically, it is the provincial Noo Hin who is acclaimed as a core inspiration of the exotic collection by the French designer, so undermining such dominant constructions of beauty. The film therefore indicates the return of intermeshed local and global discourses in the Thai film industry in a way that has been largely absent since the economic crisis of 1997, making Noo Hin not only a highly enjoyable but also a very significant and potentially progressive text in the New Thai industry.

Natthanai Prasannam

Title: *Seasons Change / Phro Akat Plianplaeng Boi*
Director: Nithiwat Tharatorn
Studio: GTH
Year: 2006

Seasons Change is Nithiwat Tharatorn's first solo work after his success as part of the six-director team for the nostalgia-driven *My Girl* (2003). The film shares the mood and tone of *My Girl*, in combination with the pacing and picture style of Adachi Mitsuru's Japanese manga, and contrasts rock and classical music genres, making this a very notable addition to Thai filmmaking in this decade.

The film is a conventional coming-of-age story about self-exploration. Defying his parents, who believe that music is not suitable for a career, and driven by his hidden love for Dao (Yuwanat Arayanimisakul), the protagonist Pom (Witawat Singlampong), a talented drummer, enters a music college for high school. Pom asks Aom (Chutima Teepanat), a female school friend who is talented at music theory but cannot perform music well, to keep his studies secret from his parents, but Aom is also secretly in love in Pom. At the same time, Pom's friends ask him to join their rock band as a drummer in order to compete in a national rock music contest, conflicting with his desire to join Dao's orchestra as a timpani player. Pom is then faced with a choice as to whether he should concentrate upon winning the competition or winning Dao's heart, as well as choosing when to reveal the truth to his family.

The film is an ideal GTH "feel good movie": the romantic sequences are not intense and represent an "innocent" form of love, while there is no antagonist at all and the family issue unfolds warmly. This focus upon classical music as the background setting for the narrative is unusual in Thai cinema and *Seasons Change* may, arguably, be the first time that classical music has been so significant in a Thai film. The use of music is also deeply symbolic; Pom plays both a rock drum set and the classical timpani. The two types of drums represent two different seasons: summer and winter, and the different seasons represent the two girls: cheerful Aom and calm Dao. Such oppositions represent the two decisions the protagonist is pulled between: to be yourself or to be "someone" else.

Yossapol Chutipanyabut

Title: *Bus Lane / Mel Narok Muai Yok Lo*
Director: Kittikorn Liasirikun
Studio: Avant
Year: 2007

In the Thai political crisis of 2006, anti-government protesters demonstrated against Prime Minister Thaksin Shinawatra's council. The situation did not just lead to a military coup d'état, but also eventually changed the sphere of political conflict in Thailand, dividing Thai people into two groups: Pro-Thaksin "Red Shirts" and Anti-Thaksin "Yellow Shirts," creating a rift that continues in the contemporary context.

Inspired by this situation, Kittiporn Liasirikun wrote and directed *Bus Lane* to stress how conflict can occur amongst those who are self-centred and not open to alternative ideas. The story takes place on a bus during the Thai New Year holiday, known locally as *songkran*. Ko (Udom Taephanit) is a sarcastic bus conductor who is annoyed at having to work during the holiday, mostly because he wants to stay with his girlfriend. The situation is made worse when Ko's boss makes him work with a moody driver (Suthep Po-ngam) whom he hates. The middle-aged man does not drive well, never stops precisely by the bus stop and curses a lot. Yet the clash really begins when a fat security guard (Kiat Kitjaroen) gets on to the bus and eventually hijacks the vehicle in a rage because the driver does not stop. Throughout this, the passengers also argue amongst themselves about who is to blame for the situation.

Although Liasirikun also worked as an assistant director to M.J. Chatrichalerm Yukol in the epic *The Legend of King Naresuan* saga (with six films between 2007 and 2015 and counting) his own films are not blockbusters. Often, like in *Goal Club* (2001), he applies a low-budget visual style together with a *luk thung* (country music) soundtrack. His film style is also highly versatile, including action films such as *The Mia* (2005), children's story *Dream Team* (2008) and the romance *Sunset at Chaophraya* (2013). However it is comedy that first launched his career with his debut film *18–80 Buddy* in 1997. Indeed, *Bus Lane* brings together three famous comedians: standup comedian Udom Taephanit, "café" stage comedian Suthep Po-ngam, and TV personality Kiat Kitjaroen. Despite this concentration upon humour, the director still manages to construct the film as an adept metaphor for the current conflicts in Thailand. For such simple stories and conversational comedies, Liasirikun received the prestigious Thai National Film Association's Suphannahong Award as Best Director in 2008.

Yossapol Chutipanyabut

Title:	*E-Tim Tai Nae*
Director:	Yuthlert Sippapak
Studio:	Sahamongkol Film
Year:	2008

Starting with his debut action-comedy *Killer Tattoo* (2003), Yuthlert Sippapak has made a name by blurring genres. *E-Tim Tai Nae* is another such example of his work, located at the intersection of Muay Thai movie and romantic comedy.

The film tells the story of adolescent Tueng (Udom Taephanit) who "performs" as a fake Muay Thai boxer in the tourist centre of Pattaya. Falling in love with the Japanese tourist Itemi (Asuka Yanagi), Tueng overcomes his painful shyness around women to initiate a romance. He introduces her to his hero Sathaan Faa, a well-conditioned professional Muay Thai boxer, yet in an impromptu bout Tueng unexpectedly faces Sathaan Faa and is roundly beaten and humiliated in front of his new love. Eager to redeem himself, Tueng accepts Sathaan Faa's invitation to become his *luksit* (student), however before his first lesson he discovers that his idol has stolen his girlfriend. Makin (Sirin Horwang), an ethnic Hmong girl selling souvenirs in Pattaya's streets, then encourages Tueng to try to win Itemi back and Tueng challenges Sathaan Faa to a Muay Thai match. What follows is a modified David-versus-Goliath tale: Tueng narrowly defeats Sathaan Faa with the help of a clever trick by Makin, yet after the bout Itemi confesses that she has also used a trick to help her new boyfriend. Disenchanted by this further betrayal, Tueng suddenly realizes that he is actually in love with Makin, and in the closing scene he wins her heart by singing a Hmong song dressed in Hmong costume.

While the film might be purely seen as light entertainment, it can also be read as a commentary on national identity in the age of globalization. Muay Thai films often portray Thai men as defenders of national identity against the threats of foreign invasion or the corruptions of modernity. Yet as a comedy, *E-Tim* plays with this genre. Teung is not the typical strong man: as a mere stage performer he is unathletic, wimpish and is accused of fighting worse than girls. Yet his sympathetic plight wins out when he triumphs against a professional boxer.

Such themes of cultural authenticity and commodification are also evident in the encounter between Tueng and Makin. Tueng disparages Makin, accusing her of merely masquerading as Hmong to make more profit from tourists. In one sequence, he makes her sing aloud the Thai national anthem, blaming her for being neither a "real" Hmong nor a "real" Thai. Ironically however, it is Tueng himself who is performing a commodified version of Thai culture for a tourist audience.

In the context of debates on the loss of Thai-ness in the face of modernity and globalization, Sipappak's depiction stands in stark contrast to the dominant nostalgic discourse found in the Muay Thai genre. Such films locate Thai-ness in the countryside and the past, associating the city and the future with moral decay. Yet in the ending of *E-Tim* Sippapak seems to suggest that genuineness and morality still persist, even in the touristy and commodified Pattaya.

Jelka Günther

Title: *Bangkok Traffic Love Story / Rotfaifa Ma Ha Na Thoe*
Director: Adisorn Trisirikasem
Studio: GTH
Year: 2009

After his success as one of the six directors of *My Girl* (2003), Adisorn Trisirikasem continued to follow up with more comedy films, including the controversial *Lucky Loser* (2006). *Bangkok Traffic Love Story* was screened in 2009 and remains his standout masterpiece, gaining huge success with mass audiences and wide acclaim from several film institutions.

The film portrays the life of Meili (Sirin Horwang), a Chinese-Thai and middle-class singleton. As a "thirty-something" singleton, Meili is pressured to find a boyfriend of her own, indeed the film's opening exposition is set at a wedding ceremony of Meili's best friend. Without romantic familiarity, Meili is fearful of loss and her own imperfections. Meili meets Lung (Theeradej Wongpuapan), a sky train engineer, when her car crashes and nearly hits Lung and his friends. Without her car Meili is forced to experience the ill-famed Bangkok traffic, which consumes her energy even more than her office work. The protagonists' relationship is developed around the Bangkok traffic and during the Songkran period. Setting up the romantic comedy, Meili tries to court Lung in various funny ways, often helped or aided by Plern, her younger neighbour. Yet Lung works a night shift, causing a temporal rift between him and Meili. When Lung is offered a scholarship to pursue a higher degree in Germany, Meili comes to realize their incompatibility. A two year gap follows, with the couple eventually reuniting on the Bangkok sky train when, in a reversal of roles, Meili goes for her night shift and Lung ends his working day.

The main targeted audience of the film was the mass of urban working women in Bangkok, with Meili's plain Chinese looks an easy source of identification for such viewers. Sirin Horwang plays Meili in her début role, while Theeradej Wongpuapan, a familiar presence on Thai television since the 1990s, plays the leading "prince charming" role of Lung. The film therefore depicts how ethnicity, class and gender are interwoven in the urban context, while strongly referencing Thai women's culture of television dramas and shopping centres. Speaking with a modern slang, Meili and her female audience share this sisterhood of "Cinderella syndrome."

With its fairy-tale resolution, the film is also influenced by Hollywood "chick flicks" and translated "chick lit" widely circulated in Thailand since the turn of the century. Meili struggles with her love life, work, consumption, urban ways and family tradition, so sharing strong similarities with similar protagonists such as those of *Bridget Jones's Diary* (2001). *Bangkok Traffic Love Story* officially gave birth to Thai chick flicks, and many films and television series framed within this formula were to follow, such as the similarly successful *30+ Single On Sale* (2011) and *Fabulous 30* (2011).

Natthanai Prasannam

Title: *Hello Stranger / Kuan Muen Ho*
Director: Banjong Pisanthanakun
Studio: GTH, Jorkwang Films, KTCC
Year: 2010

Directed by the well-known figure in Thai filmmaking Banjong Pisanthanakun and adapted from Songkalot Bangyikhun's novel *Two Shadows in Korea*, *Hello Stranger* is a romantic comedy based on the accidental relationship that develops between two Thai tourists in South Korea. Part of a corpus of romantic comedies which emerged in commercial Thai cinema from the turn of the twenty-first century, the film garnered around 4.2 million USD at the Thai Box office and was screened for eight weeks.

The light-hearted story is based upon the frictional encounters between an urbane, sophisticated woman, May (Nuengthida Sophon), and a parochial, loutish man, Dang (Chantavit Dhanasevi), who begins to soften as the two characters grow closer. May travels to South Korea as a tourist, while her male counterpart Dang is hastily placed on the arranged group tour by his friends to help him get over an unhappy relationship. After overcoming the friction from their initial encounter, the two strangers grow fond of each other as they travel around South Korea, appreciating each other pasts. Despite this budding relationship, their encounter does not evolve further into a romance given the sudden appearance of Dang's girlfriend in Seoul. The two characters therefore awkwardly revert to strangers again, with neither exchanging names or contact details. Having lost touch upon their return to Thailand, it is only after Dang randomly hears a call-in by May on a radio program that the film ends with at least the possibility of a romantic reconnection.

Yet while its love-hate relationship may seem somewhat typical, *Hello Stranger* can be distinguished from the general genre of Thai romantic comedies as the film is almost entirely set in South Korea. The production therefore becomes a cinematic caricature of the enthusiastic reception of Korean popular entertainment by Thais in the past decade. In *Hello Stranger*, the Thai tourists that the male protagonist is reluctantly travelling with are over-excited and enjoy mimicking the lifestyles and actions of the Korean artistes they see on the small screen. Such sheer enthusiasm is also exhibited by May, much to the annoyance of Dang who is forced to accompany her after missing his tour bus.

In staging this romantic comedy in South Korea, *Hello Stranger* offers a critical reversal of the cinematic gaze. Like its Southeast Asian counterparts, cinematic portrayals of Thailand are often objectified as unchanging, feudal and dangerous oriental societies by both Hollywood and East Asian cinemas. By reversing this portrayal, the Thais in *Hello Stranger* become meaningful subjects of cinematic travels and participation in the industrialized world, a modernity that is nevertheless still represented by the East Asian city of Seoul.

Liew Kai Khiun

Title: *30+ Single On Sale / 30+ Sot On Sale*
Director: Puttipong Pormsakha Na-Sakonnakorn
Studio: Sahamongkol Film
Year: 2011

This 2011 romantic comedy recalls the Thai colloquialism, *chan on sale* – "I'm on sale (for a discount)," a jovial and preemptive phrase usually associated with older single Thai women. In the opening act, the lead character Ing's (Laila Boonyasak) wealthy boyfriend of seven years, Kong, reveals that he has been cheating on Ing, and that she is not his only girlfriend. Kong becomes the first of many unsuitable men whom Ing encounters throughout the film, before she finally learns to appreciate the male lead, Jeud (Arak Amornsupasiri). Considering her beauty and charm, Ing's romantic predicament may seem far-fetched, yet it also alludes to the larger and equally unreasonable crisis facing aging female actors such as Boonyasak.

The film regards Ing's single status as somewhat abject. At her lowest point, Ing drunk-dials Kong from the stall of a crowded restroom, cursing and screaming as she reveals that Kong was her first and only sexual partner, while realizing too late that Kong abandoned his phone number and she is actually speaking to its new owner.

The motivations of the central and supporting characters are also broad. Ing cries vigorously whenever upset. Mint, Ing's promiscuous close friend, proposes to disrobe in front an attractive trainer while exercising alongside Ing. Ing's boisterous, and sassy friend Yee also provides comic relief in a sub-plot that reflects growing concerns over rapid globalization in Thailand. In an effort to protect local businesses and culture, Yee successfully leads a protest to stop the launch of a Bangkok shopping complex led by a global conglomerate. Despite her over-the-top aggressiveness, Yee wins the heart of the conglomerate's Western CEO and they marry.

Ing encounters her destined beau, Jeud, when she seeks out his quixotic services as a "grilled pork fortune teller" who interprets her bite marks on his pork. He offers to pose as Ing's boyfriend to help her seem more desirous to potential suitors, giving Jeud a reason to spend much of the rest of the film alongside Ing.

The film exemplifies how belief in karmic destiny shapes Thai romantic comedies. There are many more plot coincidences than would be unpalatable to audiences unfamiliar with the Thai nuances of this genre, all of which are explained via karma intervening to bring the leads together. In a montage, Jeud is eventually revealed to be the man who saved Ing during a rock-climbing accident, the composer of a favourite song of hers, and the stranger who answered the phone when Ing drunk-dialled Kong.

Such complex plot coincidences arguably stand-in for intricacies of character development. In an effort to appeal to the broadest possible audience, both leads (especially Jeud) have few character flaws or moral lapses. They do not kiss at any point in the film and, among many other noble acts, Jeud even literally gives the suit off of his back to a beggar. Ultimately, the film was a commercial success – grossing 2,310,687 USD domestically and 1,137,840 USD internationally, while also cementing former singer Amornsupasiri's status and viability as an actor.

Kom Kunyosying

Title: *SuckSeed / SuckSeed: Huay Khan Thep*
Director: Chayanop Boonprakob
Studio: GTH
Year: 2011

SuckSeed is a film for Thai people who were teenagers in 1990s, recalling high school life and popular music from this era. The film tells the story of high school friends Ped (Jirayu La-Ongmanee) and Kung (Pachara Chirathivat) who are entering Hot Wave Music Awards, the biggest national music contest for young talent in Thailand that has launched the careers of local rock stars such as Ka-La, Labanoon, Clash, and Bodyslam. The boys have been friends since primary school but are not academically gifted or musically talented. Most significantly for them, neither has ever had a girlfriend. Further complicating the situation, they must also compete with Kung's twin brother Kay, who is a capable musician. In order to defeat Kay's band, Ped and Kung need an exceptional guitarist; enter Ped's long-time hidden love, the beautiful and musically excellent Earn (Nattasha Nauljam), who has just transferred to their school and is interested in joining the band.

The film was released in the renaissance era of GTH, a studio well-known for its feel good movies, romantic comedies, coming-of-age themes and general deployment of nostalgia. All such signatures come together in *SuckSeed*, combined with a background of music tracks from the studio's partner GMM Grammy, a significant music label in Thailand. While this soundtrack evokes the "good old times" for viewers to sing along to, the film also surprised the audience with its famous rock bands who sing background music throughout the film. *Shonen* (Japanese comic) animation style is also a distinct influence on screen, emphasizing the importance of Japanese culture in Thailand during the 1990s.

Except for Jirayu La-Ongmanee (Ped), all other main characters are played by unknown actors. This is a strategic choice, rather than using big names the film places emphasis upon the "everyman" nature of its protagonists, who face challenges in love and friendship while seeking success in their interests and abilities. While the film was not a blockbuster, it achieved success largely through word-of-mouth with audiences for whom this nostalgia of 1990s youthful determination resonated strongly.

Yossapol Chutipanyabut

Title: *ATM / ATM: Er Rak Error*
Director: Mez Tharatorn
Studio: GTH
Year: 2012

Among the films that focus on the everyday lives of urban middle-class Thais, *ATM* stands out as one of the most creative representations of the main fantasy of many white-collar office workers: to be in a relationship with office colleagues.

ATM tells a story about the struggling love of Sue (Chantavit Dhanasevi) and Jib (Preechaya Pongthananikorn), two office colleagues who work for a Japanese bank in Bangkok. The two engage in a relationship, even though their company does not allow its employees to do so. The chaos starts when Jib has to sack two of her lower-ranking colleagues because the company has found out that they have engaged in a romantic and sexual relationship. Having to fire these two secret lovers herself, Jib becomes even more anxious that her relationship with Sue will be exposed and that both of them will get fired. The two decide to solve this problem by getting married. However, one of them still needs to resign from the company, but neither one wishes to do so. To decide who will resign, Jib challenges Sue with an urgent assignment: to fix a broken ATM and to get the over-withdrawn money back. If one of them can fix the problem, the other must resign. The film ends with an even more complicated result but still maintains a romantic twist. Jib finds the group of people who took the money, but she does not want them to be sued by the company. Sue then helps her by using his own savings to pay the bank.

While the plot of *ATM* depicts many details and events, the film largely maintains its attraction and humour through using well-known comical actors. Dhanasevi has previously played roles in many of GTH's romantic comedies, such as the highly successful *Hello Stranger* (2010). In *ATM*, while maintaining a "cool" and attractive look, his performance is also exaggerated and highly comical. Additionally, the film casts popular comedian Kornpob Janjarearn (literally translated as "Joke So Cool") to play the son of Ter and Jib's boss, who also falls in love with Jib.

Despite its light and comical nature, *ATM* offers a representation of the romantic fantasies and anxieties of many office workers in Thai urban settings. In the increasingly isolated metropolitan society of Bangkok, marriage rates have decreased amongst the younger generation. The narrative of *ATM*, in which the two lovers have to struggle against the company their work for, clearly reflects the relationship anxieties of urban middle-class people in modern-day Thailand.

Pasoot Lasuka

Title: *I Fine… Thank You… Love You*
Director: Mez Tharatorn
Studio: GTH
Year: 2014

As another exciting and creative light-hearted offering from GTH, *I Fine… Thank You… Love You* addresses social mobility through English language proficiency, a central concern of many Thai people, and turns it into a romantic comedy.

I Fine follows the struggling love life of Yim (Sunny Suwanmethanon), a factory worker who is dumped by his Japanese girlfriend, Kaya (Sora Aoi), because she has gone to America. Wanting to make the relationship work again and wanting to go to America to see her, Yim decides to go for a job-transfer interview, hoping to relocate to be with Kaya. However, because the interview is in English and Yim is afraid that he will not pass the interview, he asks Phleng (Preechaya Pongthananikorn), who is also Kaya's former English language teacher, to train him for the English language interview. Because Yim's English language skills are poor, Phleng has to employ many new strategies to teach him and spend more time with him. This leads to the development of an emotional and romantic attachment between Yim and Phleng. The crucial moment in the film, when the emotional attachment between them has reached the highest point, comes when Yim goes for the interview. Yim decides to ruin the interview and returns to Phleng to confess his true feelings for her.

Similar to other films from the GTH studio, particularly *ATM* (2012) made by the same director, *I Fine* is presented in a realistic and chronological narrative order that is easy enough for a general audience to understand. The main cast, particularly Yim, often curse, reinforcing the fun-loving and down-to-earth nature of the film and the central issue (the language barrier) is turned into an attractive story line with a romantic twist.

The film was highly successful at the box-office, earning more than 170 million baht in the week after its release, breaking the record of Tharatorn's last film, *ATM*, which had a similar cast. Most significantly, the film is also indicative of the ongoing attempt of commercial Thai cinema to attract global (or at least regional Asian) audiences, being particularly successful in China and Indonesia, both countries where English is also highly desirable in the job market. Such success represents a shift from the national "heritage" films produced in the 2000s to films that depict content and issues commonly shared by other proximate nations, therefore increasing Thai cinema's appeal in the international market.

Pasoot Lasuka

Title: *Freelance / Freelance: Ham Puay... Ham Phak... Ham Rak Mo*
Director: Nawapol Thamrongrattanarit
Studio: GTH
Year: 2015

Known among Thai hipsters as a young and trendy writer, Nawapol Thamrongrattanarit started his cinematic career crossing back and forth between mainstream and arthouse circles. Despite being part of a writing team for GTH, one of the most successful Thai studios, Thamrongrattanarit started his directorial debut on a shoestring budget with *36* (2012). His sleeper hit *Mary Is Happy, Mary Is Happy* (2013), a Biennale College-funded project, won him local and international fame before he firmly stepped into the lime light with *Freelance* (also known under an alternative English title *Heart Attack*).

Said to be based partly upon the director's own personal experience, *Freelance* explores the daily life of a freelance graphic designer, Yoon (Sunny Suwanmethanon), who is forced to choose between his high-profile portfolio and his true love. Yoon's daily life is a lonely mix of excessive work, inadequate consumption and social insecurity. One day he finds some strange rashes on his skin and goes to see a young and beautiful dermatologist who gives him a prescription that has a huge effect on his daily life. After several months of visits, Yoon loses his job but gains something else – an intimate connection and poignant memories between two souls amidst the otherwise isolating modern world.

Echoing Thamrongrattanarit's own career, the film is built upon opposites, embodying both the director's arthouse spirit and the Thai studio's requirements. Thamrongrattanarit's cinematography adopts arthouse techniques unusual for a mainstream Thai film – he uses a handheld camera in sequences depicting Yoon's chaotic life and unusual angles to depict the dermatologist. Editing and make-up is minimal while performance is subdued, in contrast to the frequent over-the-top performances by Thai stars. Likewise, while Yoon has a very modern job as a graphic designer, his home includes an old copy machine and is decorated with nineties bathroom tiles and apartment décor – all part of Thamrongrattanarit's own coming-of-age setting.

The script uses the same punchy dialogue evident in Thamrongrattanarit's own writing, much of which explains the unfailing loyalty *Freelance* received from the director's fans. This sympathetic satire pokes fun at the out-of-date ways of the life and opinions of elders, though stops short of insulting anyone, while the film's "feel-good" ending adheres to GTH's own formula.

Upon its release in Thailand, responses to *Freelance* were polarized to the extreme. While the director's fans loved it, fans of GTH weren't sure what to make of the film. Responses from audiences could be categorized into film fans, film reviewers, and Thai film buffs. Despite this mixed reaction, the film won all major awards in Thailand for that year, including Best Picture, Best Director, Best Actor, Best Actress, and Best Supporting Actress.

Anchalee Chaiworaporn

8

Queer Cinema

In June 2015 the first-ever Thai Gay and Lesbian Film Festival was held over a ten-day period in Bangkok. Commentators praised the festival as a symbolic coming-of-age for local GLBT/LGBT communities but also expressed some surprise that such an event hadn't been held much sooner, given Thailand's reputation for social tolerance and the vibrancy of its queer cultures. The use of queer vis-à-vis gay/lesbian is pointed here. While Thailand has a long history of queer – as in non-normative – gender and sexual expression, it is only in recent times that newer models of Western-style gayness as an identity-based social category have started to take root. This is an historical trajectory that can be traced in Thai cinema itself.

Ever since the first Thai talkie, *Gone Astray* (1932) titillated early audiences with its sensationalist tale of an upcountry innocent's encounter with the sexual excesses of urban modernity, Thai cinema has been an important forum for the representation of diverse and even transgressive sexuality. While homosexuality may not have been an overt aspect of these early films, it was frequently intimated as a subtextual presence. Effeminate male characters or *kathoei*, for example, featured regularly as marginal comic relief in films of the 1960s/70s and queerly gendered characters even made an occasional appearance in serious dramas such as *Mae Ai Sa-uen* (1972) or *Kaeo* (1980).

Queer representations started to move centre stage in the 1980s with a series of high profile "social realist" films, notably the *kathoei* melodrama *The Last Song* (1985), its sequel *Tortured Love* (1987) and the gay male comic drama *I Am a Man* (1987). Queer images were further mainstreamed as part of Thai cinema's post-97 revival. The international success of *The Iron Ladies* (2000) signalled the strong commercial potential of queer-themed films and generated a long line of emulative *kathoei* comedies. Meanwhile, mainstream studio films like the tense action melodrama *Bangkok Love Story* (2007) and the romantic teen hit, *Love of Siam* (2007) pushed queer themes into an ever-wider range of genres.

It is however in the area of independent film that Thai queer cinema has made greatest strides. Indie filmmakers as diverse as Apichatpong Weerasethakul, Thunska Pansittivorakul, Nitchapoom Chaianun and Tanwarin Sukkhapisit have developed a strong international profile for diverse and often politicized expressions of cinematic queerness. In a different vein, independent queer media companies have been making good use of new digital exhibition modes such as DVD/VCD, online delivery and video-sharing sites to offer a growing catalogue of niche marketed films like *Silom Soi 2* (2006) and Sarawut Intaraprom's string of soft-core "bromances": *Seng Pet* (2009), *Khru Lae Nakrian* (2014) and *Pho Lae Lukchai* (2015). That many of these films are frequently subject to suppression by state censors highlights both the power and the challenge of queer cinema in Thailand.

Brett Farmer

Title: *The Iron Ladies / Satri Lek*
Director: Yongyoot Thongkongtoon
Studio: Tai Entertainment
Year: 2000

Released in the full flush of the post-97 Thai Film Revival, *The Iron Ladies* exemplifies the newfound cultural and commercial confidence of Thai cinema in the era. Its feel-good narrative, populist sexual comedy, and slick production values propelled the film to record box office success at home, as well as considerable success abroad. It won a number of awards on the international festival circuit and was the first Thai film to secure a theatrical release in the North American market, a symbolic "David and Goliath" achievement which Thai local media made much of at the time.

Indeed, *The Iron Ladies* is a classic underdog fighting-against-the-odds tale that is arguably key to the film's mass appeal. The tale is loosely based on the true story of a volleyball team made up of transgender *kathoei* from Lampang. The team rose to national prominence and celebrity as much for their outrageous flamboyancy and on-court antics as for their sporting prowess. The two lead characters Mon (Sahaphap Tor) and Jung (Chaichan Nimpulsawasdi) are talented young *kathoei* volleyball players who are consistently overlooked for team selection because of their sexuality. Impressed by the pair's talent and fighting spirit, newly appointed Lampang head coach, Bee (Shiriohana Hongsopon), herself a lesbian and no stranger to discrimination, agrees to take the two on for the provincial team. When the other teammates walk out in transphobic disgust, Mon and Jung reach out to their friends and fill the team with a colourful assortment of gay and *kathoei* players. Combatting prejudice from sports officials and derision from spectators, the team pulls together with grit and determination. They progressively enlist fans with their camp flair and sporting zeal, progressing up the tournament ladder before eventually winning the national championship in a victorious finale.

Released in the wake of the catastrophic 1997 Asian financial crisis in which Thailand suffered unprecedented economic collapse and the international humiliation of an IMF bailout, *The Iron Ladies*' story of underdog victory struck a deep chord with the national zeitgeist. Its scenario of grassroots Thais pulling together in the face of adversity and its moral emphasis on collective cooperation, discipline, and sacrifice offered both solace and inspiration to a demoralized Thai public. *The Iron Ladies* proved so popular with domestic audiences that it became the biggest commercial hit of 2000 and the second-highest grossing Thai film to that date.

That *The Iron Ladies* cast transgendered *kathoei* as the narrative agents for its feel-good fantasy of national restoration is as notable as it is surprising. *Kathoei* had been a presence in Thai popular film for some time, but they were typically shunted to the sidelines as support characters where

Figure 19 The triumphant volleyball players of *The Iron Ladies* (2000).

they were used for added colour or comic relief. *The Iron Ladies* was one of the first films to feature *kathoei* not only as central protagonists but as sympathetic figures of audience identification. The film's success effectively helped create a bona fide new film genre, the *kathoei* comedy, that continues apace to the present day.

Brett Farmer

Title: *The Adventures of Iron Pussy / Huachai Thon Nong*
Directors: Michael Shaowanasai, Apichatpong Weerasethakul
Studio: Kick the Machine
Year: 2003

On paper, this campy pastiche of 1960s-era Thai cinema seems a singular anomaly in the oeuvre of Apichatpong Weerasethakul, the film's co-director and contemporary Thai cinema's most celebrated artistic figure. Nevertheless, it bears many of the same features that characterize the film-maker's other, more sober art-house fare: independent production, artistic collaboration, formalist experimentation, and themes of non-normative gender/sexuality, among others.

Born out of a partnership between Weerasethakul and artistic polymath Michael Shaowanasai, *The Adventures of Iron Pussy* is essentially a showcase built around a transgender performance persona, the eponymous Iron Pussy, created by Shaowanasai for an earlier series of underground video projects. An unexpected break between productions due to funding delays allowed Weerasethakul to team with Shaowanasai in bringing Iron Pussy to the big screen in a feature-length homage to the schlocky Thai exploitation cinema that both men remembered fondly from their childhood.

Modelled upon iconic 16mm era film star, Petchara Chaowarat, Iron Pussy is a mild-mannered gay convenience store worker by day and a glamourous cross-dressed crime avenger by night with big hair, big boots and an even bigger heart. Called in by the government to crack a nefarious foreign drug ring, Iron Pussy goes undercover as a maid at an upcountry estate and the scene is set for a histrionic mix of thrills, chills and high-heeled kickboxing in the wilds of the Thai jungle. With action aplenty, a sudsy romance, dashes of family melodrama, and even a handful of choreographed musical sequences, *Iron Pussy* takes the patchwork polygenericity of classic Thai cinema to parodic extremes.

The film's low budget and rushed production schedule actually proved conducive to simulating the aesthetic of 1960s Thai filmmaking. The decision to shoot on cheap digital helped achieve the grainy texture and oversaturated colour palette of 16mm, while post-production work recreated the era's raw editing styles and lurid musical underscoring. The production team even revived the period practice of post-dubbed dialogue, using many actual dubbing artists from the era.

In keeping with the filmmakers' combined reputations as visual artists of international standing, *Iron Pussy* received its principal distribution via the global arts festival market. However, the film's constitutive investment in lowbrow Thai pop culture and unpolished technical style dismayed international viewers anticipating a lyrical art film. Meanwhile, in Thailand where the film should have proved far more accessible, it failed to secure anything other than a limited theatrical release – a fate sadly common for many independent productions – though it did manage to find a modest local reception on DVD/VCD.

In a postscript befitting the repetitive seriality of popular Thai cinema, the Iron Pussy persona was resurrected a few years later when Shaowanasai teamed with another high-profile local auteur, Wisit Sasanatieng, for *Iron Pussy: A Kimchi Affair*, part of an omnibus project, *Camellia* (2010), commissioned for the Busan International Film Festival.

Brett Farmer

Title:	*Bangkok Love Story / Phuean Ku Rak Mueng Wa*
Director:	Poj Arnon
Studio:	Sahamongkol Film
Year:	2007

Securing a modest revenue of around 9 million baht, *Bangkok Love Story* is a LGBT-centric tragedy that also includes elements of crime and action. The film won The Grand Prize at the Brussels International Independent Film Festival in 2007, as well as three National Film Association Awards in Thailand in 2008 for Best Screenplay, Best Cinematography and Best Sound.

The film narrates the gay love story of hired assassin Maek (Rattanaballang Tohssawat) and his target, the informer Iht (Chaiwat Thongsaeng). When Maek refuses to kill the family oriented Iht, he is himself shot, and both men make a getaway to a desolate rooftop room, where Iht cares for the injured Maek and love begins to blossom between the two.

The film heavily commodifies the bodies of the two protagonists, whose muscle-bound torsos are regularly depicted shirtless, in a vest, in underwear, or even almost completely naked. Such a masculine depiction is very different to similar films from the same director, in which gay characters tend to appear overly effeminate. The film also depicts a notably long and passionate sex scene, in which Maek and Iht consummate their relationship. The variety of camera angles contribute to a sensual and ethereal sequence in which the love-making protagonists are reflected in the water-soaked floor.

Due to his record of serial murders, karma demands that Maek eventually dies. Yet the film is much more complex due to the depiction of Maek's tragic and abusive impoverished background, which contradicts karmic demands of retribution. Maek's mother and younger brother Mok are both infected with HIV due to abuse, and one scene shows a woman flinging a stone and uttering the profanity "Damn AIDS man!" while other scenes depict the neighborhood teenagers thumping Mok. Such injustice is ultimately not punished, so undermining Maek's eventual death as punishment for his wrong-doing.

Patipat Auprasert

Title: *Haunting Me / Ho Taeo Taek*
Director: Poj Arnon
Studio: Five Star Production
Year: 2007

Kathoei horror-comedy *Haunting Me* grossed more than 50 million baht upon its release in 2007. Such success was quickly followed up with sequels *Haunting Me 2* in 2009, *Haunting Me 3* in 2011, *Haunting Me 4* in 2012 and finally *Haunting Me 5* in 2015. Throughout the series, the main cast of actors largely remains constant, including comedians Koh-tee Aramboi, Jaturong Mokjok, singer Ekkaachai Srivichai, and Achan Yingsak.

Telling the story of three *kathoei* who run a boarding house, *Haunting Me* begins with a shocking scene in which local girl Nam-ning lies dying in the backyard. When transgender Pancake also dies after slipping on soap and knocking her head on the lavatory, both characters become ghosts that incessantly haunt the residents of the boarding house. The story follows the ageing *kathoei* owners as they struggle to exorcise the spirits, eventually working to avenge Nam-ning's death.

Throughout the film, classic Thai tropes abound in which characters are depicted fleeing comically from these resident spirits, along with the familiar spirit-exorcising shaman, again a source of comedy. The film even references *Brokeback Mountain* (2005), depicting, in silhouette, nocturnal gay visitors in cowboy outfits making love in a tent, a scene that, in typical Thai style, ends up in slapstick comedy.

Crude slapstick humour also appears through sexual innuendo: a memorable scene involves *kathoei* Taew unknowingly mistaking a phallic charm for an inhaler. Likewise in a play on words, the character name of "Koy" corresponds closely to "*khuai*," the Thai vernacular for "dick." Yet while such slapstick humour is very effective, this seeming celebration of gender diversity is somewhat dubious and even offensive to an extent; even the shaman, brought in to exorcise a spirit, utters profanities "*i tut*" – "Damn Tranny."

Patipat Auprasert

Title: *Love of Siam / Rak Haeng Siam*
Director: **Chookiat Sakveerakul**
Studio: **Sahamongkol Film**
Year: **2007**

One of the most talked about films of 2007, *Love of Siam* proved that elusive entity in Thai cinema: a film with a combined domestic and international appeal. Performing exceptionally well at the local box office and with solid returns abroad, the film was notably lucrative in the regional Asian market, garnering widespread praise from critics and receiving numerous major national awards.

Love of Siam's huge success was a surprise. The film initially entered the market as an apparently nondescript teen flick of the kind routinely churned out to cater for the multiplex youth trade. The slick marketing campaign focused on the film's lead quartet of attractive dewy-eyed highschoolers, a soundtrack heavy on chart-appealing pop, and a principal setting in Bangkok's favoured adolescent hangout of Siam Square (hence the title). But the film held a number of unexpected tricks up its candy-coloured sleeve.

Clocking in at a hefty 150 minutes, *Love of Siam*'s lengthy running time served as an immediate indication that it carried more substance than the usual popcorn fare. Moreover, its complex weblike narrative pushed the film beyond a simple schoolyard romance, embedding its teen storyline in a network of family-based drama with a host of challenging themes, including parenthood, loss, grief and questions of Thai national identity.

The film's biggest surprise, however, and the source of much of its controversial popularity came in the same-sex romance of the young male leads. Friends from early childhood, Mew (Witwisit Hiranyawongkul) and Tong (Mario Maurer) find solace in each other's company and their friendship gradually becomes romantic. This culminates in an extended on-screen kiss widely, if erroneously, reported as the first in Thai film history. This same-sex romance became a contentious topic in the Thai media, eliciting a barrage of commentary for and against and turning the two young actors into overnight celebrities.

That *Love of Siam* proved so ground-breaking is due in no small measure to the talents of writer-director Chookiat Sakveerakul. Having already proved an innovative creator of intelligent genre films with the hit horror-comedy *13 Beloved* (2006), Sakveerakul was able to leverage substantial creative licence when making *Love of Siam*. Indeed, parent studio Sahamongkol was so delighted with the film that, in something of a first for Thai cinema, they issued an extended director's cut in 2008. Meanwhile, *Love of Siam* has continued to grow in stature and popularity, emerging as a mini-cult classic and motivating a host of online fandoms. It even inspired a rare example of transnational intertextuality when, as a nod to the film's huge Chinese fanbase and a sign of the growing significance of pan-Asian cultural flows, stars Maurer and Hiranyawongku were briefly "reunited" in the closing credits of the 2012 Chinese film *Love on That Day*.

Brett Farmer

Title: *Me… Myself / Khu Hut Rak Chongcharoen*
Director: Pongpat Wachirabunjong
Studio: Mono Film
Year: 2007

Me… Myself, Pongpat Wachirabunjong's debut film, is a romantic comedy that questions the fixity of gender identity. The protagonist Tan (Ananda Everingham) has amnesia and is taken in by Oom (Chayanan Manomaisantiphap), a woman who ran him over with her car after a mugging. The police send Tan home with Oom to take care of him as he does not have any ID; he only has a piece of jewellery that spells out Tan, so this becomes his new assumed name and identity. Oom is in a bad relationship with Krit (Piya Wimookdayon) and is raising her orphaned nephew, Ohm (Monton Annupabmard). At first, Tan seems to be a burden, but Oom comes to see him as helpful and Ohm begins to look up to him.

Tan has a feminine touch that Oom appreciates. He also comes to be happy in his new situation and no longer wants to engage with his past life. But fragmentary memories come back to him and he comes to realize the truth about his past. Tan, was previously Tanya, a *kathoei* (transgender) cabaret performer. Yet he has fallen in love with Oom and seeks to recreate a new life in this new family environment.

In Tan's transition from transgender woman to heterosexual man, *Me... Myself* suggests that gender and sexual identity are not biological but enculturated (Tanya was raised by *kathoei*) and thus could be changed. As a result the film received much criticism from LGBT people and sexual diversity activists. Indeed, the Thai title suggests that this development is a form of spiritual progress, and activists were worried that parents may try to "cure" the sexual and gender orientation of their children. In response to the film The Ministry of Public Health therefore took the extraordinary step of releasing a statement warning parents not to try to remediate their children's gender/sexuality using physical "accidents."

Dredge Kang

Title: *This Area Is under Quarantine / Boriwen Ni Yu Phaitai Kan Kakkan*
Director: Thunska Pansittivorakul
Studio: ThaiIndie
Year: 2008

Thunska Pansittivorakul's densely constructed hybrid documentary – composed of archival materials, interviews, and staged sequences – uses explicit sexuality to draw attention to the systematic administrative and military violence against Muslims in Thailand's three southernmost provinces: Yala, Pattani, and Narathiwat. The film presents previously censored details of the October 2004 Tak Bai massacre, in which at least seventy-eight Muslim men were killed by the Thai Army in Narathiwat province. Amidst this situation of purportedly religious-based conflict (the "Buddhist" occupation of the majority-Muslim Thai South) Pansittivorakul explores interreligious intimacy, enacting freedom of expression also through the representation of queer bodies and desires.

Quarantine juxtaposes soft-porn sex scenes between a young Muslim Thai man and a young Buddhist Thai man with Malaysian footage of the Tak Bai massacre. The film depicts various intimate scenes, including one in which the Muslim man, Adeck (Sathit Sobree), lounges in a hotel room, Adeck's monologue about his past love life, and a more explicit conversation about the Buddhist man, Pe's (Pradit Pradinan), past. The men's accounts of their failed romantic trajectories parallel the story of a failed Thai multiculturalism and demonstrate the continued melancholy attachment to notions of coexistence. Footage of the Tak Bai massacre is inserted twice; the second time the images of soldiers rounding up Muslim men are accompanied by "Phaenpen" (Scar), the pop song that also underwrites erotic shots of Adeck at the film's beginning. However, *Quarantine* becomes most interesting when the events in the film seem to overtake the scripting. In one instance, the men's intimacy exceeds the filmmaker's directions and in another Adeck opposes the filmmaker's own opinions, refuting assumptions about Islam's sexual illiberalism and thereby correcting anti-Islamic prejudice. Through his own initiative, Adeck claims a strong position in the Thai nation for himself as both a Southern Muslim and a gay man within a Muslim community.

While *Quarantine* at first casts doubt on the viability of Buddhist-Muslim coexistence, it ultimately devises a novel way of mobilizing both the human body and the documentary form as a basis for reimagining interethnic coexistence. Aligning a Muslim subject's "performance of himself" with scenes of casual intimacy, *Quarantine*'s queer coexistential vision actualizes freedom of expression in a radical way. In doing so the film bypasses official notions of ethnic reconciliation and multicultural nationalism espoused by Bangkok governments. The incorporation of non-scripted content also intervenes into the conventions of anti-Muslim sentiment, thereby undermining globally pervasive divides between Islam's purported illiberalism and a supposedly liberal sexual modernity ("pinkwashing"). Instead, in a remarkable (and ultimately forbidden) display under the current political conditions in Thailand, the film allows queer sexual representation and advocacy for the Muslim South to enter into progressive alliance, reinfusing a stalled situation with cultural and political mobility.

Arnika Fuhrmann

Title:	*Yes or No / Yes or No: Yak Rak Ko Rak Loei*
Director:	**Saratswadee Wongsomphet**
Studio:	**Come On Sweet Co.**
Year:	**2010**

At a first glance, Saratswadee Wongsomphet's *Yes or No* (2010) seems inconspicuous. This subdued narrative follows an emerging teenage romance, tracing the blossoming relationship between two young women, Pie (Sushar Manaying) and Kim (Supanart Jittaleela). Shot on a modest budget of 400,000 USD, the film's aesthetics and tempo resemble a TV drama rather than a feature film. Yet this humble storytelling effort functioned as a surprising star vehicle for one of its leads Suspanart Jittaleela, who, with her effortless charm and a hairstyle worthy of a K-pop boyband, is now a media sensation, amassing over two million fans on Facebook and over a million followers on Instagram. Jittaleela now embodies the figure of the Thai tomboy, with *Yes or No* as the first high-grossing Thai film to openly discuss this subject.

While various romantic breakthroughs could serve as material for intense melodrama, *Yes and No* fits more comfortably in the "slice of life" genre, depicting mundane and everyday events. Most visibly incarnated in contemporary manga, the genre radiates "cuteness" and "quirkiness," of which there is no shortage in *Yes or No*. Near the beginning of the film, when Kim and Pai first meet in a dorm room they're sharing, Wongsomphet uses both setting and situation to sketch the film's mood, central narrative, and style. In a constrained shot of a dorm room Kim's feet appear in the right corner of the screen by an open door. This humble introduction is deliberately ambiguous: with sporty, casual clothes and a guitar in her hand, Kim's silhouette evokes that of a teenage boy. Only when we see her a few seconds later through Pei's eyes, do we get a slow-motion, flirty head-turn which highlights Kim's charismatic expression. This early scene encapsulates many of the film's defining features: its candid character, subtle erotic tension between Kim and Pai, melodramatic music, and humorous tone. Indeed, a huge cockroach then immediately runs over Kim's bare feet, which prompts her to shriek and charge at Pei, initiating their first physical contact.

Aimed at a young audience, *Yes or No* touches on a variety of issues close to the younger generation, depicting hope, romance, tender kisses and dreamy songs. Pie, a middle-class student from a conservative family, falls in love with Kim, a working-class tomboy, illustrating how the film cuts across more than simply gender boundaries. Yet Wongsomphet leaves little hope when it comes to initiating a dialogue between generations; a sugar-coated happy ending implies that the younger generation must make a decisive break with their parents' views in order to further social progress. While on the surface *Yes or No* could therefore seem somewhat superfluous, the film ultimately represents a quiet revolution that was nevertheless highly significant to the challenging of Thai social norms.

Bogna M. Konior

Title: *It Gets Better / Mai Dai Kho Hai Ma Rak*
Director: **Tanwarin Sukkhapisit**
Studio: **Amfine Production**
Year: **2012**

Thai cinema has certainly had its fill of transgender comedies and dramas. However, all too often the representation of *kathoei* characters has yet to evolve beyond the most obvious demeaning stereotypes used for comic relief. *It Gets Better* is one of the rare Thai films with gender-fluid characters that are rounded and complex. The film does include familiar *kathoei* themes, such the occasional larger-than-life drag queen and, indeed, the main character suffers a tragic fate in-keeping with the general lack of a happy ending that so many queer characters endure in Thai gay movies. Yet the film also touches upon a number of valid social and personal issues connected to sexuality and gender identity, from coming to terms with one's own individuality to debating the positioning of and attitudes towards transsexuals in Thai Buddhist society.

It Gets Better consists of three interwoven stories which are eventually revealed to be connected. Iconic 1980s model and actress Penpak Sirikul plays Saitarn, an ageing post-op transsexual on vacation in pastoral Northern Thailand. Din (Pavich Suprungroj) is a teenage boy who gets sent to become a novice monk after his father finds him dancing around the house dressed in his late mother's clothes. Finally, Tonmai (Panupong Waraakesiri) is a young man returning from the US to take care of the *kathoei* cabaret/nightclub he inherited from his father. Tonmai blames his father for abandoning their family, and his negative attitude to transsexuals, combined with the growing unease at discovering that he is actually sexually attracted to some of the *kathoei* peformers, makes Tonmai decide to close the business. Din transitions into Saitarn, who is eventually named as Tonmai's father, but only after we see Saitarn sacrifice her life to defend her elderly father from thugs. The fact that Saitarn's father recognizes her as Din and shows that he accepted her new identity only makes her pointless death more tragic.

While LGBT issues are at the forefront of the narrative, the film is also notable for the picturesque cinematography of Nikorn Sripongwrakul and the devilishly stylish costumes of Penpak Sirikul (who appears as though she has just stepped out of a vintage fashion magazine). The original soundtrack also features several songs by "Bell" Nuntita Khampiranon, who won the hearts of Thai audiences with her performance in Thailand's Got Talent, and who plays one of the transgender characters in the movie.

Transgender director, Tanwarin Sukkhapisit made waves with her first fully independent feature, *Insects in the Backyard* (2010), which played at several festivals, including Canada's Vancouver International Film Festival, and Italy's Torino GLBT Film Festival in 2010. Despite such success however, the film was subsequently banned by the Thai board of censors on account of its vivid portrayal of sexual acts, which were deemed a threat to the nation's morality. *It Gets Better* takes a much more subtle and commercially appealing approach to LGBT issues, which allowed for the film to be distributed theatrically in Thailand, winning moderate popularity with Thai audiences.

Katarzyna Ancuta

Title: *Supernatural*
Director: Thunska Pansittivorakul
Studio: Sleep of Reason Films, Jürgen Brüning Film
Year: 2014

Known primarily for his experimental documentary work and short films, writer-director Thunska Pansittivorakul made his narrative fiction feature film debut with *Supernatural*, a science fiction film set 100 years into Thailand's future. Pansittivorakul studied at the Department of Art Education at Chulalongkorn University and in 2007 received the prestigious Silpathorn Award from the Thai Ministry of Culture's Office of Contemporary Arts. The director's work typically delves into concerns around human rights, modes of discrimination and oppression, and the precarious nature of liminality and marginalization. Raised by his mother in Padang Besar, along the Thai-Malaysian border and openly homosexual, Thunska Pansittivorakul's politics cannot be separated from his poetics.

Supernatural's speculative fiction contests in oblique terms the pervasive power of the Thai State to shape history. Indeed the director was particularly inspired by a line from George Orwell's *1984*: "who controls the past controls the future." The film focuses on three characters who are reincarnated across three different moments of time periods. In each, the "Leader" is never seen but palpably felt. The tension between identity politics, the policies of the Thai state, and official state historiographies stretches across the citizen-subjects, as well as those whose bodies are rendered either invisible or unassimilable by the state, including homosexual Thais and refugees from displaced Karen communities along the Thai-Burmese border.

True to his own politics, Pansittivorakul challenges and disrupts the state's narrative power over Thai historiography while also integrating his fiction with contemporary popular culture and so merging the realms of fiction and reality. *Supernatural*'s speculative fiction is infused with a sensuous historiography, and history is expressed through border zones, through textures on the screen (titles, text messages), and via the gestural politics of touch (what bodies are touchable, for example). Locations include Ubon Ratchathani, located near the Thai-Lao border and Suan Phueng, in Ratchaburi, the location of Karen refugee communities.

Supernatural's future is overwhelmingly dystopian. While touch is rendered problematic and forbidden, the film's sumptuous visuals express a palpable and queer erotic tactility. This is expressed through various scenes which explore modes of touch: soft caresses of male genitalia or the slight pressures of fingertips grazing across skin. The camera communicates this language of tactile intimacy with a mixture of soft focus, extreme close-ups, and pans and tilts that, for example, run along the contours of two male bodies in contact with each other.

The film adds to the small generic corpus of Thai science fiction films, yet its incisive meditation and critique of the pillars of Thai nationalist-historiography (religion, nation and monarchy) also infuses *Supernatural* with a strong ethical sensibility. Like all of Pansittivorakul's work, the film did not obtain a general, theatrical commercial release in Thailand and instead has circulated at a number of film festivals, including as an official selection at the International Film Festival Rotterdam (2014) and the Queer Lisboa International Queer Film Festival (2016).

Sophia Siddique

9

Animation

Viewed through the lens of global feature film animation, Thai animation has an extremely limited history. Such history largely resides in the person of Payut Ngaokrachang in the pre-digital era, whose experiments with animation techniques began in advertising and short film animations in the mid-1950s (Lent, 2001). Payut would be the only animator to produce a feature-length animated film, *The Adventure of Sudsakorn* in 1979, using his own students and a camera system he built himself to adapt famous Thai poet Sunthorn Phu's *Phra Aphai Mani* to the screen. Production of this film was famously hard, with Payut going wildly over-budget and schedule, losing staff when he could no longer pay them (many of whom were his students), and even losing much of the sight in his left eye (Lent, 1997). The result was Thailand's only two-dimensional, cel-style animated film, and it shows Payut's transnational influences from Disney in its character designs, as well as the influence of Japanese "limited" animation techniques in his extensive re-use of cycles of movements. This latter technique is used to great effect when Payut's mermaid characters dance using repeated cycles of hand and body movements mimicking traditional Thai dance styles, or when the bamboo in the forest bends and wiggles the same way repeatedly during a musical number.

Payut's influence extends into the digital era of Thai animation production, and he was an advisor on the country's first Computer Generated animation feature, *The Blue Elephant* (2006), whose director calls Payut "a national treasure" (Gershon, 2006). However, viewed more complexly, Thai animation has a more varied and longer history in advertising and "in-between" animation, or outsourcing. Rather than simply being a one-man industry, the long-standing existence of companies like Kantana Productions, which was founded as a radio company in 1951 but quickly moved into post-production for film and television thereafter, shows that there was a basic grassroots infrastructure for animation in Thailand even before the explosion of Thai animation culture in the post-digital world.

This explosion was a product of Thai government policies, industrial diversification and the expansion of outlets for animated works since the popularisation of digital animation from the mid-1990s onwards. The boom in digital animation hit Thailand from 2002 onwards, with both the creation of several new government initiatives intended to support animation production and the increased international demand for high quality "clean up" work for digital animation that was flowing into Thailand from North America and from around Asia (Niracharapa, 2014). As a result, new companies have emerged from larger existing companies, all with a broad production profile. These include Imagimax and Vithita Animation (Bendazzi, 2016, pp. 282–283) as well as smaller boutique-style animation studios like Monk Studios, whose short film, *Nine Lives* (2014), a mix of two-dimensional backdrops and three-dimensional characters, has been performing well at international film festivals. From a single, great-man history of animation, Thailand's animation industry now boasts thousands of animators and dozens of companies.

Rayna Denison

Title: *The Blue Elephant* / *Khan Kluay*
Director: Kompin Kemgumnird
Studio: Kantana Animation
Year: 2006

On its release in 2006, *The Blue Elephant* was saddled with great expectations. It was Thailand's first Computer Generated (CG) animated feature film, and the first Thai feature-length animation since 1979. After becoming the year's top-grossing box office film, the film exceeded such expectations and offered a new model for animation production in Thailand. Its overseas sales have paved new pathways for subsequent Thai animation successes, and, as the origin point for a transmedia franchise, *The Blue Elephant* has shown how Thai animation can be profitable if its reach is extended across borders and media platforms.

However, despite its technical prowess and animal protagonists, *The Blue Elephant* is still a very traditionally Thai film in many respects. Not only does the film start with an aesthetic homage to Thai shadow puppetry, but the story is also based on the historical sixteenth century of Ayutthaya-era Thai history and follows the life of King Naresuan, one of Thai culture's most renowned kings, beginning with his childhood through to major battles fought against the Burmese in the mid-1550s. However, the introduction of the elephants as fantastical, rainbow-hued characters more developed than any of their human counterparts soon shifts the focus away from Thai history and towards the family-centred fantasy of an elephant's coming-of-age story in a time of war. Khan Kluay (Banana Stem) is introduced as a tiny blue baby elephant whose famous father, a war elephant for the Thai royal family, is missing. The story parallels Naresuan's decision to go to war with Burma with Khan Kluay's decision to fight in defence of his country, for his family and his king. This portrayal is also married to a set of subtle voice performances, led by Phoori Hiranyapruk's nuanced performance as the adult Khan Kluay, all of which marks the film as a new benchmark for Thai animation.

It is in this fantasy of youth that director Kemgumnird demonstrates Kantana Production's advancements in Thai CG animation. *The Blue Elephant* contains beautifully realized forests, action montages and battle sequences, not least of which is a montage showing elephants wearing boxing gloves on their trunks in an homage to Thailand's first animated film *The Adventure of Sudsakorn* (1979). The forests team with light and life, as shown in an early scene where butterflies scatter in the wake of a young elephant, making the screen literally glow. While character animation, particularly of humans, suffers from over-caricaturing and extremes of exaggeration, the plethora of elephant characters, which are all carefully differentiated, are where the film really shines. Moreover, the battle sequences between the elephants contain a realistic sense of gravity and weight, both of which are difficult to produce in CG animation, adding to the emotional resonance of the film. This central theme of war was not without its problems though: when the film travelled to North America, the reproduction cut early sequences explaining the death of Khan Kluay's father, and another where a young elephant peers down the barrel of a rifle, all of which add emotional weight in the Thai version.

Rayna Denison

Title: *Nak*
Director: Natthapphong Rattanachoksirikul
Studio: Sahamongkol Film, Baa-Ram-Ewe, beboydcg
Year: 2008

Nak, a 2008 variation on the often remade tale of Mae Nak, is noteworthy not only as one of the few Thai feature-length animated films but also for its distinctive updating of, and elaborations upon, its classic narrative source. The film notably eschews some of the grimmer and more "adult" dimensions of the Mae Nak lineage, making the tale much more appropriate for a family audience. There are few scenes of outright horror or gore, and no image of horrific childbirth. The figure of Nak's husband, moreover, is completely absent, something which allows an erasure of the unsettling erotic dimensions of the tale (although these arguably make a return in the inexplicably slender and buxom cartoon rendering of Nak). Indeed, the overall tone of the production – its largely light-hearted comic approach and exaggerated cartoon imagery – suggests a kind of juvenilization of the Nak narrative, though this is at the same time contradicted by the increasingly apocalyptic nature of the plot. This inconsistency in tone or approach may indeed be part of what led to the film's inability to achieve the box office success (or international DVD distribution) of 2006's *The Blue Elephant*.

In this version, Mae Nak is no longer a horrific, dangerous, and erotically charged figure and instead becomes a kind of Thai national heroine, not a monster to be feared but a defender of the public. This new Nak narrative also takes place in a fictive present, in which rural human and ghost communities live side by side in peace and cooperation. The plot gains momentum when, at a local temple fair, a monstrous spirit appears and kidnaps a village boy. It turns out that this crime has been perpetrated by urban ghosts in preparation for a larger planned take-over of the human world; members of the local ghost community, understanding the gravity of the turn of events (and also having their consciences prodded by Nak), agree to head to Bangkok to aid in the child's rescue.

Nak thus deploys another classic Thai narrative trope, that of rural innocents (in this case both children and traditional ghosts) exposed to the dangers of the hyper-developed, internationalized city, where traditional mores have been lost. After some initial comic situations, the film takes on a darker tone in its latter half, as Bangkok is set upon by highly militarized waves of modern urban ghosts (inescapably suggestive imagery at a time of real-world political unrest). As might be expected, however, Nak and her fellow spirits are able to come to the rescue, rendering Bangkok and Thailand at peace once again.

Adam Knee

Title: *Yak: The Giant King / Yak*
Directors: Prapas Cholsaranont, Chaiporn Panichrutiwong
Studio: Workpoint Entertainment
Year: 2012

Written and co-directed by Prapas Cholsaranont and Chaiporn Panichrutiwong, *Yak: The Giant King* is a testament to the entry of all kinds of transmedia production companies into the animation industry in Thailand. Prapas is the co-founder and current Vice-Chairman of Workpoint Entertainment. The film was the first feature for Workpoint, better known in Thailand as a television production company, and it is perhaps unsurprising that the company chose to launch their filmmaking branch through the re-telling of a traditional story from the *Ramayana*, which has a long history in Thai cultural traditions and arts. Indeed, the title character of *Yak*, Na Keow, is seemingly a combined mixture of religious figures from the traditional giant temple guardians (known as Yakshas) and the many-armed *Ramayana* character Totsakan. However, the story itself has little relationship to the *Ramayana*, with the exception of minor character design elements like the tiny robots living in Na Keow's head, or the character Peak's Hanuman-style monkey tale-cum-chain and prominent eyebrows. Rama, instead, is the near-villain of the film, forcing Peak into an adversarial relationship with the gentle giant Na Keow and seeming to threaten the far-future Earth's robot culture with annihilation.

Such a convoluted description does the film a disservice, as the animation quality rivals that of US films like *Robots* (2005), to which *Yak* owes some aesthetic debt. Like *Robots*, *Yak* uses contrasting sizes and character shapes to create truly distinctive aesthetics, which it marries to a carefully selected palette of colours that makes Na Keow stand out as an emerald gem amongst predominantly red-toned robots. Movement is constant too, and occurs along every imaginable axis, with Na Keow's climbing of the sky ladder towards the film's end supplying vertiginous views of the world, while the initial literal chaining of Na Keow and Peak creates an unusual heroic montage as the two try to sever their bonds, becoming heroes by chance along the way.

The choice of robots as characters instead of human beings is both helpful and problematic. The filmmakers, who reportedly stopped work on the project after Pixar's *Wall-E* (2008), began *Yak: The Giant King* again having decided that their combination of traditional storytelling and science fiction imagery would create something new (Parinyaporn, 2012). The long gestation period on *Yak: The Giant King* (as with other Thai animation) also suggests a considerable challenge for Thai animators, whose ideas are at risk of being outpaced by their international competitors. Indeed, the filmmakers' insistence that it was the use of traditional storytelling and Thai aesthetics that made *Yak* different to its better-known US predecessors shows how difficult it is for Thai animators to carve out a unique space in the global animation marketplace.

Rayna Denison

10

Independent Cinema

It is the global acclaim of Apichatpong Weerasethakul, whose films are discussed in this section, that has raised the international profile of independent filmmaking in Thailand. Such culture continues to thrive, and directors such as Pimpaka Towira, Aditya Assarat, Anocha Suwichakornpong, Sivaroj Kongsakul, Nawapol Thamrongrattanarit, Lee Chatametikool, Kongdej Jaturanrasamee, Thunska Pansittivorakul, Sompot Chidgasornpongse and Uruphong Raksasad are part of a small but increasingly well-known active independent filmmaking community within Thailand today. This movement is supported and sustained by a small number of organizations including the Thai Film Foundation, a non-profit organisation established in 1994 by film activists to promote film culture in Thailand; the Thai Short Film and Video Festival; the Bangkok Experimental Film Festival and the Thai Film Archive. There are also a small number of production and distribution companies that play a key role in ensuring that the films reach a wider, international audience (Musikawong, 2007). These include Mosquito Films Distribution (a sales and festival distribution company founded in 2014 by Apichatpong Weerasethakul, Pimpaka Towira, Aditya Assarat, Anocha Suwichakornpong, Soros Sukhum, and Lee Chatametikool) and the Bangkok-based production companies Kick the Machine (founded in

1999 by Apichatpong Weerasethakul, Eric Chan, Gridthiya Gaweewong, Michael Shaowanasai and Suaraya Weerasethakul), Electric Eel Films (founded in 2006 by Anocha Suwichakornpong), Extra Virgin (founded by Pimpaka Towira in 2008) and Pop Pictures (founded in 2006 by Aditya Assarat, Soros Sukhum, and Jetnipith Teerakulchanyut.).

However, as Chalida Uabumrungjit (Director of the Thai Film Foundation and of the Thai Short Film and Video Festival) has described, independent filmmakers in Thailand continue to struggle; firstly to find the funds to produce their films and secondly, to screen them (Uabumrungjit, 2012, p. 61). Producing creative work under a military dictatorship is not easy, and censorship continues to place restrictions on freedom of expression (Ingawanij, 2012, p. 167; Uabumrungjit, 2012, pp. 55–56; Khumsupa and Musikawong, 2016). In 2008, the "Free Thai Cinema" campaign was instigated by Weerasethakul in response to the censor's demands for him to cut scenes from his film *Syndromes and a Century* (2006). The campaigners petitioned the government to introduce a ratings system instead of relying on an outdated and paternalistic system that had not been updated since the Film Act of 1930 (Weerasethakul, 2007; Ingawanij, 2008). A new bill was introduced (the Film and Video Act) but was no more progressive as it continued the right of the Ministry of Culture to censor films if they touched on sensitive issues such as the country's turbulent past, the history and legacy of state violence, or for dealing with other issues considered to be "inappropriate" by the board, particularly regarding the representation of Buddhism or of nudity and sexuality (Uabumrungjit, 2012, pp. 55–56; Khumsupa and Musikawong, 2016).

The transnational circuit of arthouse cinema at film festivals plays a vital role in this respect; several of the films discussed in this section have won awards in competitions including the "New Currents Award" at the Busan International Film Festival and the "Tiger Award" at the International Film Festival Rotterdam. Through this network, they have also, crucially, received funding from overseas including the Hubert Bals Fund and the Busan Asian Cinema Fund, both of which have played a vital role in supporting independent Southeast Asian film culture. With such continuing support and acclaim, it seems that the future for Thai independent filmmaking and, likewise, that from around the region, grows brighter every year.

Philippa Lovatt

Title: *Mysterious Object at Noon / Dokfa Nai Mue Man*
Director: Apichatpong Weerasethakul
Studio: 9/6 Cinema Factory, Firecracker Film
Year: 2000

Before the 1997 Asian Financial Crisis, Thailand appeared in various Western media representations of East Asia, such as Jon Bon Jovi's music video "This Ain't a Love Song" (1995), the *Mortal Kombat* (1995) film, and Danny Boyle's adaptation of the famous backpacker novel *The Beach* (1996). In such representations, "Thailand" functions as an exotic yet primitive backdrop for stories designed for Western audiences, all supported by the Thai National Film Association, the Tourist Authority of Thailand, and the Amazing Thailand campaign that sought new sources of capital to develop the national image. Between 1997 and 1999, the project for *Mysterious Object at Noon* built on the director's earlier experimental critiques such as *Third World* (1997) and sought to re-map Thailand from within by jumping across the nation-state's culturally diverse landscape. The simplicity of the film's black-and-white 16mm celluloid and a soundscape of cassettes, megaphones and everyday noise forces the unaccustomed viewer into the gritty yet extraordinary livelihoods of the Thai urban street and rural countryside.

The film opens in mid-movement, as a fruit vendor truck circles the streets of Bangkok. When the truck stops at a construction site, one of the vendors narrates her traumatic story of sexual servitude in an informal economy that brings young girls into Bangkok to restructure rural debt. Her monologue plays over a montage of politician billboards that display the men who prey on the continued victimhood of sexualized labor. An off-screen voice asks, "Do you have any other stories to tell us? It can be real or fiction." The travelling film crew thus begin to formulate a narrative about a similar-aged Dorkfah, a rural tutor who instructs her wheelchair-bound student about the outside world. The film's "mysterious object" is culture and people in movement between the worlds of modern melodrama, historical memory, and global media, but also the local traditions that contradict the territorial discourse of a uniform nation-state (Winichakul, 1994). As the film crew moves around more provinces and regions, they ask each new group to continue the story of Dorkfah by playing back the cassette tape transcripts of prior recordings. Encountering a group of young Karen men, two deaf high school students, a theatrical troupe in a Northeastern village, children in Southern Thailand, and several others, Dorkfah transforms from tutor into miraculous crash survivor, evil twin, and space alien. Such movement destabilizes narratives and contradicts the notion of Thai nationhood, a construction that relies on fixed perceptions of territorial identity in a global hierarchy that prefers Thailand to be a passive object of its imagination. After viewing the film, the well-known fiction writer Uthis Haemamool (2001) wrote that *Mysterious Object* is not Thailand "ready-made," but Thailand as a project. As the project continues, Weerasethakul's debut feature film will remain a cornerstone of experimentation in independent Thai filmmaking.

Noah Viernes

Title: *Blissfully Yours / Sut Saneha*
Director: Apichatpong Weerasethakul
Studio: Kick the Machine, Anna Sanders Films, La-ong Dao
Year: 2002

Made early in the now-renowned director's career, *Blissfully Yours* is an exquisite masterclass in Apichatpong Weerasethakul's characteristic "slow" aesthetic. This film style privileges duration over narrative-driven cuts, allowing moments on screen to unfold in real time. Now synonymous with Weerasethakul's auteur style, the technique demonstrates the influence that American avant-garde and structuralist filmmakers such as Andy Warhol, Chris Marker and Bruce Baillie have had on his work. *Blissfully Yours* premiered at the Cannes Film Festival in 2002 where it was awarded *Le Prix Un Certain Regard*. This marked a turning point in Weerasethakul's career, since then he has risen to become a much-celebrated global arthouse phenomenon.

Blissfully Yours, like *Tropical Malady* (2004) and *Syndromes and a Century* (2006) later, follows a clear two-part structure. Set in a small town close to the Burmese border, the film tells the story of the relationship between a young female factory worker named Roong (Kanokporn Tongaram) and her lover Min (Min Oo), an illegal Burmese immigrant, as well as a middle-aged woman named Ong (played by Weerasethakul's regular collaborator and muse Jenjira Jansuda – now Pongpas). Min suffers from a severe skin complaint and when the two women fail in their attempt to get him treatment from the local clinic, they prepare homemade concoctions of moisturizing creams and freshly chopped vegetables to help soothe the itching. In the first part of the film, Min rarely speaks, trying not to reveal his Burmese identity to various authority figures. In this respect, he occupies a child-like position where the two women attempt to "mother" him in a rather awkward and sometimes uncomfortable love triangle.

In the second part of the film the characters journey into the jungle, relieving some of the pressures of their everyday lives. The rural idyll offers a space in which to escape their mundane routines and it is here that Min begins to take the lead, guiding Roong through the forest to a river bank where they have oral sex in the glistening sunshine. Ong also has sex with her lover in a field nearby (a colleague of her husband who possibly is later found dead in *Tropical Malady* – the only clue to the connection being the yellow underpants worn in both scenes).

While Min has experienced loss through his displacement from his homeland and also (as we learn later) his separation from his wife and child, Ong is similarly quietly grieving for a child she lost some time ago. This melancholic mood pervades the film, despite the general focus on sensual pleasures and escapism. Min's voice-over (in Burmese) towards the end of the film provides an insight into his own experience of displacement and marginalization, revealing that his silence in the first part of the film was a form of protection due to his illegal status. The experience of migrant workers is a theme Weerasethakul continues in the short film *Mobile Men* (2008) which was made as part of the Stories on Human Rights collection produced to mark the 60th anniversary of the Universal Declaration of Human Rights.

Philippa Lovatt

Title: *One Night Husband / Khuen Rai Ngao*
Director: Pimpaka Towira
Studio: GMM Pictures
Year: 2003

One Night Husband is a unique feminist, arthouse, slow-burning mystery produced by GMM Grammy, Thailand's largest entertainment company. GMM Grammy's longstanding association with the film industry emerged in four phrases, each with a different affiliated production company: Grammy Film (1995–2000), GMM Pictures (2002–2004), GTH (2004–2015), and GDH 559 (2016–). GMM Pictures collaborated with key industry players to generate commercial hits such as *My Girl* (2003), yet also continually greenlighted in-house projects, including *One Night Husband*.

Premiered at the Berlinale film festival, *One Night Husband* is supported by a range of talents, including director Pimpaka Towira, known for *Mae Nak* (1997), a short film made with the Goethe-Institut's experimental film workshop under the mentorship of filmmaker Christoph Janetzko. Pimpaka invited Janetzko to be cinematographer on her debut feature, and co-wrote the story with Laddawan Ratanadilokchai and novelist Prabda Yoon, choosing Weerasethakul's right-hand man, Lee Chatametikool, for editing.

One Night Husband touches upon topics rarely portrayed on local screens, including domestic violence and intimacy between women. As the title implies, the film depicts the journey of Sipang (popular singer Nicole Theriault) a "one night" wife whose husband disappears after their wedding night. Sipang's search for her husband leads her to meet her new brother-in-law and his wife Bussaba (played by *Transistor Love Story*'s Siriyakorn Pukkavesh), with whom she strikes up a budding companionship. Despite the stark contrast between Sipang, a modern woman, and Bussaba, a desperate housewife, the film suggests that the two women are two sides of the same coin, who together reflect the state of the half-liberal, half-conservative Thai woman who must negotiate her life under patriarchal rules.

The film is stylistically ambitious, mixing neo-noir and European arthouse aesthetics while subverting space and time and granting agency to environmental entities, specifically water. The innovative climatic sequence is depicted through a split-perspective flashback and so the film becomes a hybrid of two temporalities. A long take of Sipang consoling Bussaba mid-film is a remarkable slow sequence that was rarely seen in Thai cinema at the time (other than in Weerasethakul's work), though years later the style would come to characterize the work of young independent filmmakers.

One Night Husband has two versions: the international cut (118 minutes) and the local cut (96 minutes). In the latter, which was released on DVD, scenes are shortened to clarify the story for local viewers. Though not a box-office success, the film marked Pimpaka as a significant figure in Thai cinema. She would later become one of the most prolific figures on the Thai film circuit, working as a festival programmer, feature documentarian, and independent film distributor. In 2015 Pimpaka returned to fictional features with the road movie *The Island Funeral*.

Graiwoot Chulphongsathorn

Title: *Tropical Malady / Sat Pralat*
Director: Apichatpong Weerasethakul
Studio: Kick the Machine, Anna Sanders Films
Year: 2004

A meditation on death, loss and desire, Apichatpong Weerasethakul has described his second feature film, *Tropical Malady* as "the evil twin" of *Blissfully Yours* (2002). The Thai title, *Sat Pralat*, translates as "Strange Creature" or "Monster" and is indicative of the Thai horror and folklore traditions to which the story is indebted. Filmed on location in Petchaburi and Khao Yai national park, the film was inspired partly by the jungle adventure stories of Thai novelist Noi Inthanon and partly by the Khmer folk tales that are well known across the region. Such stories inform several narrative strands across Weerasethakul's body of work, merging together elements of Theravada Buddhism, Hinduism, animism and ancestor-spirit worship.

Tropical Malady begins with a black screen and a distinct hissing sound reminiscent of static on old film, highlighting its connection with the history of cinema. The narrative is made up of two separate but interrelated strands, the first of which is the portrayal of a romance between Tong, a young male villager (played by Sakda Kaewbuadee who also appears in

Uncle Boonmee Who Can Recall His Past Lives, 2010, *Syndromes and a Century*, 2006 and several other of Weerasethakul's short films), and an army patrol soldier named Keng (played by Banlop Lomnoi who later appears again as a soldier suffering from a mysterious sleeping sickness in *A Cemetery of Splendor*, 2015). Situated in a bustling small town, the lovers go on dates to the movies, a restaurant, and the market while also spending time together in the countryside around Tong's family home.

Midway through the film however, Tong disappears without explanation. Perhaps, we are left to wonder, he has been killed by the mysterious animal that has been slaying local livestock? The tone of the film then changes: the setting moves to the dimly lit jungle and an ambient environmental soundscape of animal, insect and bird life plays alongside the deep, electronic drones of sound designers Akritchalerm Kalayanamitr and Koichi Shimizu. Keng tracks a shaman who has taken on the form of a tiger but, as he makes his way further into the darkness of the jungle, the tables are turned, and *he* ends up being hunted instead.

Tropical Malady won the Prix du Jury at the Cannes Film Festival in 2004, the Age d'Or Prize, Cine Decouvertes, in Belgium, the Grand Prize at Tokyo Filmex, Best Film. But the accolades did not end there. In 2005, the film also won the Special Jury Prize at the XX International Gay and Lesbian Film Festival in Turin in 2005 and the Special Jury Prize at the Singapore International Film Festival.

Philippa Lovatt

Title: *Syndromes and a Century / Saeng Satawat*
Director: Apichatpong Weerasethakul
Studio: **Anna Sanders Films, Backup Films, CNC**
Year: **2006**

In the opening scene of *Syndromes and a Century*, a female physician administers a psychological test to a new male hire at a military-run medical clinic. The conversation inaugurates the director Apichatpong Weerasethakul's re-imagination of his parents' early career courtship in two slow-moving parts of the film. The first part unfolds in the lush Northeastern Thai province of Khon Kaen, in which the rational examinations and medical protocols of the rural medical clinics contrast with the green landscapes and carefree dialogue. Here, the distance between people is countered by the development of friendships that connect doctor with patient and open up space for a possible romance. Such intimacy allows the director's would-be parents to meet, for monks to play guitars while imagining other lives, and for a dentist to perform love songs in the clinic's adjacent night market.

These scenes of community that decorate the first half of the film then abruptly fade to a second part set in a veteran's hospital amid the skyline of dystopian Bangkok sometime in the future. Repeating the simple plot in a new setting, the same two doctors repeat the psychological test. In the hospital, disciplined tracking shots, factory-like aerobics sessions, and hospital orientation are interrupted by either silence or conversations about work relocation. Meanwhile, patients move around in colour-coded rehabilitation teams and sincere honesty is relegated to the hospital's basement level where doctors drink whiskey and lament their obligatory appearances on public television as the moral exemplars of an ethical society. In two significant montage sequences, the oppressive space of Bangkok's impersonal division of labor unfolds amid low angle shots of royal statues that line the hospital, regimented teams that move through the hospital corridors, and the eerie drone of Koichi Shimizu's sound design (a pitch-stretched ship whistle originally recorded for an art installation about the city's abandoned buildings).

Syndromes is known for its visual meditation on the unique rural-urban divisions built into the Thailand's modernization cycles, and for the rigid censorship board that banned the film in the wake of the 2006 coup. With the ban conditionally lifted, Weerasethakul screened the film with over seven minutes of blacked-out cuts demanded by the board, which included a monk playing guitar, a visibly aroused doctor, the afore mentioned whiskey scene, royal statues, and monks controlling a flying saucer in a park. Benedict Anderson described the film as a unique window into Thailand's current political stalemate, while assistant director Sompot Chidgasornpongse further engaged with the aesthetics of censorship in the short film "Diseases and a Hundred Year Period," which is available with several versions of the DVD.

Noah Viernes

Title:	*Wonderful Town* / *Mueang Ngao Son Rak*
Director:	Aditya Assarat
Studio:	Pop Pictures
Year:	2007

Aditya Assarat is part of a new generation of Thai directors who emerged in the early 2000s following the success of Apichatpong Weerasethakul at international film festivals. Educated in the US from a young age and communicating fluently in Thai and English, Assarat has a distinct advantage in his ability to access a network of arts institutions for film funding. *Wonderful Town*, the director's first feature film, was supported by the Rotterdam International Film Festival's Hubert Bals Fund, along with the Sundance Institute's Annenberg Film Fellowship and the Busan International Film Festival's Asian Cinema Fund. The film was also financed by the Thai Ministry of Culture and some private financiers, who have begun to support indie movies after their critical success overseas.

Set in a small town in the South of Thailand, the film tells the story of Ton (Supphasit Kansen), an architect who has agreed to travel from Bangkok to oversee the (re)construction of a seaside resort at Takua Pa after the 2004 Tsunami. Ton stops at a gas station on the edge of the town and stays in a nearby hotel, where he meets Na (Anchalee Saisoontorn) the owner's daughter, who runs the hotel. The two individuals soon find attraction and comfort in each other amidst the quietness of this small faraway town. Yet after learning that Ton is not the type to settle down and marry, Na's brother (who has noticed his sister's new radiant glow) gathers his gang of local delinquents to disrupt the relationship, and viewers are finally left to ponder how the characters will continue living their lives after this disturbance.

The film portrays fleeting moments of joy through the eyes of a visitor, one who treats the landscape with tenderness and genuine wonder, while the actual residents warn him of boredom and constraining local customs. *Wonderful Town* takes time to reveal the problematic issues of family obligations and social conformity which permeate the routine lives of a close-knit Southern community. The post-Tsunami town becomes a transit space that residents and outsiders alike traverse, with many appearing again in Assarat's subsequent film. This motif coincides with the director's own sense of self as an outsider in both Thailand and the US, something Assarat mentions in several interviews. The locations also offer a nice addition to the recurring views of Bangkok, the North and Northeastern cities in commercial and independent Thai films from this period.

It is the portrait of the hotel's concrete rooftop, a place where characters openly contemplate their own desires which connects the film with other urban East Asian and Thai movies from the last two decades. These including Wong Kar-wai's *2046* (2004) and Nawapol Thamrongrattanarit's *36* (2012). Such poignant visuals and social reflections certainly contribute to *Wonderful Town*'s critical success; the film won the Tiger Award from Rotterdam and the Best Picture award from Thailand's National Film Association. Such recognition later enabled the director to continue making a more personal movie in *Hi-So* (2010).

Wikanda Promkhuntong

Title: *Mundane History / Chao Nokkrachok*
Director: Anocha Suwichakornpong
Studio: Electric Eel Films
Year: 2009

As the winner of the VPRO Tiger Awards at the International Film Festival Rotterdam and of another five awards from various film festivals and screenings in more than forty cities around the world (including a DVD release in the UK and the Netherlands), *Mundane History* is a key Thai film in the transnational age. The film was partially supported by the Hubert Bals and Asian Cinema Funds and was the feature debut from the first Thai director to have a short film (*Graceland*, 2006) selected in Cannes's *Cinéfondation*.

Originally shot with RED and 16mm film camera (then transformed to 35 mm film) the feature takes place in an ancient Thai bourgeoisie house. The house belongs to a father whose adolescent son, Ake (Phakpoom Surapondsanuruk), was paralyzed by an accident. Since Ake cannot take care of himself, the father hires a male nurse to look after his stubborn son. At first, Ake greets his nurse with resistance, but he later embraces his new companion tenderly. This simple narrative is complicated by an abstract structure of non-linear editing (from Weerasethakhul's regular editor Lee Chatametikool), resulting in chaotic allegorical fragments that perplexed global and local spectators. The unchronological main story is cross-cut with a tale of a bird with a broken wing, a cine-essay of Ake's empty house, an image of a bursting star, and documentary footage of Thai political protestors.

This dysfunctional family becomes a metaphor for a class-based nation in crisis. The film therefore reflects the wider mood of Thailand at the time, when ongoing political turmoil indicated the end of this particular era. Yet the film also goes beyond such overtly political context, becoming a meditation on time and impermanence. *Mundane History* laments that all things are born, live, and die, be it a single cell, an animal, a human, a nation, a civilization, a star, or even a universe, and the film tellingly ends with the sign of a new beginning, albeit ambiguous.

By placing male bodies at the centre of the gaze, Suwichakornpong impressively avoids the familiar trope of a woman director telling a woman's story. The film observes several modes of male bodies: fragile, full-frontal, impotent, caring. There is much use of "haptic visuality" (Marks, 2000) in which the close-up lens transforms human skin into an abstract landscape. Indeed Suwichakornpong chose to work with a range of filmic mediums: the images from RED camera are vivid, the 16mm footage creates a poetic visual essay and the digital visual effects of the bursting star are spectacular. Soundtracks from the rock bands Furniture and The Photo Sticker Machine add an appropriate sonic landscape to match the visual.

Graiwoot Chulphongsathorn

Title:	*Uncle Boonmee Who Can Recall His Past Lives / Loong Boonmee Raluek Chat*
Director:	Apichatpong Weerasethakul
Studio:	Kick the Machine
Year:	2009

Winning the highly prestigious Palme d'Or in Cannes, *Uncle Boonmee Who Can Recall His Past Lives* brought worldwide attention, exposure and acclaim to Apichatpong Weerasethakul and to Thai independent cinema. This is all the more remarkable given the film's central premise, which follows a subtle mediation upon sensitive Thai regional and national issues. As a fictional feature, the film was also part of a wider art project by Apichatpong Weerasethakul that includes a graphic novel, an art exhibition and several short films. Transnationally co-produced by Weerasethakhul's Kick the Machine company (and supported by several independent European companies) the film was well received at festivals and in cinemas worldwide, placing its director firmly among the ranks of internationally acclaimed arthouse auteurs.

The film is set during the last days of Boonmee (Thanapat Saisaymar), an aging man who lives in the Thai Northeast. While dying of kidney failure, Boonmee confronts his past as a soldier, a father and a husband, reencountering his long-lost son, who has become a monkey ghost, and his late wife, who returns as a translucent spirit and comforts him in his fear of dying. The story is interspersed with scenes of a roaming buffalo wandering in the jungle, as well as the tale of a princess from a bygone era, who mourns her lost youth and mates with a catfish. These beings might be understood as Boonmee's previous lives, however the connections between these scenes ultimately remain unexplained.

The film's strange, opaque and non-linear narration transcends the individual protagonist, instead evolving into a universal contemplation of the fleetingness of existence. Teeming with all kinds of spirits, ghosts, human-animal relations and hybrids, as well as near-death visions, an out-of-body-experience, and reincarnation, *Uncle Boonmee Who Can Recall His Past Lives* focuses on transgressions between the living and the dead, blurring the borders between these realms.

This narrative style also enables the film to reflect on political issues indirectly. As in much of Weerasethakul's work, the Thai Northeast features prominently. A region with a long, troubled history of marginalization by the central Thai government, the film invokes the bloody prosecution of communists by government forces that took place here during the Cold War era. Dialogue alludes to these acts of violence, while the ghost characters reference the silenced, traumatic history of the subaltern that has never been acknowledged in official accounts of the state.

The film's focus upon themes of reincarnation can also be linked to a meditation on classical cinema as a dying art form and the suggestion of its resurrection. As a reaction to the impending digitalization of cinema, several scenes and characters in *Uncle Boonmee Who Can Recall His Past Lives* refer to Thai melodrama and ghost movies of the 1960s, as well as to pop culture of more recent eras.

Natalie Boehler

Title: *Eternity / Thirak*
Director: **Sivaroj Kongsakul**
Studio: **Pop Pictures**
Year: **2010**

Director Sivaroj Kongsakul previously worked as an assistant director for Pen-Ek Ratanaruang, Wisit Sasanatieng and Aditya Assarat, and also completed the cinematography for Apichatpong Weerasethakul's 2005 short film *Worldly Desires* (co-directed by Pimpaka Towira). Kongsakul made his first short film *Always* in 2006, followed by *Silencio* in 2007, which received a special mention at the Clermont-Ferrand Short Film Festival. His debut feature *Eternity* was supported by the Hubert Bals Fund and Busan's Asian Cinema Fund.

Beginning with a lingering shot of misty mountains, *Eternity* displays a similar fascination with Thailand's rural landscapes as can be found in the films of Weerasethakul. Indeed, the frequent long takes are reminiscent of Weerasethakul's "slow," contemplative style, while the film has also been compared to Aditya Assarat's *Wonderful Town* (2007). *Eternity* is a dream-like semi-autobiographical exploration of memory and grief inspired by the death of the director's father. The film is part love story, part ghost story and is divided into three sections that are all connected by the theme of loss. Shot largely at dusk, the twilight depictions have an "other-worldly" quality which evokes the liminality of this world and the next. Although melancholic, there is an intimacy and a poignancy that suggests a deep affection between the filmmaker, his characters, and the rural landscape in which the narrative unfolds.

Eternity takes place across three parts, all of which are connected by a metaphorical "darkness" associated with the death of a loved one. The first part of the film features Wit (Wanlop Rungkamjad), a middle-aged man who, having recently died, returns on his motorcycle looking for his family home. This follows a traditional Thai belief that the dead will return home after three days to reconnect with their loved ones. The action then moves seamlessly back in time to Wit's youth when he fell in love with a young teacher named Koi (played by Namfon Udomlertlak), and becomes a re-enactment of the stories Sivaroj's mother told him about when she first met his father. As Wit courts Koi (who is from Bangkok) he takes her to meet his parents, shows her around his family's rural home, and visits a Buddhist temple on the hillside. Koi spends time with Wit's family and seems to develop a fondness for them and for the farming village in which they live. Although Koi is unsure whether she truly wants to live in the countryside, she eventually agrees to marry Wit. The final part of the film then shows the family, recently bereaved, but still able to feel Wit's spirit around them, as the now widowed Koi continues to raise her children.

The film won the prestigious Tiger Award at the Rotterdam Film Festival in 2011 and, following this success, Kongsakul went on to make another short entitled *Our* in 2014. This was followed by another feature film, a Chinese/Singapore/Thai co-production *Distance* in 2016, an omnibus project co-directed by Xin Yukan and Tan Shijie, and produced by Anthony Chen (award winning director of *Ilo Ilo*, 2013).

Philippa Lovatt

Title: *Hi-So*
Director: **Aditya Assarat**
Studio: **Pop Pictures**
Year: **2010**

Hi-So, translating roughly as "high society," is a familiar word amongst Thais. It is used, often derogatively, to refer to upper-class people who can lead a luxurious jet-set life. The subject is intimately and open-mindedly explored through the life of a young Hi-So, Ananda (Ananda Everingham), who grew up in Thailand, went abroad and has now returned to the country to establish his own career. The film was intended to be Aditya Assarat's first feature after finishing his studies in the US, and the parallel connections with the director's own life are evident.

The story begins in the South of Thailand, similar to Assarat's first feature *Wonderful Town* (2007). This time the outsider protagonist is played by the half-Australian half-Laotian actor who grew up in Thailand. Ananda, the character, lands himself a job as an actor, as commonly occurs to young Western-looking Thais, despite not being able to speak the language fluently. He is visited by an Asian American girlfriend, Zoey (Cerise Leang). Despite their cheerful reunion and physical intimacy, Zoey struggles to come to term with Ananda's new life in his homeland and his new role as an actor. Feeling disconnected from the film set and Ananda's new grown stardom, Zoey finds retreat in a company of hotel staff who modestly enjoy themselves with folk music and local whiskey. The low-season empty hotel rooms and trance music create a soundscape that captures Zoey's sense of isolation and disconnection from her surroundings.

Such moments again recur in the second half of the film. In Bangkok, Ananda develops an intimate relationship with May (Sajee Apiwong) who works in a film company and later moves to live with him. A mirror image of Zoey, May cannot speak English and relies on Ananda to connect with his world of overseas-educated cool kids. Like the empty hotel rooms in the film's first part, Ananda lives in a once-prosperous apartment building in central Bangkok owned by his mother. The place is now run by a high class lady manager and a close-knit group of workers from the Northeast. As the year ends, characters are drawn into their own worlds. May decides to visit her family in Chiang Mai, while Ananda finds himself alone at an airport.

The film is produced by Assarat's own company, which went on to produce Nawapol Thamrongrattanarit's movies. The transit space, in which people do not belong anywhere, is a recurring theme in these films, and while *Hi-So* is Assarat's own personal project, it can also be connected to a troupe of Thai films that could be described as "rooftop melancholy." Each of these representations offers a snippet of people from all walks of life who intersect amongst the fast-changing capital city of Thailand. Indeed, the lyrical tone and melancholic soundscape of *Hi-So* closely resonates with

Thamrongrattanarit's *36* (2012), and the unique sounds of Shimizu Koichi and Desktop Error permeate these films and other Thai New Wave movies from this period.

Wikanda Promkhuntong

Title:	*36*
Director:	Nawapol Thamrongrattanarit
Studio:	Pop Pictures
Year:	2012

Originally from a publishing background, director Nawapol Thamrongrattanarit has written numerous scripts for the notable Thai studio GTH, including the blockbuster *Bangkok Traffic Love Story* (2009). After making a series of short films including *Cherie Is Korean-Thai* (2010), which won the Grand Prize at the Thai Short Film Festival and was selected to screen at the Rotterdam International Film Festival, the director ventured into filmmaking with *36*. Self-funded, the film was produced by Aditya Assarat's Pop Pictures following the success of his own movies at international film festivals.

The story revolves around the developing relationship between Sai (Vajrasthira Koramit), a location scout, and Oom (Wanlop Rungkamjad), an art director, who have started working on the same project: visiting rundown buildings to survey a possible film location. With minimal but carefully crafted dialogue and lyrical acoustic guitar tracks, the two quiet characters bond through their rumination on the history of deserted hotels and their means of recording personal events. Sai takes as many photos as possible and keeps them in portable hard disks, allowing her to revisit them for a new project and share them with others. Oom however opts for an analogue film camera and rarely gives developed photos to others as promised.

Two years later, Sai revisits the same hotel as a possible location for a new movie. This time she is accompanied by an intern, since Oom has moved on with a new job. Sai's mission is to find a location based on a photograph from the film's director. She later discovers that the actual building has been demolished for a new condo, but in the process Sai also finds out that her hard disk with old photos of Oom is broken.

36 is ultimately a reflection on special, short-lived moments and the unreliability of technology to record and recall precious memories. Connecting this theme of memory with various technologies and film language, the film is formed through 36 shots (similar to the number of photos in a roll of film) connected together by quirky intertitles. This play upon intertwining texts, dialogue and different forms of image-making recur again in Thamrongrattanarit's second feature film *Mary Is Happy, Mary Is Happy* (2013). The concrete buildings and rooftop iconography in the film also resonate with works of the film's producer Aditya Assarat. Together, these form a kind of urban realism, emerging through reflecting upon how people keep up with the fast changing city life.

Strategically, Thamrongrattanarit released the film through ad-hoc screenings advertised through his Facebook page. The film was warmly welcomed by a community of Bangkok-based cinephiles and artists. Sold-out sessions at the Bangkok Art and Culture Centre, where audiences sat on office chairs based on their heights, led to more screenings and film festival invitations. Subsequently, *36* won the Fipresci Prize and New Currents Award at the Busan International Film Festival and was nominated for the Tiger Award at the Rotterdam International Film Festival.

Wikanda Promkhuntong

Title: *In April the Following Year, There Was a Fire / Sin Me Sa Fon Tok Ma Proi Proi*
Director: Wichanon Somumjarn
Studio: Electric Eel Films
Year: 2012

Wichanon Somumjarn is a clear example of how the success of Apichatpong Weerasethakul has paved the way for a new generation of Thai directors who might otherwise have chosen a very different career path. Somumjarn studied engineering before shifting to filmmaking after winning a scholarship from a local short film competition, a subject that is briefly mentioned in *In April the Following Year, There Was a Fire*.

The film employs a "returning home" narrative that is common in Thai cinema; the protagonist decides to leave their work in the concrete city of Bangkok, where people have less time to care for one another, in order to return to their home town in the provinces. The story revolves around the character of Nhum (Uhten Sririwi) a construction foreman who visits his home town in the Northeast of Thailand during the Thai New Year in mid-April. Deciding to stay with his father and look for a new job, Nhum meets up with old friends, many of whom are also jobless. After attending the wedding of a classmate, Nhum meets Joy (Jinnapat Ladarat) his senior high school crush and despite their separate lives the two rekindle their connection. With time on his hands, Nhum revisits his old school and reflects on the changes in the now "modernized" town. As with other indie Thai films of this generation, the melancholic story line is accompanied by soulful electric guitar music as the protagonist contemplates his future. Local folk songs are also used as the characters drink and sing to forget their worries.

Shot in Khon Kaen where both Somumjarn and Weerasethakul are originally from, the film references recurring elements in Weerasethakul's works, including the scene of Nhum visiting a hospital and of his father watering orchids, similar to the hobbies of Weerasethakul's mother. Significantly, the political conflict in Thailand acts as a backdrop for the films of both directors. Bangkok continues to haunt Nhum through both his search for a new job and the regular news of clashes between officers and the mainly Northeastern protesters. The story is also intercut with footages of people celebrating the water festival and sequences of an interview with Nhum's father who tells childhood stories of Nhum's encounter with a jelly fish and a house fire.

As Somumjarn's debut does not make explicit connections to specific traditions of art cinema, its critical reception was limited to a network of international film festivals and those interested in the politics and culture of maginalized people in Thailand. However, this did not prevent Somumjarn from continuing to make film with available resources. His follow-up project *Somewhere Only We Know* (2014) is a short film crowdfunded through Somumjarn's own Facebook campaign, ensuring that his work continues to explore the lives of working class people striving to make a living in Bangkok.

Wikanda Promkhuntong

Title: *Mekong Hotel*
Director: Apichatpong Weerasethakul
Studio: Kick the Machine
Year: 2012

In this hour-long semi-documentary, Apichatpong Weerasethakul revisits some of his key concerns and motifs. These include the Thai Northeast and its troubled history as a borderland, the political issues of this region, and Thai spirit lore, including ghosts that act as carriers of traumatic Thai memories. *Mekong Hotel* was co-produced by Weerasethakul's own independent company Kick the Machine and several European Producers. This production mode allows the filmmaker much more artistic freedom than the mainstream Thai industry and its confines would usually allow. As with so many of Weerasethakul's productions, the film was screened internationally, notably in a special program at the Cannes Film Festival.

Set in an old hotel at a far end of the Thai Northeast, with a terrace overlooking the Mekong river, *Mekong Hotel* is narrated through a series of loosely connected episodes, melding documentary and fictional narration while also offering fragments of its own "making-of." The film interweaves a budding romance between a young man and woman, a conversation between a mother and her grown-up daughter (who is the woman in the previous love story), and a ghost story revolving around a *phi pop*, a spirit common in Thai ghost lore, who appears as the mother. Another narrative strand features the director of the film and the musician who provides the film's score, both appearing as themselves and discussing the film's music.

As a key border river, the Mekong has seen much unrest since colonial times. *Mekong Hotel* broaches this issue of water and border politics in various ways: the mother-ghost tells the younger characters stories of the region's past, mentioning the flow of refugees from Laos during the

Cold War as well as the state-enforced training of the local population, who were required to shoot enemy troops during border conflicts. The film also touches on the present-day issues of dams built across the Mekong, many of which form a serious threat to the region's environment. Such initiatives were planned by Thailand in collaboration with China, and the film links these problems to the severe floods that ravaged Thailand in 2010, which occurred while the film was being shot. Thus, *Mekong Hotel* connects the past with the present day, revealing unofficial versions of Thai history told from a regional perspective. Once again in Weerasethakul's work, these spirit and ghost characters convey complex political subtexts in a subtle, non-offensive way.

The general slow-paced style adheres to the filmmaker's previous work. This slow pace is underlined by the guitar music score that accompanies all scenes and the constant watery presence, all of which lend the film a dreamy, fluid atmosphere. Yet Weerasethakul also pays homage to post-war Thai cinema and its B-horror films through humorous references and exaggerated acting as well as a cinematography that employs long, static takes. The ending scene, especially, takes this style to its extreme by showing a 16-minute take of the hotel's view over the Mekong and the Thai-Lao Friendship Bridge.

Natalie Boehler

Title: *Concrete Clouds / Phawang Rak*
Director: **Lee Chatametikool**
Studio: Vertical Films, Far Sun Films, Kick the Machine
Year: 2013

Lee Chatametikool's debut feature *Concrete Clouds* is an intimate commentary on the fragility of human dreams and desires, set against the backdrop of the Asian Financial Crisis of 1997. The film reconstructs the past on both a narrative and metatextual level, assembling a nostalgic array of archival stock footage photos, fragments of television broadcasts, commercials, and music videos from the 1990s, as well as including stylized "dream sequences" shot to resemble 1990s karaoke pieces. Through invoking this archive of images and music, the film examines how memories are made and how such a construction contributes to the recording of both a real and imaginary past.

The film opens with a scene showing a middle-aged man listening to radio reports about the collapsing economy. Taking one final look at the blueprints of a building that will never be built, the man jumps off the roof of his apartment and ends his life. His older son, Mutt (Ananda Everingham), who is a currency trader in New York, and has therefore, ironically, contributed to Thailand's economic downfall, returns to Bangkok for his father's funeral. Mutt attempts to act as a role model for his younger brother Nic (Prawith Hansten) but the two fail to bond. Nic seems decidedly more affected by their father's death and is also preoccupied by his budding relationship with a pretty neighbour, Poupee (Apinya Sakuljaroensuk), who he would have to leave if he is to follow his brother to America. Meanwhile, Mutt spends time with his childhood friends and reconnects with his former girlfriend Sai (Janesuda Parnto) who is trying to establish herself as a businesswoman but is also suffering from the economic downturn. Identified as Mutt's first true love, Sai is placed in contrast with Mutt's American wife with whom Mutt does not seem to feel much connection. However Sai and Mutt ultimately fail to rekindle their affair, as Sai questions the sincerity of Mutt's emotions and accuses him of being in love with a fantasy.

Lee Chatametikool is known in Thai independent cinema as the editor of all Apichatpong Weerasethakul's films since 2002 and Anocha Suwichakornpong's award-winning *Mundane History* (2009). He has also collaborated on commercial Thai productions, including *Shutter* (2004), and romantic comedy *Midnight My Love* (2005). *Concrete Clouds* was Chatametikool's directorial debut and was supported by various cinema funds, including Visions Sud East from Switzerland, the Busan Film Festival's Asian Cinema Fund and the Hubert Bals Fund of the International Film Festival Rotterdam.

Chatametikool's better-known collaborators also produced the film, including Apichatpong Weerasethakul, Anocha Suwichakornpong, Thai independent film producer Soros Sukhum, and Taiwanese veteran filmmaker Sylvia Chang. *Concrete Clouds* completed a successful run on the international festival circuit, and despite its limited theatrical release within

Thailand, quickly captured the hearts of local film critics, perhaps illustrating how resonant memories of the 1997 crisis remain even ten years later. In 2015, the film won three Thai National Film Association Awards for Best Picture, Best Director and Best Supporting Actress and was nominated in eight more categories.

Katarzyna Ancuta

Title: *Mary Is Happy, Mary Is Happy*
Director: Nawapol Thamrongrattanarit
Studio: Pop Pictures
Year: 2013

After his successful debut feature film *36* (2012), Nawapol Thamrongrattanarit's second film gained international support from the Biennale College Cinema. The film includes elements of absurdity, parody and intertexual homage to contemporary Thai and East Asian auteurs, including Apichatpong Weerasethakul and Wong Kar-wai. Continuing to experiment with film language and digital technology, the script of *Mary Is Happy, Mary Is Happy* was developed from 140 consecutive tweets of a user called "Mary Malony" who followed Thamrongrattanarit on Twitter. The director constructs the story around Mary's insightful observation of objects, things and feelings. Each tweet appears on the screen in quirky interactions with the protagonist's actions, marking a unique approach to digital storytelling.

The fictional Mary (Patcha Poonpiriya) is a final year high school girl who hangs around with her best friend Suri (Chonnikan Netjui) during their last semester together. Wanting to create history and mark their moments together, Mary proposes a plan to make a school year book with the fund allocated by the art teacher (Prabda Yoon, who is a well-known writer with his own followers in Thailand). However, Mary's life begins to spin out of control when she finds a bag full of cash and develops a crush on a mysterious boy she meets at a pancake stall near the school. Strange things then begin to happen at school as the art teacher quits his job, the headmaster suddenly passes away, and the institution is turned into a totalitarian boarding school. Mary's procrastination with her minimalist year book (as she will only take photos of friends during the "magic hour" with best natural lighting) then leads to a new teacher (Krissada Sukosol, a singer well-known in the Thai indie music scene) taking over the project.

The film offers a glimpse into Thai high school life, with its push and pull between freedom and restriction. Mary's year book project becomes a reflection on the making of an artistic work, with its ideal visions and unpredictable constraints. Through his film, Thamrongrattanarit therefore suggests a means by which one can thrive both within and outside the system. The combination of East Asian arthouse attitude and playful genre characteristics of Asian high school drama and Thai pop culture, ensured the film became a cult hit amongst Thai high school audiences. Online media reported that Thamrongrattanarit's fans queued up to buy both movie tickets and the special edition T-shirts similar to those worn by students in the film.

After the success of the film, Thamrongrattanarit went on to make *Freelance* (2015) funded by the notable local studio GTH, a studio now famous for blurring the indie and commercial divide in Thai filmmaking. In between making feature films, Thamrongrattanarit also directs quirky TV commercials and works on various story-telling related projects.

Wikanda Promkhuntong

Title: *Paradoxocracy / Pracha Thip'Thai*
Director: Pen-Ek Ratanaruang, Pasakorn Prammolwong
Studio: TangkwaMatograph
Year: 2013

Veteran director Pen-Ek Ratanaruang is known for setting trends in Thai cinema, but his experimental foray into documentary filmmaking will likely be remembered as one of his more risky endeavours. A socio-political documentary, *Paradoxocracy* chronicles Thailand's troubled relationship with democracy since the establishment of a constitutional monarchy in 1932. Beginning with the Siamese Revolution of 1932, the film addresses several major political movements, uprisings, and military coups until the present day. A voice-over narration of Thai political history accompanied by archival footage is intercut with interviews with fifteen major thinkers, scholars, and political activists.

Produced in the aftermath of civil unrest and the military crackdown on protesters in 2010 (and anticipating further political turmoil that eventually led to the military coup of 2014), *Paradoxocracy* openly asks the questions that seem to dominate the everyday lives of contemporary Thais but are rarely voiced in public. Given Thailand's strict lese majeste laws that impose harsh punishments for any form of expression deemed defamatory to the monarchy (which includes members of the royal family past and present), contesting history is an impossible task in Thailand and one that requires great sensitivity. To meet this challenge, Ratanaruang teamed up with his long-time friend and producer, Pasakorn Pramoolwong, but despite engaging in heavy self-censorship that practically eliminated 80 percent of their research, they were still required to cut parts of the film. Ironically, these last minute adjustments imposed by the Thai board of censors largely misfired, as they provided the directors with an opportunity to engage with the notion of censorship on an artistic level. The film thus included several scenes where the audio track is abruptly removed and the English subtitles awkwardly crossed out, so highlighting that which cannot be said out loud.

Perhaps the most unexpected turn of events, however, was the resistance *Paradoxocracy* met from its distributors. The film was scheduled for two weeks of limited screenings in two Bangkok cinemas. However, the cinema chain not only refused to advertise the film but actively tried to prevent the audience from attending. Several people reported not being able to buy the tickets because the cinema denied that the film was being shown. As a result, Ratanaruang pulled the film from theatres after a few days and it was never shown again, although a limited double-disc DVD edition was made available in local DVD stores. The directors also refused to release the film for international festival screenings to avoid accusations that they had made it to win favours with foreign critics.

In an interview given to *Hollywood Reporter*, Ratanaruang and Pramoolwong explained that they made the film because they felt the need to understand what democracy means to them on a personal level. Asked whether they were worried about possible legal consequences, Ratanaruang responded "We weren't concerned at all; we were too naive. And we made this film for ourselves" (Brzeski, 2013). The film ends with the promise of a sequel and the directors have confirmed their willingness to continue the topic. At the same time, however, they have also admitted that even if the second part of the film is made, given the current political situation in Thailand, the audience may never get to see it. Even if this is the case however, the courage and determination of the directors should only be applauded.

Katarzyna Ancuta

Title: *The Last Executioner / Phetchakhat*
Director: Tom Waller
Studio: De Warrenne Pictures
Year: 2014

Based on the true life story of state executioner Chavoret Jaruboon, the last man to execute prisoners in Thailand with a sub-machine gun, *The Last Executioner* is a striking portrayal of a subject matter and individual that may at first glance seem somewhat salacious. Despite its sensational topic however, the film ultimately blends a measured and deeply personal biographical narrative with poetic, if at times surreal, ruminations on the nature of duty, humanity, and karma. Don Linder's original script, largely based on extensive interviews with Jaruboon's wife, children, and close friends, pieces together asynchronous fragmentary stories from Jaruboon's early days as a musician and Elvis impersonator to his time at Bangkok's Bang Kwang prison, where, between 1984 and 2002, Jaruboon executed 55 prisoners. Unlike most other countries, Thailand's executions by firing squad were carried out by a single executioner who used a sub-machine gun to shoot the condemned from a distance of about four metres with up to 15 bullets. All executions were carried out by the same team, which meant they all involved the same executioner.

Similar to the British biopic of a similar story *Pierrepoint* (2005), *The Last Executioner* portrays Jaruboon (Vithaya Pansringarm) as a "good man" for whom the decision to join the ranks of Bang Kwang's prison guards and, subsequently, take the role of the official executioner, is merely a career choice, motivated by the need to provide for his family. However, despite his declaration of faith in the infallibility of the Thai judicial system, Jaruboon suffers from guilt, an emotion materialized in the film under the guise of The Spirit (David Asavanond), who appears out of nowhere to taunt Jaruboon with recurring memories of executions that suddenly seem more barbaric and unnecessary than before. This is especially the case with the death of a female convict (based on the 1979 case of Ginggaew, a maid who helped to kidnap the son of the wealthy family) who had to be brought back from the morgue for a second execution after the first did not kill her, and who additionally maintained her innocence throughout.

The Last Executioner is the third feature film directed by Tom Waller. Waller is known as the producer of smaller locally made films like *Butterfly Man* (2002) and *Ghost of Mae Nak* (2005) as well as some larger multinational productions such as *Mechanic: Resurrection* (2016) and *Battle of Memories* (2017). Born to a Thai Buddhist mother and Irish Catholic father, Waller's films often centre upon issues of faith and religiosity, with particular preoccupation over guilt and sin. His first film, *Monk Dawson*, shot in the UK in 1998, was an exploration of priesthood against the background of rewards and temptations offered by civilian life. His later production *Mindfulness and Murder* (2011) was a neo-noir crime story set against a background of Thai monastery life. In *The Last Executioner* Waller explores Buddhist teachings on death, karma and responsibility by weaving these into a narrative that examines the motivation of the main character Jaruboon and the consequences he must face for such a career choice.

The Last Executioner received several awards, including the *Tukkata Thong* or Golden Doll awards for Best Picture and Best Screenplay, given by the Thai Entertainment Reporters Association (2015), as well as Best Director and Best Actor awards at Dhaka International Film Festival (2016). In 2014, Vithaya Pansringarm won Best Actor award at Shanghai International Film Festival, where the film was additionally nominated for Best Film and Cinematography.

Katarzyna Ancuta

Bibliography

Ainslie, M. (2009). The monstrous Chinese "Other" in the Thai horror movie *Zee-Oui*. In R. Cheung & D.H. Fleming (Eds.), *Cinemas, identities and beyond* (pp. 97–114). Newcastle: Cambridge Scholars Publishing.

────── (2011). Contemporary Thai horror: The horrific incarnation of Shutter. *Asian Cinema* 22(1), 45–57.

────── (2015). Thai horror film in Malaysia: Urbanization, cultural proximity and a Southeast Asian model. *Plaridel: A Philippine Journal of Communication, Media, and Society* 12(2).

────── (2017). Post-war Thai cinema: Audiences and film style in a divided nation. *Film International* 15(2).

Ancuta, K. (2011). An interview with Pen-Ek Ratanaruang. *Asian Journal of Literature, Culture and Society* 5(1), 209–219.

────── (2013). Ghost skins: Globalising the supernatural in contemporary Thai horror film. In G. Byron (Ed.), *Globalgothic* (pp. 14–156). Manchester: Manchester UP.

────── (2016). The smiling dead, or on the empirical impossibility of Thai zombies. In D. Fischer-Hornung & M. Mueller (Eds.), *Vampires and zombies: Transnational transformation* (pp. 21–42). Jackson, MS: University Press of Mississippi.

Ancuta, K. & Ainslie, M., eds. (2014). Special Issue on Thai Horror Film. *Horror Studies* 5(2).

Bendazzi, G. (2016). *Animation: A world history volume III: Contemporary times.* Boca Raton, FL: CRC Press for Taylor and Francis.

Brauenlein, P. & Lauser, A., eds. (2016). *Ghost movies in Southeast Asia and beyond.* Leiden: Brill.

Brzeski, P. (2013). Thailand's Pen-Ek Ratanaruang on risking it all to film the paradoxes of Thai democracy (Q&A). *Hollywood Reporter*, 7 August. Retrieved from http://www.hollywoodreporter.com/news/thailands-pen-ek-ratanaruang-risking-581674.

Chaiworaporn, A. (2001). Thai cinema since 1970. In D. Hanan (Ed.), *Film in South East Asia: Views from the region* (pp. 141–162). Hanoi: South East Asia Pacific Audio Visual Archives Association.

────── (2006). Home, nostalgia, and memory: The remedy of identity crisis in New Thai Cinema. *Asian Cinema* 17(1), 108–122.

Bibliography

Chaiworaporn, A. & Knee, A. (2006). Thailand: Revival in an age of globalization. In A.T. Ciecko (Ed.), *Contemporary Asian cinema* (pp. 58–70). New York: Berg.

Fuhrmann, A. (2009). Nang Nak- ghost wife: Desire, embodiment, and Buddhist melancholia in a contemporary Thai ghost film. *Discourse: Journal for Theoretical Studies in Media and Culture 31*(3), 220–247.

—— (2016). *Ghostly desires: Queer sexuality and vernacular Buddhism in contemporary Thai cinema*. Durham and London: Duke University Press.

Gershon, J. (2006). Comeback tale. *The Hollywood Reporter: International Edition 394*(32), 6 June, p. 90.

Haemamool, U. (2001). Mysterious object at noon. *Thai Film Quarterly 3*(11), 99–107.

Hamilton, A. (1994). Cinema and nation: Dilemmas of representation in Thailand. In W. Dissanayake (Ed.), *Colonialism and nationalism in Asian Cinema* (pp. 141–161). Bloomington: Indiana University Press.

Harrison, R. (2005). Amazing Thai film: The rise and rise of contemporary Thai cinema on the international screen. *Asian Affairs 36*(3), 321–338.

Higson, A. (2003). *English heritage, English cinema*. Oxford: Oxford University Press.

Ingawanij, M.A. (2007). *Hyperbolic heritage: Bourgeois spectatorship and contemporary Thai cinema* (Doctoral dissertation). University of London, London.

—— (2008). Disreputable behaviour: The hidden politics of the Thai film act. *Vertigo 3*(8). Retrieved from http://www.vertigomagazine.co.uk/showarticle.php?sel=bac&siz=1&id=927.

—— (2012). The Thai short film and video festival and the question of independence. In M.A. Ingawanij & B. McKay (Eds.), *Glimpses of freedom: Independent cinema in Southeast Asia* (pp. 165–181). Ithaca, NY: Cornell University Press.

Ingawanij, M.A. (2006). Un-Thai sakon: the scandal of teen cinema. *Southeast Asia Research 14*(2), 147–177.

Khumsupa, M. & Musikawong, S. (2016). Counter-memory: replaying political violence in Thai Digital Cinema. *Kyoto Review of Southeast Asia*). Retrieved from https://kyotoreview.org/issue-20/counter-memory-replaying-political-violence-in-thai-digital-cinema.

Kitiarsa, P. (2007). Muai Thai cinemas and the burdens of Thai men. *South East Asia Research 15*(3), 407–424.

Knee, A. (2005). Thailand haunted: The power of the past in the contemporary Thai horror film. In J. Schneider and T. Williams (Eds.), *Horror international* (pp. 141–159). Detroit: Wayne State University Press.

Lent, J.A. (1997). "A screw here, a crank there": Payut Ngaokrachang and the origins of Thai animation. *Animation World Magazine* 2.1. Retrieved from http://www.awn.com/mag/issue2.1/articles/lent2.1.html.

―― (2001). Thai animation: Almost a one-man show. In J.A. Lent (Ed.), *Animation in Asia and the Pacific* (pp. 185–191). London: John Libbey.

Loos, T. (2008). A history of sex and the state in Southeast Asia: class, intimacy and invisibility. *Citizenship Studies* 12, 27–43.

Marks, L.U. (2000). *The skin of the film: intercultural cinema, embodiment, and the senses*. Durham: Duke U Press.

Musikawong, S. (2007). Working practices in Thai independent film production and distribution. *Inter-Asia Cultural Studies* 8(2), 248–261.

Ngoenwichit, S. (2008). In conversation with Pakhpum Wonjinda. *Asian Journal of Literature, Culture and Society* 2(1), 124–135.

Niracharapa, T. (2014). Competitiveness of animation industry: The case of Thailand. *World Academy of Science, Engineering and Technology* 8(7), 2257–2262.

Parinyaporn, P. (2012). Animating an epic. *The Nation*, 5 October.

Ruth, R.A. (2011). *In Buddha's Company: Thai Soldiers in the Vietnam War*. Honolulu: University of Hawaii Press.

Songsri, C. (2000). *63 pi khong phap thi mi ... khang lang* [63 years of painting which has ... something behind]. *Matichon,* 8 December, p. 20.

Uabumrungjit, C. (2003). Resurrection of The Knight. Thai Film Festival. Tokyo: The Japan Foundation Asia Center, 40–45.

―― (2012). The age of Thai cinema: Looking back on the first decade. In M.A. Ingawanij & B. McKay (Eds.), *Glimpses of freedom: Independent cinema in Southeast Asia* (pp. 47–61). Ithaca, NY: Cornell University Press.

Weerasethakul, A. (2007). The folly and future of Thai cinema under military dictatorship. Thai Film Foundation. Retrieved from http://www.thaifilm.com/articleDetail_en.asp?id=.

Winichakul, T. (1994). *Siam Mapped: A History of the Geo-body of the Nation*. Honolulu: University of Hawaii Press.

Index

13 Beloved, 1, 123–124, 201
13 Sins, 124
16mm era, 3, 18, 24, 147, 197
16mm film, 9, 19, 28, 36, 37, 40,
    41, 56–57, 107, 126, 197, 217,
    225, 226
2046, 225
30+ Single On Sale, 169, 183, 185–186
35mm film, 10, 24, 36, 37, 40, 41, 51,
    59, 63, 147
36, 190, 225, 231–232, 237
6ixtynin9, 14, 15, 76, 78–80, 89
9/6 Cinema Factory, 217

Abat, 13
adaptation, 14, 20, 38, 39, 49, 55, 59,
    61, 97, 98, 105, 119, 144, 217
Adventure of Sudsakorn, The, 58–59,
    209, 211
Adventures of Iron Pussy, The, 196–198
advertising, 7, 11, 14, 77, 83, 86, 109,
    119, 144, 145, 209, 210
Alone, 13, 132–133, 136, 143
Amarttayakul, Akara, 160
Amazing Thailand campaign, 217
America
    filmmakers, 28, 30, 36, 218
    Latin America, 22, 164
    New York, 15, 236
    South America, 19
    United States of, 19, 30, 36, 41, 45,
        50, 51, 52, 55, 69, 71, 72, 73, 81,
        118, 124, 127, 143, 189, 195, 236

American era, 41
Americanization, 29, 51, 52, 72
Amfine Production, 205
Amornsupasiri, Arak, 133, 142, 185
Anderson, Benedict, 223
Andre, Peter, 72
animation, 5, 58–59, 115, 162, 178,
    187, 209–214
Anna Sanders Films, 218, 221, 222
Annupabmard, Monton, 202
Aoi, Sora, 189
Apiwong, Sajee, 230
Applause Pictures, 98, 99
Aramboi, Koh-tee, 199
Arayangkoon, Monthon, 130, 135
Arayanimisakul, Yuwanat, 179
Arjsamat, Oraphan, 136
Arnon, Poj, 198, 199
art cinema, 22, 151, 233
"art for life" movement (or *sinlapa
    phuea chiwit*), 66, 83
Art of the Devil 2, 120–122, 160
Asano, Tadanobu, 15, 85, 88
Asavanond, David, 241
Asia
    East, 1, 21, 35, 77, 79, 89, 112, 117,
        167, 169, 170, 184, 185, 217, 225,
        237, 238
    South, 1
    Southeast, 1, 9, 10, 22, 27, 35, 89,
        170, 184, 216
Asian Financial Crisis, 5, 72, 77–78,
    81, 84, 94, 95, 96, 101, 102, 104,

Index

106, 108, 119, 151, 178, 195, 217, 235, 237
Assarat, Aditya, 215, 216, 224, 228, 229, 230, 231, 232
ATM, 187–189
Atsawet, Fay, 77
Aubaret, Gabriel, 106
audience
  international, 8, 17, 24, 25, 34, 108, 124, 131, 215
  national, 7, 17, 38, 93, 142, 152, 195
Aumporn Cinema, 32
Australia, 23, 85, 88, 157, 230
auteur, 1, 9, 14, 21, 23, 86, 89, 130, 156, 198, 218, 227, 237
Avant, 133, 135, 149, 179
avant-garde, 1, 21, 29, 76, 218
awards
  Asian Film Award (Bucheon), 124
  Dragons and Tigers Award (Vancouver), 17
  Fipresci Prize, 86, 232
  Golden Doll (*Tukkata Thong* or Saraswati Award), 24, 25, 61, 241
  New Currents Award (Busan), 216, 232
  Oscars (Academy Awards), 15, 25, 67, 89, 104
  Palme d'Or (Cannes), 21, 108, 226
  Silpathorn Award (Thai Ministry of Culture), 9, 17
  Suphannahong (Thailand National Film Association Awards), 70, 180
  Tiger Award (Rotterdam), 216, 225, 229, 232

Baa-Ram-Ewe, 12, 152, 157, 163, 164, 212
Backup Films, 222
Bacon, Kevin, 12
Baillie, Bruce, 218
Ban Phi Pop, 64–66
Bang Rajan: The Legend of the Village Warriors, 95–97, 153, 160
Bangchang, Thavi Na, 35
Bangkok, 2, 27, 28, 34, 41, 51, 52, 55, 56, 63, 66, 78, 79, 83, 86, 87, 114, 124, 132, 147, 154, 160, 164, 165, 170, 174, 178, 183, 188, 200, 213, 217, 223, 225, 230, 233, 234
  Bang Kapi, 55, 56
  Bang Kwang, 240
  Siam Square, 200
Bangkok Art and Culture Centre, 232
Bangkok Critics Assembly, 69
Bangkok Daily Mail, The, 30
Bangkok Dangerous, 139
Bangkok Film Company, 31
Bangkok Kung Fu, 18
Bangkok Love Story, 194, 198–199
Bangkok Traffic Love Story, 169, 182–183, 231
Bangyikhun, Songkalot, 183
Banluerit, Ekphan, 65
Battle of Memories, 241
Beach, The, 217
Beautiful Boxer, 150–152
beboydcg, 212
Behind the Painting, 20, 97–98
Benjamas, Patcharasri, 176
Bhanomyong, Pridi, 33–35
Bhirombhakdi, Piyapas, 100
Big Boss, The, 162
Black Silk, 10, 39–41
Blissfully Yours, 21, 22, 218–219, 221
blockbuster, 11, 36, 71, 94, 111, 116, 180, 187, 231
Blue Elephant, The, 210–212
Body #19, 133–134, 138
Bodyguard, The, 155–156
Bodyslam, 186

248

Index

Bollywood, 13
Bon Jovi, 217
Boonchu Phu Narak, 63–64
Boonkasemsanti, Phassaporn, 135
Boonkasemsanti, Wisut, 135
Boonprakob, Chayanop, 186
Boontawee, Kampoon, 59
Boonyakiart, Passorn, 66
Boonyaruk, Mahasamut, 86
Boonyasak, Laila, 111, 139, 185
Boonyasak, Sinitta, 85
Born to Fight, 148, 154–155
Bowring, John, 106
box office, 7, 24, 47, 55, 60, 64, 71, 81, 86, 96, 98, 104, 109, 116, 138, 142, 143, 145, 149, 158, 164, 169, 175, 184, 189, 194, 200, 211, 212, 221
Boyle, Danny, 217
Bradley, Dan Beach, 106
Bridget Jones's Diary, 183
British Film Institute (BFI), 55
Brokeback Mountain, 18, 199
Buacharoen, Panisa, 177
Buddhism
    Buddhist, 19, 13, 39, 40, 84, 99, 110, 126, 152, 168, 169, 171, 172, 175, 203, 206, 229, 241
    monk, 8, 36, 38, 39, 40, 53, 56, 70, 88, 149, 158, 171, 175, 206, 223
    religion, 7, 16, 39, 84, 150, 143, 175, 208, 216, 221
Buppha Ratri: Flower of the Night, 18, 111–113, 118, 149
Buranajan, Pasith, 120
Burma, 34, 57, 96, 100, 148, 153, 154, 155, 207, 211, 219
Bus Lane, 179–180
Butch Cassidy and the Sundance Kid, 167

Butterfly and Flowers, 60–62
Butterfly Man, 241

Cambodia, 121, 126, 127
Carabao, 63
Caravan, 63, 67
Cathay Studios, 147
Cemetery of Splendour, 22, 222
censors, 2, 16, 141, 194, 202, 206, 239
censorship, 2, 13, 16, 22, 90, 115, 216, 223, 239
Chaianun, Nitchapoom, 194
Chaibancha, Mitr, 17, 28, 41, 44, 46, 48, 49, 147
Chalermthai Studio, 114
Champagne X, 72, 78
Chan, Eric, 216
Chan, Jackie, 152, 157
Chang, Sylvia, 236
change
    cultural, 5, 56
    economic, 5, 54
Changthom, Prangthong, 113
Chantaraviboon, Sayan, 51
Chanthonsiri, Pha-un, 8
Chaowarat, Petchara, 28, 41, 45, 46, 48, 197
Charoenpura, Inthira, 113, 135
Charoenpura, May, 100, 140
Charuchinda, Sakka, 24
Chatametikool, Lee, 215, 220, 226, 235–236
Chatree, Sorapong, 24, 54, 55, 62, 63
Charoenphol, Parinya (or Nong Toom), 150
Charuchinda, Narong, 67
Chaungrangsri, Suporntip, 129
Chen, Anthony, 229
Cherdchai Films, 55, 70
Chern-Yim, Note, 175
chick flicks, 183

249

Index

Chidgasornpongse, Sompot, 215, 223
Chienthawon, Sirachuch, 125
China, 1, 35, 38, 119, 169, 183, 190, 201, 229, 235
Chirathivat, Pachara, 186
Chitmanee, Sonthaya, 160
Chocolate, 11, 12, 148, 161–163
Cholsaranont, Prapas, 213
Christensen, Lena, 115
Chung, Christy, 8, 99
Chungking Express, 78
Chupong, Dan (or Chupong Changprung), 148, 154, 155, 158, 159
Chutintaranond, Sunait, 100
Cinemascope, 40
Cinemasia, 8, 81, 83, 85
cinephiles, 2, 3, 9, 12, 21, 29, 232
Citizen Dog, 16, 17, 86–88
CJ Entertainment, 88, 89
Clash, 186
class
  hi-so, 229
  inequality, 20, 83, 94, 113, 161, 174
  lower class, 9, 46, 111, 116, 159, 175
  middle class, 46, 86, 108, 126, 143, 144, 160, 161, 175, 180, 182, 187, 188, 205
  working class, 21, 67, 87, 113, 160, 167, 205, 234
Click, 13
CNC, 222
Cold War, 7, 36, 50, 56, 73, 227, 235
collaboration, 8, 12, 21, 63, 137, 163, 197, 235
Come On Sweet Co., 204
comedian, 18, 50, 149, 155, 156, 175, 180, 188, 199
Coming Soon, 136–137, 143
commercials, 7, 15, 16, 77, 83, 235, 238

Concrete Clouds, 235–237
Coppola, Francis Ford, 23, 25
co-production, 12, 28, 72, 78, 85, 88, 229
Cordero, Maria, 88
Country Hotel, 10, 37–38
Couple in Two Worlds, A, 68–70
crisis
  economic, 5, 72, 77, 78, 81, 94, 95, 96, 101, 102, 104, 106, 108, 119, 123, 151, 178, 195, 217
  political, 22, 179, 226, 235, 237
Cronenberg, David, 132

Dang Bireley's and Young Gangsters, 5, 7, 16, 86, 93, 94–95, 98, 109, 166
De Palma, Brian, 132
De Warrenne Pictures, 240
Dead Ringers, 132
Dean, James, 95, 166
Dedicate, 88, 89
Desktop Error, 231
Dhanasevi, Chantavit, 137, 184, 188
division
  political, 16
  social, 20, 160, 170, 223
Dorm, 125–126
Double Luck, 28, 31–32
Doyle, Christopher 78, 85, 86, 88
Duangporn, Noppadol, 84
Dusit, Sake, 49
Dynamite Warrior, 148, 158–160

Electric Eel Films, 225, 232
Elephant Keeper, The, 24, 62–63, 99
Elephant White, 12
Eternity, 228–229
ethnicity, 183
ethnography, 60, 80
E-Tim Tai Nae, 181–182
Europe, 19, 21, 34, 220, 227, 234

Index

Everingham, Ananda, 116, 164, 201, 229, 236
experimental film, 6, 8, 24, 25, 162, 164, 207, 217, 220
Extra Virgin, 216
Eye, The, 113, 114

Fable from an Uncle: The Magical Ring, A, 32–33
Faivre, Florence, 105
Falling in Love with You, 25
Far East Film Ltd, 10, 35, 36
Film Bangkok, 80, 95, 105
Film Factory, The, 15, 86, 129
film festivals, 9, 23, 71, 75, 83, 89, 109, 115, 124, 160, 195, 197, 210, 216, 227, 232, 239
   Asia-Pacific Film Festival, 8, 35, 36
   audiences, 2, 5, 86
   Bangkok Experimental Film Festival (BEFF), 215
   Bangkok Gay and Lesbian Film Festival (BGLFF), 193
   Bangkok International Film Festival (BKKIFF), 86, 89
   Berlin International Film Festival (Berlinale), 15, 77, 80
   Brooklyn Film Festival, 80
   Brussels International Independent Film Festival, 198
   Bucheon International Film Festival (BiFan), 124
   Busan International Film Festival (BIFF), 198, 216, 224, 232, 236
   Cannes Film Festival, 15, 17, 21, 80–81, 83, 108, 218, 222, 225, 226, 234
   Clermont-Ferrand Short Film Festival (Clermont ISFF), 228
   Deauville Asian Film Festival, 17
   Dhaka International Film Festival (DIFF), 241
   Fantasia International Film Festival, 17
   Hawaii International Film Festival (HIFF), 61
   Hong Kong International Film Festival (HKIFF), 80
   International Film Festival Rotterdam (IFFR), 21, 22, 208, 216, 224, 225, 229, 231, 232, 236
   Manila International Film Festival (Cinemanila), 60
   market, 197
   Queer Lisboa, 208
   San Francisco International Asian American Film Festival (CAAMFest), 17
   Shanghai International Film Festival (SIFF), 241
   Singapore International Film Festival (SOIFF), 222
   Thai Short Film and Video Festival, 21, 215, 216
   Three Continents Festival, 55
   Torino GLBT Film Festival (TGLFF), 206
   Toronto International Film Festival (TIFF), 17, 98, 113
   Vancouver International Film Festival (VIFF), 7, 17, 206
   Venice Film Festival, 15
film style, 10, 16, 29, 33, 51, 79, 81, 83, 86, 111, 165, 180, 197, 204, 218, 221, 228, 235
Firecracker Film, 217
Five Star Production, 56, 59, 60, 63, 67, 77, 78, 80, 86, 120, 126, 139, 142, 160, 164, 199
Focus Film, 88, 89

Index

folk tales, 8, 59, 221
folklore, 21, 52, 53, 64, 107, 125, 136, 221
Fortissimo Films, 88, 89
Free Thai Cinema movement, 22
Freelance, 190–191, 238
Fun Bar Karaoke, 14, 77–78, 80
funding
    Asian Cinema Fund, 216, 224, 225, 228, 236
    Biennale College, 190, 237
    Hubert Bals Fund, 21, 22, 216, 224, 225, 228, 236
    Sundance Institute's Annenberg Film Fellowship, 224
    Thai Khemkhaeng (Stronger Thailand Project), 25
    Visions Sud East, 236
Furniture, 226

Gangster, The, 149, 166–168
Gate-Uthong, Saengthong, 86
Gaweewong, Gridthiya, 216
gay, 18, 142, 176, 177, 193, 194, 195, 197, 198, 199, 203, 205, 222
GDH 559, 14, 220
genre
    action, 5, 11, 12, 17, 25, 28, 37, 49, 61, 81, 88, 95, 147–168, 173, 174, 180, 181, 194, 197, 198, 211
    comedy, 4, 5, 12, 13, 14, 18, 25, 37, 38, 42, 45, 50, 61, 64, 65, 68, 70, 71, 72, 78, 80, 83, 84, 88, 103, 110, 112, 113, 115, 116, 122, 124, 139, 140, 143, 145, 147, 151, 155, 158, 169–191, 194, 199, 201, 236
    documentary, 6, 7, 16, 21, 59, 63, 166, 202, 203, 207, 226, 234, 238
    drama, 25, 37, 39, 57, 70, 79, 80, 84, 89, 98, 103, 104, 113, 148, 194, 200, 205
    fantasy, 16, 21, 49, 83, 102, 141, 151, 195, 211, 236
    film noir, 10, 40, 143, 165, 220, 241
    historical, 19, 29, 34, 66, 93, 94, 96, 100, 105, 106, 110, 118, 153, 168, 169, 211
    horror, 1, 2, 4, 5, 8, 12, 13, 14, 16–19, 29, 53, 61, 107–146, 147, 149, 160, 169, 170, 199, 201, 221, 235
    gangster, 7, 18, 40, 93, 95, 143, 148, 162, 165, 167
    melodrama, 16, 30–31, 38, 42, 49, 57, 63, 66, 67, 80, 81, 130, 170, 194, 197, 204, 218, 228
    musical, 28, 37, 41, 42, 48, 49, 64, 87, 104, 105, 113, 197
    queer cinema, 5, 138, 193–208
    romance/romantic comedy, 11, 12, 14, 17, 18, 25, 37, 38, 42, 45, 63, 70, 113, 139, 145, 169–191, 197, 200, 201, 204, 205, 234, 236
    short film, 21, 215, 228, 231
    slapstick, 18, 29, 38, 65, 110, 111, 115, 116, 124, 145, 156, 158, 159, 170, 173, 174, 199, 200
    superhero, 17, 49, 50, 113, 115, 149, 158, 159, 165
    thriller, 8, 11, 38, 80, 88, 107, 138, 142, 143
    versatility, 11, 180
    Western, 16, 18, 38, 86, 164, 167
ghost, 2, 13, 14, 18, 19, 45, 46, 53, 58, 65, 66, 107, 108, 111, 112, 117, 118, 123, 125, 127, 141, 144, 145, 199, 212, 213, 227, 228, 234, 235
Ghost Game, 121, 126–127
Ghost of Guts Eater, 52–53, 128
Ghost of Mae Nak, 241

Index

Ghost of Valentine, 19, 127–128
GMM Pictures (also GMM Grammy), 71, 72, 116, 150, 187, 220
Godfather, The, 167
Gojiew, Vitcha, 101
Golden Age, 28, 36, 45, 107, 147
Golden Eagle, 49–50, 147
Gomarchun, Saneh, 38
Gone Astray, 193
Goodfellas, 167
gothic, the, 16, 125, 126, 130, 143
Group Four Production, 64
GTH (or GMM Thai Hub), 14, 83, 101, 125, 132, 133, 136, 137, 143, 145, 173, 176, 179, 182, 183, 186, 191, 220, 231, 238

Haemamool, Uthis, 218
Hansten, Prawith, 236
Hanuman Film, 10, 35, 36, 37, 39, 42
Haunting Me, 199–200
Hello Stranger, 14, 169, 183–185, 188
Heritage, 2, 4, 8, 25, 39, 55, 57, 71, 72, 76, 93–106, 118, 119, 123, 158, 169, 190
His Name Is Khan, 24, 54–55
Hi-So, 225, 229–231
Hitchcock, Alfred, 9, 37
Hiranyapruk, Phoori, 211
Hiranyasap, Toon, 88
Hiranyawongkul, Witwisit, 201
Hollywood, 9, 10, 17, 23, 24, 28, 29, 30, 36, 41, 78, 107, 130, 148, 152, 166, 183, 184
  blockbuster, 116
  filmmakers, 10, 23
  remake, 13, 108, 118
  studios, 10, 28, 36
Hollywood Reporter, 239
Holy Man, The, 170, 175

Hong Kong, 88, 99, 147, 167, 169
  cinema, 7, 18, 78, 140, 148, 152, 153, 156, 157
  filmmakers, 8, 88, 156, 162
  performers, 8, 88, 99
Hongsopon, Shiriohana, 195
Horwang, Sirin, 181, 182, 183
Hounsou, Djimon, 12
House, The, 135–136
House of the Peacock, 19
Hunger Games, The, 127
Hunsat, Orpreeya, 176

I Fine… Thank You… Love You, 169, 189–190
I-Aem, Suchada, 65
Ilo Ilo, 229
imagined community, 5, 158
immigration, 29
In April the Following Year, There Was a Fire, 232–234
independent film, 2, 5, 20, 21, 72, 194, 196, 198, 206, 215, 216, 217, 218, 221, 225, 226, 236
India, 1, 43, 44, 46, 47
Indonesia, 1, 190
Ingawanij, May Adadol, 71, 76, 93, 95, 216
Inpornwijit, Kritteera, 134
Insects in the Backyard, 206
Insee, Adisorn, 177
Inthanon, Noi, 221
Invisible Waves, 15, 78, 88–89
Iron Ladies, The, 1, 83, 138, 151, 176, 194–196
Iron Ladies 2, The, 138
Isan (*see also* Thailand, Northeast)
  dialect, 59, 60
  people, 19, 159
  region, 59, 159, 175, 177

Index

Islam
   Muslim, 8, 19, 61, 171, 172, 202, 203, 204
   religion, 203
   It Gets Better, 205–206

Jaa, Tony (Japanom Yeerum), 12, 148, 152, 153, 154, 155, 157, 162
Jaengmeesuk, Meesuk, 176
Jan Dara, 8, 98–99, 171
Janetzko, Christoph, 220
Janjarearn, Kornpob, 188
Jansuda, Jenjira (later Jenjira Pongpas), 219
Japan, 1, 14, 85, 97, 118
   cinema, 17, 18, 19, 169
   culture, 108, 167, 187, 209
   imperialism, 34
   occupation, 28
Jaruboon, Chavoret, 240, 241
Jaturanrasamee, Kongdej, 172, 215
Jayasvasti Jr, Thienchai, 176
Jenaksorn, Montri, 57
J-horror, 112, 117, 130
Jindachote, Ploy, 127
Jirabenterng Film, 58
Jirakul, Focus, 101
Jitnukul, Tanit, 95, 96, 153, 160
Jitsomboon, Charwin, 101
Jittaleela, Supanart, 204
Jorkwang Films, 183
Jürgen Brüning Film, 207

Kaewbuadee, Sakda, 221
Ka-La, 186
Kalayanamitr, Akritchalerm, 222
Kampaengphet, Prince, 30
Kang, Hye-jung, 88
Kansen, Supphasit, 224
Kantana Animation, 210, 211
Kaomoolkadee, Pattamawan, 66

Kasetsart University, 72
kathoei, 1, 18, 150, 151, 169, 193, 194, 195, 196, 199, 200, 202, 205, 206
Kaweechai Pappayon, 45
Kemglad, Somchai, 149, 166
Kemgumnird, Kompin, 210, 211
Kendara, Kong, 126
Khampiranon, Nuttita, 206
Khamsing, Somrak, 155
Khamuan, Maneerat, 138
Khao Pappayon, 31
Khiaogao, Phaibunkiat, 77, 78, 80
Khmer, 121, 126–127, 221
Khomsiri, Kongkiat, 120, 142, 143, 160, 161, 166, 167, 168
Kick, The, 12, 148, 163
Kick the Machine, 196, 215, 218, 221, 226, 227, 234, 235
Kill Bill, Vol. 1 162
Killer Tattoo, 18, 148–150, 181
King Chulalongkorn (Rama V), 32, 104, 105
King and I, The 106
King Mongkut (Rama IV), 70, 105, 106
King of the White Elephant, The, 33–35
King Naresuan, 211
King Rama VI, 30
King Rama VII, 32
Kitjaroen, Kiat, 180
Kitsuwon, Supakorn, 82, 115
Kittikachon, Thanom, 55
Kongsakul, Sivaroj, 215, 228, 229
Koramit, Vajrasthira, 231
Kounavudhi, Vichit, 56, 57
Kraisri, Phadung, 177
Kritayakon, Renu, 34
KTCC, 183
Kuga, Tomono, 88
Kuhontha, Suwanee, 54
kuman thong, 114

Index

Kun Anurakrathakarn (or Pleng Sookviriya), 28, 30, 31

Labanoon, 186
Ladarat, Jinnapat, 233
Ladda Land, 136, 143–144
Lampang, 195
Lamwilai, Ornjira, 133
La-ong Dao, 218
La-Ongmanee, Jirayu, 186, 187
Last Executioner, The, 240–241
Last Life in the Universe, 8, 15, 78, 85–86, 88, 89
Last Song, The, 194
Lawo Films, 24, 41, 54
Leang, Cerise, 230
Lee, Bruce, 148, 152, 157, 162
Leenutapong, Pimpaporn, 172
Legend of King Naresuan, The, 25, 67, 100, 180
Legend of Suriyothai, The, 25, 99–101
Lertkasemsap, Kalaya, 69
Liasirikun, Kittikorn, 179, 180
Library of Congress, 35
Limtrakul, Rashane, 163
Linder, Don, 240
Local Color Films, 164
Lomnoi, Banlop, 222
Love of Siam, 12, 194, 200–201
Luang Boonyamanop (Saengthong), 31
Luang Konkarnjenjit, 31
luk thung, 46, 47, 49, 180
Lumière Brothers, 27
Lyovarin, Win, 15

Macau, 15, 88
MacDonald, Ray, 77, 78
MacRae, Henry Alexander, 28, 29, 30
Mae Nak (or Nang Nak), 2, 14, 38, 39, 108, 109, 110, 145, 212
Mae Nak Phra Khanong, 38–39

Magic Shoes, The, 11
Mahagan Films, 111
M.A.I.D.: Mission Almost Impossible Done, 170, 173–174
Malako, Kaew, 65
Malaysia, 1, 61, 171, 203, 207
Maligool, Jira, 83–83
Malucchi, Stella, 80
Manaying, Sushar, 204
manga, 115, 178, 204
Mangpong, 111
Manomaisantiphap, Chayanan, 201
Manopet, Jaran, 64
Marker, Chris, 218
martial arts, 12, 18, 113, 148, 152, 154, 157, 162, 163, 164
Mary Is Happy, Mary Is Happy, 190, 232, 237–238
masculinity, 56, 102, 145, 148, 160, 161, 167, 168
Matching Motion Pictures, 118, 119
Maurer, Mario, 145, 201
Me… Myself, 201–202
Meat Grinder, 140–141
Mechanic: Resurrection, 241
Mekhong Full Moon Party, 83–84
Mekong Hotel, 234–235
Mekong River, 22, 234, 235
Mercury Man, 113
Metanee, Sombat, 28, 43, 53, 147, 148
Metrosexual, 138, 176–177
Midnight My Love, 12, 236
Miike, Takashi, 143
Mindfulness and Murder, 241
Ministry of Culture, 9, 17, 25, 106, 207, 216, 224
Miramax, 81
mise-en-scène, 10, 40, 41, 51, 57, 78, 90, 93, 95, 104, 113, 117, 159
Miss Suwanna of Siam, 28, 29–30
Mission Impossible, 148

255

Index

Mitsuru, Adachi, 178
Modern Dog, 89
Moeithaisong, Tiwa, 140
Mom Ubol Yukol Na Ayudhya, 23
Money Money Money, 41–42
Mongkolthong, Songsak, 139, 140
Monk Dawson, 241
Mono Film, 201
Monrak Lukthung, 28, 47–49
monster, 45, 130, 141, 212, 221
monstrous feminine, 116
Morris, Greg, 148
Mortal Kombat, 217
Mosquito Films, 23, 215
Mountain People, 56–57
Muay Thai, 1, 11, 12, 60, 115, 147–168, 147, 148, 150, 151, 152, 154, 160, 161, 162, 163, 18181
Muay Thai Chaiya, 148, 160–161, 167
Muay Thai Nai Khanom Tom, 96
Muen and Rid, 19, 70–71
Muengderm, Mai, 55
Mukdasanit, Euthana, 60, 61, 71
Mundane History, 225–226, 236
music video, 7, 8, 11, 22, 62, 83, 86, 87, 164, 217, 235
My Girl, 101–103, 177, 178, 182, 220
Mysterious Object at Noon, 21, 217–218
mythology, 9, 35, 115

Na Lumpang, Panalak, 174
Na Songkhla, Pornchita, 174
Nadee, Isara, 120
Nai Khanom Tom, 148
Nak, 212–213
Nakomthai Picture, 111
Nakornsawan, Apaporn, 156
Nakprasitte, Napakpapha, 120
nam nao films, 54
Namwong, Aranya, 52
nang bu, 49, 50, 147, 148

nang kathoei, 150, 151
nang naeo, 16, 17
Nang Nak, 8, 16, 39, 80, 86, 98, 108, 109–110, 111, 113, 118, 171
nang phi, 107
nang sayong khwan, 107, 142
Naowarach, S., 52
National Film Heritage registry, 55, 57
nationalistic, 5, 10, 20, 72, 76, 94, 95, 96, 106, 158, 161, 164
Nauljam, Nattasha, 187
Netjui, Chonnikan, 237
New Thai Cinema, 25, 75–92, 116
New York Times, 34
Ngamdee, Jaran, 96
Ngamsan, Chartchai, 80
Ngaograjang, Nantana, 55
Ngaokrachang, Payut, 58, 209
NGR, 126
Ngu Phi, 44–45
Nguyen, Johnny, 157
Nimibutr, Nonzee, 5, 7–9, 16, 18, 39, 76, 80, 83, 93, 94, 98, 108, 109, 166, 171
Nimpulsawasdi, Chaichan, 195
Nixon, Richard, 10
Noo Hin: The Movie, 177–178
North, Robert 10, 36
nostalgia, 4, 5, 7, 8, 16, 29, 49, 56, 59, 71, 83, 93, 94, 95, 101, 102, 106, 108, 123, 130, 161, 178, 182, 187, 235
novel, the, 8, 15, 17, 20, 33, 55, 56, 60, 72, 83, 86, 97, 98, 105, 124, 172, 173, 183, 217, 227
Nymph, 15

Ochiai, Masayuki, 108
October 14 Uprising, (*14 tula*), 24
OK Baytong, 8, 170, 171–172
One Night Husband, 220–221

Index

Ong-Bak: The Thai Warrior, 1, 11, 12, 96, 103, 124, 148, 152–154, 155, 157, 158, 159, 161, 162, 163
Oo, Min, 219
Oradee, Makut, 60
Orwell, George, 207
Overture, The, 8, 103–104

Pachimsawat, Kulnadda, 176
Pakdeevijit, Chalong, 148
Pan Kam, 45
Pang Brothers, 139
Panichrutiwong, Chaiporn, 213
Panpeng, Rangsiroj, 105
Pansittivorakul, Thunska, 194, 202, 203, 207, 208, 215
Pansringarm, Vithaya, 240, 214
Pantural, Pakasit, 125
Panyopas, Jaruwan, 51
Panyopas, Lalita, 78, 80, 89, 90
Paovarat, Vailaikorn, 57
Paradoxocracy, 15, 16, 238–240
Parnto, Janesuda, 236
Pataweekarn, Patiparn, 72
Pattamasiri, Jarupus, 174
Pattani Kingdom, 8
Payakarun, Samart, 156
Pee Mak, 14, 108, 143, 145–146
Permpoonpatcharasuk, Kantapat, 138
Pestonji, Ratana, 9–11, 36, 37, 39, 40, 41, 42, 43, 44, 81
Petchrung, Nualchawee, 135
Pew-on, Piyaphong, 155
Phanpakdee, Thawatchai, 160
Phenomena, 116
phi, 107, 114, 129
   phi krasue, 19, 52, 53, 127, 128
   phi pop, 64, 65, 66, 237
   phi tai hong, 114
   phi tai thang klom, 114
Phibunsongkram, Plaek, 104

Phloengtham, Utsana, 98
Phobia, 13, 133, 137–139
Phobia 2, 13, 133
Pholyiam, Wasana, 61
Phongnithi, Seree, 120
Photo Sticker Machine, The, 226
Phra Aphai Mani, 58, 209
Phranakorn Film, 140, 175
Phu, Sunthorn, 58, 59, 209
Pierrepoint, 240
Pinijkhar, Surapong, 105, 106
Pinkaew, Prachya, 11–13, 70, 124, 148, 152, 154, 157, 158, 161, 163, 164
Pisanthanakun, Banjong, 13–14, 108, 116, 120, 132, 133, 137, 145, 183
Pisat Saneha, 45–47
Plengpanich, Chatchai, 66, 67, 142
Ploy, 15, 80, 89–91
Ployangunsri, Jenjira, 135
Pohphay, Nattapol, 138
Polanski, Roman, 23
Polasit, Kara, 97
Polsap, Yosapong, 120
Ponethon, Ong-art, 60
Po-ngam Suthep, 115, 149, 180
Pongprapaphan, Chatchai, 132
Pongsuwan, Pongsak, 149, 175
Pongthananikorn, Preechaya, 188
Poomatfon, Weerapon, 163
Poonpiriya, Patcha, 237
Pop Pictures, 216, 224, 228, 229, 231, 237
popular culture, 14, 25, 151, 207
Poster, Piak, 24, 28, 51, 97
postmodernism, 16, 81, 156
Potranan, Pakkaramai, 139
Pormsakha Na-Sakonnakorn, Puttipong, 185
Pradinan, Pradit, 203
Prammolwong, Pasakorn, 238
Pramoj Na Ayudhya, Achita, 139

Index

Praphaphom, Prim, 44
Presley, Elvis, 150
Pridi Productions, 33
Prince Anusorn Mongkolkarn
 (or Anusornmongkolkarn),
 23, 41, 66
Prince Chatrichalerm Yukol (or Than
 Mui), 23–25, 54, 62, 66, 99,
 100, 180
production value, 14, 41, 62, 83, 85,
 109, 113, 151, 194
Prommitr Production Co., Ltd
 (previously Prommitr Film), 24,
 62, 66, 99, 103
Promsiri, Santisuk, 64, 68, 70
propaganda, 28, 34, 42, 100, 161, 164
 anti-communist, 10, 36
prostitution, 20, 61, 66, 91, 95, 142
Protector, The, 11, 96, 148, 157–158
Pukkavesh, Siriyakorn, 82, 220
Pulp Fiction, 80
Purikitpanya, Paween, 133, 137

Queen Sirikit, 101
Queen Suriyothai, 100
Queens of Langkasuka, 8

Rachjaibun, Buranee, 118
radio, 7, 184, 210, 236
Raging Phoenix, 148, 163–164
Rajjanavatchra, Vorakarn, 137
Rakkandi, Tirak, 65
Raksasad, Uruphong, 60, 215
Ramayana, 213, 214
Rangkhavorn, Poonpan, 35
Ratanabhand, Ratanavadi, 40
Ratanadilokchai, Laddawan, 220
Ratanaruang, Pen-Ek, 14–16, 18, 76,
 77, 78, 79, 80, 81, 83, 85, 86, 88,
 89, 228, 238, 239
Ratanasopha, Premsinee, 120

Rattanachoksirikul, Natthapphong, 212
realism, 8, 11, 21, 24, 33, 57, 59, 110,
 135, 152, 189, 232
Red Bike Story, 71–73
Red Eagle, 130, 149, 164–165
 character, 164
Reservoir Dogs, 78
Ring, The, 109, 117, 137
Rising Sun Productions, 47
Rittakol, Bhandit, 63, 64
Rittichai, Ron, 70
Rittikrai, Panna, 12, 148, 153, 154, 155,
 157, 163
Robots, 214
Ronin Team, The, 120
Rope, 37
Royal State Railways Department, 30, 31
Royal Thai General System of
 Transcription (RTGS), 4
RS Film, 130
Rungkamjad, Wanlop, 229, 231
Rungrattana, Metta, 43
Rungreuang, Preeya, 38, 39, 43
Rungsuwan, Chakhrit, 155
Running Man, The, 127
Russia, 35
 cinema, 105

Saetthaaphakdee, Ratana, 44
Sahamongkol Film, 12, 97, 103, 113,
 122, 123, 127, 154, 155, 157, 158,
 166, 171, 172, 181, 185, 198, 200,
 201, 212
Saisaymar, Thanapat, 227
Saisikaew, Putipong, 120
Saisoontorn, Anchalee, 224
Sakakorn, Pitchanart, 131
Sakdaphisit, Sophon, 132, 136, 143
Sakhonrat, Serm, 135
saksi luk puchai (or "the honour of
 men"), 167

Index

Sakuljaroensuk, Apinya, 236
Sakveerakul, Chookiat, 123, 124, 200, 201
Saneh Silp Pappayon, 38
Sangkapreecha, Saharat, 69, 70
Sangsingkaew, Wasu, 167
Santi-Vina, 35–36
Sapanpong, Anuchit, 84
Sarasin, Pornwut, 90
Sars Wars, 114–116
Sasanatieng, Wisit, 8, 16–17, 18, 76, 77, 80, 81, 86, 129, 130, 164, 165, 198, 228
Satayawon, Sutasit, 37
Sayew, 12, 172–173
Scar, The, 19, 55–56, 97
Scared, 122–123
Screen at Kamchanod, The, 139–140
Seasons Change, 178–179
Seneewongse, Tassawan, 129
Shaowanasai, Michael, 176, 196, 197, 198, 216
Shimizu, Koichi, 222, 223, 231
Shinawatra, Thaksin, 179
Sheewanun, Naiyana, 54
Shutter, 1, 13, 19, 108, 111, 112, 116–118, 120, 132, 133, 136, 137, 138, 143, 236
Siam, 8, 30, 31, 32, 71, 105, 106, 158
Siam Niramai Company, 29
Siam Renaissance, The, 19, 105–106
Siam Sakkhee, 29
Siamese Environment Club, 23
Siamese Revolution of 1932, 98, 238
Siburapha (Kulap Saipradit), 97
Sick Nurses, 12
Sikamana, Achita, 116, 123
Silapabanleng, Sorn, 104
Singapore, 1
Singlampong, Witawat, 179
Sippapak, Yuthlert, 2, 17–19, 76, 111, 127, 128, 149, 181
Sirikul, Penpak, 206
Siriphaibun, Wimon, 105
Siriraj Forensic Medicine Museum, 119, 135
Siriwan, Sarinthip, 37
Sisters, 132
Sleep of Reason Films, 207
Slice, 142–143, 167
slice of life, 56, 60, 204
"slow" aesthetics, 218, 228, 235
Sobree, Sathit, 203
social problem films, 24, 25, 29, 56, 71
social realism, 24, 56, 57, 59, 62, 67, 83, 172, 194
social reflectionist films (*nang sathon sangkhom*), 56, 66
Somnuk Pappayon, 49
Somsri #422R, 67–68
Somumjarn, Wichanon, 232, 233
Son of the Northeast, 59–60
Song of Chaophraya, 66–67
"songs for life" (*phleng phuea chiwit*), 63, 67
Songsanant, Kiat, 172
Songsri, Cherd, 19–20, 55, 70, 71, 97, 98
Sophon, Nuengthida, 184
Sorasak, Noi, 32
South America, 19
South Korea, 1, 14, 169, 184
  cinema, 8, 88, 108, 143, 148
spirits, 15, 33, 107, 109, 114, 122, 135, 136, 144, 199, 213, 227
Sri Krung Press, 31
Sripongwrakul, Nikorn, 206
Sripoomseth, Krit, 111
Sririwi, Uhten, 233
Srisawat, Saiyon, 64
Sri-Sayam Production, 52
Srisuriyawongse, Chaophraya, 106

Index

Sri-Ubon, Chana, 37, 81
Srivichai, Ekkaachai, 199
Sriwilai, Rayvadi, 35
S.T.A.B., 148
Stone, Oliver, 96
subtitles, 2, 3, 70, 239
SuckSeed, 186–187
Sugar Is Not Sweet, 10, 42–44
Sugmakanan, Songyos, 125
Sukapatana, Chintara, 70, 125
Sukchaloen, Jirat, 125
Sukhum, Soros, 215, 216, 236
Sukkhapisit, Tanwarin, 194, 205, 206
Sukosol, Krissada, 123, 124, 166
Sumo Sam-ang, 103
Sunset at Chaophraya, 180
Supapprom, Krisada, 166
Supernatural, 207–208
supernatural, 44, 45, 47, 53, 107, 108, 109, 110, 122, 133, 138, 144, 145
Suphayang, Pimolwan, 176
Suppakarnkitjakul, Kochakorn, 177
Suprungroj, Pavich, 206
Surapondsanuruk, Phakpoom, 225
Suriyan, Chaiya, 51
Suthamsamai, Sakarin, 166
Suthat Na Ayutthaya, Nida, 118
Suwan, Asanee, 150, 151
Suwan Film, 51
Suwanatat, Sulaleewan, 53
Suwanmethanon, Sunny, 189, 190
Suwichakornpong, Anocha, 215, 216, 226, 236
Swimmers, The, 136
Syndromes and a Century, 21, 22, 216, 219, 222–223

Taephanit, Udom, 180, 181
Tai Entertainment, 68, 105, 109, 194
Tak Bai Massacre, 2004, 202, 203
talok-phi-kathoei, 18

Tan Shijie, 229
TangkwaMatograph, 238
Tang, Patrick Kazu, 163
Tarantino, Quentin, 78, 80
Tate Modern, 23
Tears of the Black Tiger, 8, 16, 17, 80–81, 86, 130
teen movies, 8, 11, 29, 61, 68, 69, 71, 72, 76, 95, 99, 194, 200
Teepanat, Chutima, 179
Teerakulchanyut, Jetnipith, 216
Teerasaroch, Sombatsara, 129
television, 7, 9, 15, 16, 24, 25, 61, 67, 68, 70, 71, 103, 105, 156, 177, 183, 210, 213, 223, 235
Temple of the Emerald Buddha, 30
Tepkorn Pappayon, 44
Thai film, 116
  history, 2, 9, 10, 14, 16, 17, 19, 24, 27, 29, 30, 31, 33, 36, 39, 45, 52, 55, 58, 108, 145, 194, 201, 210
  museum, 2, 3
  studios, 2, 12, 21, 75, 108, 190, 210
Thai Film Archive, 35, 215
Thai Film Board, 13
Thai Film Censorship Board, 22
Thai Film Directors Association, 8
Thai Film Foundation, 21, 215, 216
Thai Film Studio, 33
Thai National Film Association, 217
Thailand, 19, 20, 22, 27, 28, 33, 42, 45, 46, 48, 49, 150, 184, 185, 187, 188, 193, 195, 204, 215, 217, 223, 226, 228, 233, 236, 238, 239, 240
  Chiang Mai, 22, 230
  Chonburi, 24
  Khao Yai, 221
  Khon Kaen, 20, 21, 22, 222, 233
  Lampang, 195
  Narathiwat, 202, 203
  Nong Khai, 84

Index

Nonthaburi, 7
North, 62, 206, 225
Northeast, 20, 21, 57, 59, 64, 84, 154, 158, 159, 171, 174, 175, 177, 178, 218, 222, 225, 227, 230, 233, 234
Pattani, 202
Petchaburi, 24, 221
Phuket, 88, 89
Ratchaburi, 208
Rayong, 59
South, 8, 19, 60, 61, 64, 79, 160, 171, 172, 202, 203, 204, 218, 224, 230
Thai-Burmese border, 154, 207, 219
Thai-Lao border, 208, 235
Thai-Malaysian border, 61, 171, 207
Ubon Ratchathani, 177, 208
Udon Thani, 139
Yala, 202
Thai-ness, 5, 16, 20, 55, 56, 81, 83, 93, 94, 95, 96, 108, 130, 158, 164, 182
Thai-thae (or "authentic Thai"), 7, 30
Thammasat University Massacre, 1976, 141
Thamrongrattanarit, Nawapol, 190, 191, 215, 225, 230, 231, 232, 237, 238
Thamthrakul, Art, 120
Thanarat, Sarit, 41, 167
Tharatorn, Mez, 187, 189
Tharatorn, Nithiwat, 101, 178
Thatsanapayak, Rangsi, 28, 47
Theriault, Nicole, 220
This Area Is under Quarantine, 202–204
Thongdee, Bhandit, 113, 114
Thongkongtoon, Yongyoot, 137, 138, 173, 176, 194
Thongsaeng, Chaiwat, 198
Thongviset, Wannasa, 100
Thongyooyong, Witthaya, 101
Three, 8

Tiensuwan, Suphavadee, 57
Tinphairao, Phintusuda, 115
Tohssawat, Rattanaballang, 198
Tonahongsa, Rungrawan, 177
Tone, 28, 51–52
Tongaram, Kanokporn, 219
Tongkumnerd, Namo, 139
Tongmee, Natthaweeranuch, 116
Tor, Sahaphap, 195
tourism, 30, 85, 88, 115, 181, 182, 184
Tourist Authority of Thailand, 217
Towira, Pimpaka, 215, 216, 220, 228
Trairat, Charlie, 101, 125
Transistor Love Story, 8, 14, 15, 76, 81–83, 220
transnational, 8, 17, 22, 37, 78, 83, 85, 151, 152, 157, 201, 209, 216, 225, 227
travelling cinema, 28
Trisirikasem, Adisorn, 101, 182
Triwimol, Komgrit, 101, 177
Tropical Malady, 21, 219, 221–222
Tsang, Eric, 88
tsunami, 2004, 224
Twentieth Century Fox, 36

Uabumrungjit, Chalida, 39, 216
Udomlertlak, Namfon, 229
Udomroj, Udom, 68, 70
Uekrongtham, Ekachai, 150, 151
Umarin, Wiyada, 24
Unborn, The, 113–114
Uncle Boonmee Who Can Recall His Past Lives, 21, 108, 222, 226–228
United Kingdom (UK), 9, 23, 35, 37, 163, 214, 225
Universal Studios, 29
university, 37, 73
    Chulalongkorn University, 13, 101, 103, 207
    Kasetsart University, 72

Index

university (cont.)
  Khon Kaen University, 20
  Pratt Institute, 15
  School of the Art Institute of
    Chicago (SAIC), 20
  Silpakorn University, 7, 16
  Thammasat University, 141
  University of California Los Angeles
    (UCLA), 23
Unseeable, The, 16, 129–130
Untold Story, The, 140
US Information Service (USIS), 36

vampire, 58, 69, 130
Vasudhara, Sunh, 33
Vichailak, Ittisoontorn, 8, 62, 103
Victim, The, 130–132, 135, 136
Vietnam, 1
Vietnam War, 29, 45, 51
Virayasiri, Porniti, 59

Wachirabunjong, Pongpat, 201
Wall-E, 214
Waller, Tom, 240, 241
Wanglayangkoon, Wat, 83
Wantha, Taweewat, 114
Waraakesiri, Panupong, 206
Warhol, Andy, 218
Wasukraipaisan, Vittaya, 132
Wasuwat Brothers, 31
Wattaleela, Adirek, 95
Wattanajinda, Siraphan, 129
Wattanapanich, Marsha, 132
Weerasethakul, Apichatpong, 1, 20–23, 60, 76, 108, 194, 196, 197, 215, 216, 217, 218, 219, 220, 221, 222, 223, 224, 226, 227, 228, 232, 233, 234, 235, 236, 237
Weerasethakul, Suaraya, 216

Wichiensarn, Sarawut, 126
Wilaisak, Pisamai, 53
Wimookdayon, Piya, 202
Wisaneesarn, Senee, 40
Wisawachart, Tom, 40
Witsanukon, Thawi, 53
Wonderful Town, 224–225, 228, 230
Wong, Anthony, 140
Wong Kar-wai, 78, 86, 225, 237
Wongjinda, Pakphum, 122, 123
Wongkamlao, Petchai (or Mum Jokmok), 149, 153, 155, 156, 157
Wongpim, Chalerm, 158, 160
Wongpoom, Parkpoom, 13, 108, 116, 120, 132, 133, 137
Wongpuapan, Theeradej, 97, 182, 183
Wongsomphet, Saratswadee, 204, 205
Workpoint Entertainment, 213
World War II, 3, 28

Xin Yukan, 229
Xing Jin, 157

Yak: The Giant King, 213–214
Yanagi, Asuka, 181
Yanin, Jeeja (or Jeeja Yanin Vismitananda), 148, 162, 163
Yaowananon, Pitisak, 127
Yaowasang, Suriya, 61
Yes or No, 204–205
Yihong Duan, 119
Yingsak, Achan, 199
Yojimbo, 156
Yoon, Prabda, 220, 237
Young, Tata, 72

Zee-Oui, 118–120
zombie, 115

www.ingramcontent.com/pod-product-compliance
Lightning Source LLC
Chambersburg PA
CBHW071811300426
44116CB00009B/1276